MARRIAGE CONTRACTS AND COUPLE THERAPY

Marriage Contracts
and
Couple Therapy

Hidden Forces in Intimate
Relationships

By

CLIFFORD J. SAGER, M.D.

Clinical Professor of Psychiatry,
Mt. Sinai School of Medicine,
City University of New York

Psychiatric Director,
Jewish Family Service, New York

BRUNNER/MAZEL, *Publishers* • New York

Library of Congress Cataloging in Publication Data

Sager, Clifford J.   1916-
  Marriage contracts and couple therapy.
  Bibliography: p. 325
  Includes index.
    1. Marital psychotherapy.   2. Marriage.   I. Title.
RC488.5.S17   301.42   76-21842
ISBN 0-87630-130-8

Published by
BRUNNER/MAZEL, INC.
19 Union Square West, New York, N. Y. 10003

To
MARGE

Contents

vii

Introduction

MARRIAGE AS THE PRIME institution of society for procreation and early care of the young, as well as for fulfillment of the emotional and security needs of adults, is being sorely questioned as it is subject to the pressures generated by our changing world. The need to find ways to understand how and why marriages do not fulfill their purposes, and to prevent or alleviate misery, is self-evident. At our pressent marriage and divorce rates, half the marriages in the United States are destined for the divorce courts; in addition, untold numbers of people suffer because of ungratifying or destructive unions.

The purpose of this book is threefold: 1) to offer a series of hypotheses that will contribute to an understanding of why people behave as they do in marriage—and in other committed relationships; 2) to offer an approach tc therapy that is based on those hypotheses; and 3) to clarify the mistaken idea that marital therapy is a modality valuable only for the treatment of marital problems and is not indicated for treating individual distress. *The central concept is that each partner in a marriage brings to it an individual, unwritten contract, a set of expectations and promises, conscious and unconscious.* These individual contracts may be modified during the marriage but will remain separate unless the two partners are fortunate enough to arrive at a single joint contract that is "felt" and agreed to at all levels of awareness, or unless they work toward a single contract with professional help.

The emotional and behavioral problems of women and men can be treated effectively by utilizing the power of the marital interaction even when the individual's symptoms are not manifested primarily within the marital relationship. Conjoint treatment need not be reserved solely for the treatment of marital disharmony. Manifestations of distorted perceptions, repression, transferentially determined feelings and actions, mechanisms of defense and unrealistic expectations of one's spouse that exist in many marriages can rapidly provide a source of excellent therapeutic leverage. Working with the couple together often provides an opportunity to treat individual symptomatology and its etiological sources as well as marital disharmony.

Another concept of the book, uniting the others, is that every committed couple develops an operational, interactional contract. This contract is the creation of their marital system, the conscious and unconscious ways in which the two people work together, or against each other, to try to fulfill the terms of their individual contracts.

HISTORY OF CONTRACT CONCEPT

It may be of interest to the reader to know the history of the ideas presented here and something of the way they developed through my own work and through a series of fruitful collaborations with colleagues.

In 1961, while Dr. Jay Fidler was waiting for an elevator on the thirteenth floor of Metropolitan Hospital in New York City (the elevators were so slow that we often had our most productive conferences while waiting), I was telling him about a couple I was treating without much success. He grasped the problem and as the elevator door opened he walked in and threw over his shoulder, "Sounds like they signed different marriage contracts—he's operating on one set of terms and she on another. No wonder they have trouble." His remark was right to the point! From this quick observation I began to generalize, to test and develop the notion of the unwritten contracts. My associates on the Marriage Research Committee of the Society of Medical Psychoanalysts—Drs. Ralph H. Gundlach, Helen S. Kaplan, Malvina Kremer, Rosa Lenz, and Jack R. Royce*— played with the idea with me and we incorporated it into our research program. Together we published an article on the marriage contract concept in *Family Process*, 1971.

Since then I have extended the concept so that it can be used as a basis for organizing data to make the mysteries of marital interaction more comprehensible. It serves as a guideline for a typography of marital interactions and for the treatment of marital disharmony. The approach developed in this volume is intended to enhance the effectiveness of most theoretical and clinical approaches to work with couples.

ORGANIZATION OF THE BOOK

The concept of these marriage contracts and applications to marital therapy are discussed in Chapter 1. In Chapter 2, the specific terms of individual contracts and the levels of awareness at which they exist are described in detail. Chapter 3 deals with the interactional or operational contract that arises out of the marital system. This system is unique for each couple even though it may have aspects of marital systems each person had known previously. It is not immutable and it changes as various internal and external forces impinge on the couple.

The specific uses of both individual and interactional material in therapy are outlined in Chapter 4. What is important to emphasize here is that all these data and the therapist's interpretations are to be used dynamically in the service of the ultimate goal of the contract concept: the attainment of a single joint contract, understood by, satisfactory to, and workable for both partners. Chapter 5, the history of one couple who used marriage contracts intensively in therapy, shows how the concept helped their marriage progress toward a single contract. It also illustrates how a variety of theoretical and technical approaches can be drawn upon to form a holistic and practical approach to therapy.

Chapter 6 contains categorizations of individual behavioral profiles.

---

* Deceased.

These are not meant to be absolutes of personality types, but rather serve as useful diagnostic and therapeutic tools for marital therapy. The major profiles are those of equal, romantic, parental, childlike, rational, companionate, and parallel partners. How each of these most typically interacts in various partnership combinations is dealt with in Chapter 7; the following chapter describes the contractual clause combinations that can lead to congruence, complementarity, or conflict in the working out of the marriage contracts.

Chapter 9 discusses in depth the therapeutic principles and some of the techniques that may be used in working with the concept of contracts in marital therapy. Its purpose is to help the therapist evolve an eclectic and dynamic approach to his or her work by drawing on many theories and modalities and to demonstrate how the contract concept may be employed within one's own theoretical bias. A good deal of this material is implicit throughout the book; in this chapter it is made as explicit as possible for the use of psychiatrists, psychologists, social workers, marriage counselors, students of the behavioral sciences, and those in allied fields.

Chapter 10 deals with sexual components of the contracts—the sexual expectations of partners within the context of a committed relationship. It is included here to put into perspective the changing views of sexuality within marriage. Data from developments in sex therapy have recently caused some therapists to become more aware of the role of sex in marriage, to revise drastically their earlier opinions about how sexual components may be used to evaluate the quality of a relationship, and to reassess the priorities to be established for treating sexual problems vis à vis other aspects of marital disharmony.

Chapter 11 uses six different case histories to illustrate the many possible outcomes of marital therapy in the light of a variety of couples' contracts. Chapter 12 deals with applications of the contract concept to other relationships and, even more important, the use of the concept in education and prevention. This final chapter is meant to point the way to prevention of marital disharmony and disaster by helping young people understand and learn to deal with this vital area of their adult lives. Appendix 1 is the reminder list of the common significant areas of many marriage contracts for the use of therapists and couples and the worksheet for their data. Appendix 2 organizes the descriptive data commonly found in each of the behavioral profiles.

ACKNOWLEDGMENTS

I am indebted to so many people that I can select only a few to list. I am particularly grateful to Dr. Helen S. Kaplan, whose conceptual and technical innovations in sex therapy have provided me with models that were extremely helpful in extending my theoretical and technical approaches in working with other marital problems. Special thanks are reserved for Bernie Mazel, friend and publisher, for the persistence and faith that assured my completion of the work. If he were willing to risk, then I could too. Thanks are also due to Ms. Susan Barrows whose editorial help and encouragement were so helpful.

I owe Sanford Sherman, executive director of Jewish Family Service, a great deal for his encouragement and his astute, constructive criticism of the draft of the book. I am grateful to Drs. Kitty La Perriere, Harold I. Lief and Ralph H. Gundlach for their helpful criticism of the manuscript. Ms. Mary Heathcote was extremely skilled, patient, and considerate of my feelings as author in her editing of the manuscript. Ms. Caryl Snapperman was most helpful in the early phase of the work.

To those too numerous to mention, thanks for the thousand ways you have helped me as family, patients, colleagues, friends, and students. I am especially grateful to all the participants in my seminars at Jewish Family Service and Mt. Sinai Hospital and Medical School whose discussion and questions helped clarify my thinking.

CLIFFORD J. SAGER

New York City
June 1976

MARRIAGE CONTRACTS AND COUPLE THERAPY

1

The Concept of Marriage Contracts and Its Applications to Therapy

WRITTEN MARRIAGE CONTRACTS have existed throughout the history of man's civilization. The *New York Times* (1971) reported two scholars' translation of a marriage contract between Tamut, a former slave woman and newly converted Jew, and her husband, Ananiah bar Azariah, an official of the Jewish temple at Elephantine, an island in the Nile, in 449 B.C. Infrared photography and other new techniques revealed that Tamut must have bargained hard and successfully because the contract, written on papyrus, was erased and corrected in several places, and all corrections were to Tamut's advantage. For example, originally she was to inherit one-half of Ananiah bar Azariah's estate at his death—this was changed to all. Her son Pilti could not be reclaimed by her former master except on payment of 50 shekels, a prohibitive sum. Other changes increased the value of the dowry that she brought with her. The struggle for women's rights did not begin with George Sand!

LEGAL CONTRACTS

Legal codes throughout the ages have institutionalized personal and property rights of marriages, usually to the advantage of the male.

1

But such legal agreements are only a small part of the marriage contracts we are dealing with here. Sussman, Cogswell and Ross (1973) have recently combined their interdisciplinary talents as sociologists and law scholars to undertake a study of marriage contracts that are being used today. The contracts that contemporary couples sign together usually include the following provisions: 1) division of household labor; 2) use of living space; 3) each partner's responsibility for child rearing and socialization; 4) property, debts, living expenses; 5) career commitment and legal domicile; 6) rights of inheritance; 7) use of surnames; 8) range of permissible relationships with others; 9) obligations of the marital dyad in various life sectors such as work, leisure, community and social life; 10) grounds for splitting or divorce; 11) initial and subsequent contract periods and negotiability; 12) sexual fidelity/relationships beyond partnership; and 13) position regarding procreation or adoption of children.*

Contractual terms of this sort would usually be included, but not as formally, in the contracts discussed here, which are primarily unwritten, unspoken contracts between marriage partners and other partners in committed relationships. The formal contract that two partners may sign expresses their ideology and summarizes their principles. It is a concrete expression of feelings and attitudes to the extent that the individuals are aware of them. Such attitudes are also expressed in a more symbolic fashion when couples omit the phrase "and obey" from the woman's part of the marriage oath. That small omission signifies great change in husband-wife relationships.

Written contracts should be encouraged, but, appropriately, they are not designed to deal with the emotionally determined needs, expectations, and obligations that exist in all intimate partners at a variety of levels of awareness. In fact, the contracts that one encounters in therapy are not really contracts. The essence of the relationship is that the partners have not negotiated a contract but each spouse acts as if his own program for the marriage were a contract that had been agreed upon and signed by both partners. Each has

---

* I note the absence among these areas of one that deals with methods for resolving differences that the two are unable to settle by themselves. Some system of third-party arbitration or help on a peer level or with a professional would seem to be important.

only his or her own contract in mind, although each is unaware even of parts of that. Thus they are not true contracts at all, but two different sets of expectations, desires, and obligations, each set existing only in the mind of one partner. These non-contracts represent the most classic, common, and devastating example, in terms of their damage to the human condition, of lack of effective communication, lack of self-awareness and lack of accurate perception of others. Each partner feels that *in exchange for what he will give to the other he will receive what he wants*. However, each partner is operating on a different set of contractual terms, and each is unaware of the other's terms. Further, contractual terms change as the marriage goes on, different stages of the life cycle are attained, and outside forces impinge on the couple as a pair or on either individual. Hence, contractual terms or the rules of the game are often changed by one spouse without discussion, and certainly without the consent of the other. Under these circumstances it is not surprising that in 1975 there were a million divorces in the United States and about one divorce for every two marriages.

What is surprising, since marriage is the most complex of human relationships, is that psychiatry and psychology have only recently begun to turn from studying and treating the individual to studying and treating the two mates within the context of their marriage. Marital therapy has advanced beyond the stage of mere advice and counseling only since about 1930 (Sager, 1966a, 1966b). The current status of this area of therapy has been summarized by Berman and Lief (1975), who indicate that conjoint treatment—working with the two partners together—has become the common modality for marital therapy, but that there is still no comprehensive or generally acceptable diagnostic or theoretical system to describe and explain what factors contribute toward establishing and maintaining good or poor marriages. Although there is an increasingly large literature on marriage and marital therapy, no unifying concepts have evolved. In a recent critical overview of marital and family therapy, Olson (1975) confirms the lack of a solid theoretical base.

As a step in developing a means of conceptualizing and making order out of the myriad intrapsychic and transactional factors that contribute to determining the quality of marital interaction, my colleagues and I several years ago developed the concept of marriage contracts (Sager et al. 1971). Now this present volume deals with my further work in extending and elaborating this concept as it applies to both understanding and treating malfunctioning relationships, and using the leverage of the marital interaction to help each spouse with his individual malfunctioning.

INDIVIDUAL MARRIAGE CONTRACTS

In work with marital couples and families, the concept of individual marriage contracts has proven extremely useful as a model for the elucidation of interactions between marital partners. Specifically, we seek to understand these interactions in terms of the congruence, complementarity, or conflict of the partners' reciprocal expectations and obligations. These "contractual dynamics" are powerful determinants of the individual's behavior within the marriage, as well as of the quality of the marital relationship. Thus it is logical to assume that analysis of marital transactions according to this model may clarify otherwise inexplicable behavior and events within the marriage, and also may provide a focus around which to organize effective therapeutic intervention when an individual, a marriage, or a family is in trouble.

The term *individual contract* refers to a person's expressed and unexpressed, conscious and beyond awareness concepts of his obligations within the marital relationship, and to the benefits he expects to derive from marriage in general and from his spouse in particular. But what must be emphasized above all is the reciprocal aspect of the contract: What each partner expects to give and what he expects to receive from his spouse in exchange are crucial. Contracts deal with every conceivable aspect of family life: relationships with friends, achievements, power, sex, leisure time, money, children, etc. The degree to which a marriage can satisfy each partner's contractual expectations in these areas is an important determinant of the quality of that marriage.

The terms of the individual contracts are determined by deep needs and wishes that each individual expects the marital relationship will fulfill for him. These will include healthy and realistically plausible, as well as neurotic and conflictual, needs. It is most important to realize that, while each spouse may be aware of his own needs and wishes on some level of awareness, he does not usually realize that his attempts to fulfill the partner's needs are based on the covert assumption that his own wishes will thereby be fulfilled. Furthermore, while each spouse is usually at least partly aware of the terms of his contract, and some of the needs from which these terms are derived, he may be only remotely aware, if at all, of the implicit expectations of his spouse. Indeed, a partner may assume there is mutual agreement on a contract when in fact this is not so; the individual then behaves as if an actual contract existed and both spouses were equally obliged to fulfill its terms. When significant aspects of the contract cannot be fulfilled, as is inevitable, and especially when these lie beyond his own awareness, the disappointed partner may react with rage, injury, depression, or withdrawal, and provoke marital discord by acting as though a real agreement had been broken. This response is particularly likely to occur when one partner believes that he has fulfilled his obligations but that his spouse has not.

In my own practice the contents of the individual marriage contract are developed by both the patients and the therapist in three categories of information, or contractual terms: expectations of the marriage; intrapsychic or biological determinants of the individual's needs; and the external foci of marital problems, the symptoms produced by problems in the first two categories. Each of these categories contains material from three different levels of awareness—conscious and verbalized; conscious but not verbalized; and beyond awareness. As a general rule the therapist is able to elicit contractual terms at the first and second levels of awareness from the partners themselves. By the time couples come to therapy, they are usually prepared to verbalize not only what has been expressed previously but what has been conscious but unexpressed because of fear or anxiety. To discover the contractual material that lies beyond awareness it is necessary to depend in part on the therapist's interpretation of the patients' productions. In addition, spouses are often helpful in shedding light on each other's terms in this area.

APPLICABILITY OF THE CONTRACT CONCEPT

Many techniques and approaches may be used in marital therapy, as long as they are consonant with the therapist's own theoretical views and preferences. The concept of the marriage contract can be adapted for use with most theoretical approaches. Specifically, the therapist who utilizes the contract approach assumes that contractual disappointments are a major source of marital discord. Accordingly, he tries to clarify the significant terms of the contracts, aware of the psychic determinants of most clauses, and if these are being violated, he tries to help the couple renegotiate and develop more acceptable terms. Understanding and change may take place concurrently, but change may occur without understanding, and often understanding alone is not enough to produce change. Because we do not always know how to produce change most effectively, the therapist needs to have available a wide variety of theoretical and technical approaches.

It is useful to introduce the individual contract concept early in treatment and to emphasize the mutually satisfying elements of a couple's contracts at the outset. The concept may often be introduced in the first session. An emphasis early in treatment on positive contractual elements makes the couple aware of the valuable features of their marriage and helps to motivate them for the difficult therapeutic task that lies ahead. It is important that the therapist not lose sight of the positive elements in the relationship, including the positive complementarity that exists between two people.

A patient usually experiences relief when he attains insight into the reasons for his smoldering rage and irritability, which may have been puzzling and disturbing. On the other hand, confronting a spouse with the deep disappointments he has suffered in marriage can be upsetting, and the therapist must be sensitive to the potentially disruptive effects of his interpretations upon the relationship. The ultimate aim of treatment is to improve the marital relationship, family functioning and the growth of the individuals. Since this may require open communication between the spouses on all levels, each spouse is encouraged to verbalize to the other the unspoken aspects of their contracts. Nevertheless, contractual material, especially when it reflects unconscious dynamics or an attempt to deal with an intrapsychic difficulty, requires the therapist's greatest sensitivity and skill both in eliciting it and in using it effectively. The interpretation of the unconscious contractual material can evoke intense reactions that are potentially highly constructive but may also have a negative effect on either spouse or the marital system. Such material has to be handled with respect, as in any other form of psychotherapy.

Advances in conceptualization and technique make it possible to deal with intrapsychic problems in conjoint therapy in ways that were not even developed 15 years ago. Thus, the clarification of contractual transactions in therapy sheds light on intrapsychic factors and changes them, just as intrapsychic factors brought to light can help in clarifying and changing contractual terms. The therapist's efforts are guided by his knowledge of both variables.

When a marriage is viable, clarification of the individual marriage contracts may lead to dramatic improvement in the couple's relationship and in the growth and development of each spouse. At some point in therapy each partner is confronted with realities that were previously beyond his awareness: "I can't get A in this relationship, but I do get B and C," or, "My wishes are unrealistic, and no one can give me what I want." When such insights occur they tend to lead to increasing commitment to the marriage and to the decision to accept its realistic limitations, which, in turn, facilitates the resolution of presenting problems.

Occasionally, however, exposure of the terms of the marriage contracts results in the discovery of serious disappointments and incompatibilities, which were previously denied and which may hasten dissolution of a marriage. One partner comes to the realization that "I can't get what I want from this marriage no matter what I give," or, "I can only satisfy him if I am destructive to myself." A couple's decision to dissolve the marriage on the basis of realistic and comprehensive understanding that they cannot give each other what is wanted is not a treatment failure. Under such circumstances dissolution of an empty or painful marriage can be a constructive experience for both. Moreover, the agonizing and destructive experiences that often accompany divorce may be minimized.

The concept of individual marriage contracts helps to familiarize each marital partner with his own and his spouse's needs and willingness to give and to point out troublesome aspects of the relationship;

couples are usually highly receptive to this way of structuring their problems. The technique is particularly valuable in conjoint sessions. Communication is facilitated, and spouses are better able to understand themselves, each other, and their relationship, when the terms of their contracts are revealed. The reasons for their unhappiness, apparently irrational behavior, and bickering or bitterness then become clear. Once they gain some understanding of the contractual disappointments each has suffered, marital partners often feel less helpless and are able to seek more realistic and effective solutions to their problems.

The couple's reciprocal expectations are powerful behavioral determinants. Psychodynamic insight and learning theory methods may be employed, along with a system-transactional approach, as the therapist actively intervenes in the troubled marriage by trying to alter crucial aspects of the processes that are a product of these reciprocal interactional expectations. The individual contracts and the interactional contract provide an ongoing guide for setting therapeutic goals and for intervention.

The contract concept integrates the two parameters of behavioral determinants, the intrapsychic and the transactional. Individual contractual clauses derive from needs and conflicts that can best be understood in intrapsychic and culturally determined terms and are often adaptive attempts to resolve conflicts by means of specific interactions. The consequent interactional process, the interactional contract itself, then becomes a crucial determinant of the quality of the marriage or relationship.

The individual contracts provide us with a dynamic basis for improving our understanding of marital functioning. This concept provides indications for why, how and under what circumstances marital disharmony smolders and becomes exacerbated. The dynamic diagnosis changes as therapy changes the marital system. As the separate contracts more clearly approach a single contract, whose terms are known to and agreed upon by both partners, we may expect a healthier, more fulfilling give-and-take between the partners. Under these circumstances the individual contracts have become syntonic with the purposes of the marital system as well as for the needs of each partner.

2

The Individual Contract

UNWRITTEN MARRIAGE CONTRACTS contain clauses that cover most aspects of feelings, needs, activities, and relationships. Some of the clauses are known to the contract maker, others are beyond awareness. Not all areas need to be dealt with clinically, since disharmony within a marriage is usually characterized by a few major issues in the relationship. Some issues may be important to one partner but not to the other and can readily become the basis for quid pro quo trade-offs when they come out into the open. Possible contractual clauses are here listed and organized for the therapist's consideration, so that he or she may select for study the areas that pertain to the particular case at hand.

The partners enter the marital relationship with their own contracts and must then work toward the development of a single joint contract. The clinician helps to make the goals of the marital system explicit to the couple. In some areas the couple may already share a common goal; in others they may have to seek compromise goals that take into account the strongest wishes of each. Each spouse should try to state his goals and purposes clearly, unequivocally, and without ambivalence, so that areas of concurrence and disagreement will become apparent. Because it is difficult, if not impossible, to be a full and collaborative partner if one senses that the relationship is operating counter to one's interest, the first task is to work out common objectives, goals, or functions in hitherto conflictual areas. When objectives are clear, it is easier to allocate tasks and responsibilities. The efficiency of the system in moving toward the fulfillment of goals and purposes can then be examined and evaluated. As new and different needs emerge in the marital life cycle, the objectives of the marital system have to change to reflect these changing needs; otherwise the marriage is in trouble.

Professionals who do marital therapy have widely varying lists of the kind and number of areas considered significant for evaluating the quality of a marriage. In treating marital discord over the past 15 years I have found, from examining material gathered from patients in clinical sessions and by means of the written contracts if these have been used, that the areas discussed below are the most important.

An almost unlimited number of areas might be included in a marital contract, but to attempt to include all possibilities would be an unnecessary task. For our purposes, the contractual terms can be divided into three categories.*

> *Category 1. Parameters based on expectations of the marriage.* The act of becoming married, whether or not actually approved by church or state, denotes an important level of commitment not only to a mate but to a new entity, the marriage. Each part-ner marries for certain purposes and with specific goals, and brings to the marriage the expectations he has of the institution itself. Generally not all of these purposes and goals are fully conscious.

> *Category 2. Parameters based on intrapsychic and biological needs.* Some of an individual's needs are of biological origin and others develop from the familial and the total cultural en-vironment. Both kinds influence the expectations one has of a committed relationship. The person who inherits a schizophrenic diathesis may be more susceptible than others to losing trust in a partner. He may therefore emphasize the importance of trust and display a suspicion of other people. This example would be considered biological and also intrapsychic. Although, as we try to isolate areas in this category, we are not concerned here

---

* These categories and their parameters are listed in Appendix 1 in a slightly dif-ferent form which is designed to be more accessible for a couple's own use.

with the etiology of particular needs, some such factors have often been part of the personality of the individual for a long time. Other factors have been only potential and required interaction with a particular mate to become realized. There is usually no sharp line but rather a shading, an area of overlap, that separates the category of intrapsychic and biological needs from the other two. Much of the material is beyond awareness and becomes clear through deduction from the patient's total productions and actions and those of the spouse. Although the descriptions of what we see in this category will vary somewhat with the therapist's orientation, some aspects will be perceived similarly by the clinician and the patients themselves, regardless of biases.

Category 3. Parameters that are the external foci of problems rooted in categories 1 and 2. After examining 750 couples who came for help with their marital situations, Greene (1970) found 12 complaints to be the most common. In order of frequency, these are lack of communication, constant arguments, unfulfilled emotional needs, sexual dissatisfaction, financial disagreements, in-law trouble, infidelity, conflicts about children, domineering spouse, suspicious spouse, alcoholism, and physical attack. These complaints are not the central problem but symptoms of it. They describe possible disturbances of transactional behavior patterns but not the underlying cause. Hence the complaints that most commonly cause couples to seek help are derivative and we must seek the underlying difficulties in category 1 or 2.

CATEGORY 1. EXPECTATIONS OF THE MARRIAGE

In addition to the expectations each partner has of what marriage will give him and what he is willing to give to it, the marital system itself, like any other system, may modify existing goals or create new ones. The most common areas of initial expectation may include:

1. A mate who will be loyal, devoted, loving, and exclusive, offering the kind of relationship with a person that one may have hoped for as a child but did not receive, or had and lost. Someone with whom to grow and develop.
2. A constant support against the rest of the world. Spouses are expected to stand by each other in times of need, whether the adversity derives from external sources, such as loss of a job or an encounter with the law, or from within, as in the case of physical or mental illness.

3. Companionship and insurance against loneliness.
4. Marriage as a goal in itself rather than a beginning. Some people do not think beyond the wedding day. Instead of regarding marriage as one point along the continuum of a relationship that is constantly evolving new goals, they assume that in some magical fashion they will live happily ever after once they are actually married.
5. A panacea for the chaos and strife in one's life. All will now be calm and orderly.
6. A relationship that must last "until death do us part." Marriage has traditionally been viewed as a lifelong commitment. This concept is now changing for many.
7. Sanctioned and readily available sex.
8. Creation of a family and the experience of reproducing and participating in the growth and development of children.
9. A relationship that emphasizes the family rather than just a mate. This concept is somewhat akin to that of the "good corporation team member." We have contradictory mainstreams in the United States today, one stressing the primacy of the individual, the other the primacy of the family unit.
10. Others to be included in the new family—parents, children, friends, even pets.
11. A home, a refuge from the world.
12. A respectable position and status in society. Many people feel that there is a certain status in being married, in being or having a wife or husband.
13. An economic unit.
14. A social unit. The family as an economic and social unit contributes to a sense of continuity, of building and planning for the future, which in itself gives meaning and purpose to a person's life. Marriage lends purpose to the lives of most people. Without it, many believe (correctly or not) that they do not have a purpose.
15. An umbrella image to sanctify one's desire to work, build, and accumulate wealth, power, and position.
16. A respectable cover for aggressive drives. Competitive and hostile characteristics are rationalized as being for the good of the family. Marriage supplies a socially acceptable channel for aggressive impulses, since providing for and protecting one's family, home, and possessions are sanctioned and encouraged.

CATEGORY 2. INTRAPSYCHIC AND BIOLOGICAL DETERMINANTS

These parameters are based on the needs and desires that arise from within the individual. They are determined in large part by intrapsychic and biological factors rather than the marital system per se, although the latter may have a great modifying effect. Thus, these parameters derive from the individual as a system, while those discussed in the first category are intimately related to marriage as the system. These "individual" parameters are important because here the mate, as distinguished from the institution of marriage itself, is the subsystem that is expected to fulfill the needs of the other subsystem. The reciprocal nature of the individual contracts, both conscious and beyond awareness, is especially important in this area: "I want so-and-so and in exchange I am willing to give such-and-such."

1. *Independence-dependence.* This crucial area involves the individual's ability to take care of and function for himself. Does he or she require a spouse to complete the sense of self or to initiate what he cannot do himself? Is there a feeling of inability to survive without the mate? Is his sense of worth dependent on his spouse's attitude or feeling toward him? Is he dependent on his mate to initiate plans, to set their taste, pace, and style?

2. *Activity-passivity.* This parameter concerns the individual's desire and ability to take action necessary to bring about what he or she wants. Can he be active in deed as well as in idea? If passive, is he hostile to an active mate? For example, will he exercise veto power without suggesting alternative proposals?

3. *Closeness-distance.* Does anxiety increase with closeness or exposure of feelings, thoughts, and acts to one's mate? Communication patterns and problems are frequently related to the ability or inability to tolerate closeness. Is communication open enough to make needs known, to solve problems, to share feelings and experiences? "Tell me what you are thinking" can be an intrusive, controlling inquiry or an invitation to an open, intimate, and honest dialogue. What defenses against closeness does each mate exhibit? How imperative is the need for one's own living space? How strongly will he resist intrusion upon it? These can be telling blows to a good relationship.

4. *Use-abuse of power.* The relationship of power and the need for it color most marriages. Can power be shared in the marriage or can one partner only delegate to the other? Once acquired, power can be employed directly or indirectly, delegated, or abdicated. Can the individual accept and use power without ambivalence and anxiety? Is he or she so fearful of not having power that he must be in control, or is he even paranoid about his mate's having power? Conversely, does he have a need to renounce his own desire for power and an expectation that the partner's power will be used in his behalf?

5. *Dominance-submission* continuum or the seesaw configuration (if one is up, the other must be down). This may be consistent with the independence-dependence area. Who submits? Who dominates? Or are matters resolved in other ways by this couple? This parameter overlaps with the power parameter just as the independence and power parameters overlap each other.

6. *Fear of loneliness or abandonment.* To what extent is "love" for the mate motivated by fear of being alone? What is the mate expected to do to prevent loneliness and to alleviate the spouse's fear of desertion? How do such fears make the individual function in the relationship? Has he chosen a mate who is likely to stay with him, or someone who is bound to feed into his fears about desertion?

7. *Need to possess and control.* Does the individual have to control or possess his mate in order to feel secure? This area could be subsumed under the parameter of power, but used separately it elicits much useful information.

8. *Level of anxiety.* For physiological and/or psychological reasons some people experience a higher level of anxiety than others. Anxious people often show their anxiety openly and directly. How does the overt anxiety or defense against anxiety affect the mate? Can the mate accept the partner's anxiety without accepting blame for it? Does he or she respond in a way that decreases or increases the anxiety?

9. *Mechanisms of defense.* What are each mate's characteristic ways of dealing with anxiety and other distressing mental states? How does his or her style affect the other? The therapist should look for the most common mechanisms of defense: sublimation, altruistic surrender, repression, regression, reaction formation, perceptual defense (and/or denial), inhibition of impulses and affect, introjection (in-

corporation and identification), reversal (turning against self), displacement, projection, isolation and intellectualization, undoing (magic), and fantasy (to sustain denial). (For further discussion of these defenses see Chapter 3.)

10. *Gender identity.* "Gender identity," according to Money and Ehrhardt (1972), "is the sameness, unity, and persistence of one's individuality as male or female (or ambivalent) in greater or lesser degree, especially as it is experienced in self-awareness and behavior. Gender identity is the private experience of gender role, and gender role is the public expression of gender identity." Is the individual secure in gender identity? Does he depend on his wife to reassure him that he is a man? Does she need him to make her feel like a woman? How defensive and aggressive is each in affirming gender?

11. *Characteristics desired in one's sex partner.* These include, for example: gender, personality, physical characteristics and grace, and role requirements; need to receive and give love; feelings, attitudes, ability to function sexually and to enjoy sex with the mate; level of achievement of mate, survival ability and skills, etc.

12. *Acceptance of self and other.* Does each partner have the ability to love himself as well as the other? Does narcissism interfere with object love? Is love equated with vulnerability and therefore to be eschewed?

13. *Cognitive style.* Cognitive style may be defined as the characteristic way a person selects information to take in, how he processes it, and the way he communicates the outcome to others. As B. and F. Duhl (1975) explain, "While cognitive usually is used to define conscious thinking, we are using it in a broadened meaning in which all mental processes, conscious or otherwise, are given equal importance in a system of taking in and processing information or data." Spouses often approach and work on problems differently or view situations differently. They select or perceive a variety of data and may come up with very different conclusions; direct argument between them rarely resolves the difference. All too often they do not respect the value of the mate's style and of having two sets of perceptions or processes to work with. Difference in cognitive styles, which includes sensory intake differences and thought process differences, is the source of a great deal of marital conflict and unhappiness. Instead of exclaiming "*Vive la dif-*

férence!" as we are prone to do when referring to gonadal differences, few couples learn how to capitalize on culturally determined differences in cognitive style. The therapist should direct his attention and that of the couple to examining the cognitive area to see if differences there are the source of problems. It is especially important to examine this area because cognitive style differences between spouses have not received as much professional notice as some of the other parameters.

Intelligence may properly be included in cognitive style. A wide discrepancy in intelligence can increase style differences and communication problems between mates and can lead to a host of other dissatisfactions whose cause is not readily apparent to either spouse.

CATEGORY 3. EXTERNAL FOCI OF MARITAL PROBLEMS

External foci symptoms often seem to be the core of the marital disharmony, but in reality they are usually secondary manifestations of problem areas originating in expectations of the marriage or the biological and intrapsychic category. The more concrete complaints of category 3 often surface first, but they generally call attention to more significant sources of disharmony that are often outside of awareness.

1. *Communication.* To what degree is there openness and clarity in the giving and receiving of information and "messages"? Can there be overt expression of love, understanding, anxiety, anger, desires, and so forth?
2. *Life-Style.* Do the similarities pave the way to compatibility or, conversely, do the differences, and one's perception of differences, lead to constant strife or subjugation? Do the partners go different ways, leading parallel lives? Is one a "day person," the other a "night person"? Is one a social being, the other a loner? Is one the indoor, the other the outdoor type? Does one prefer meat and potatoes, the other gourmet cooking? What are other significant differences in taste? Do these reflect more basic differences?
3. *Families of origin.* One partner may harbor resentment toward the mate's family or toward particular members of that family (mother, father, or a sibling). How does the couple handle family visits? How successful are they in making decisions that involve their current relationship with

both families of origin? A partner's overattachment to his original family frequently causes severe problems. Some individuals attempt to retain a childlike role; others assume and exercise parental responsibility toward their own parents or siblings.

4. *Child rearing*. The philosophy of child rearing is perhaps not as important as actual practice on a daily basis. Who has authority with the children? How are decisions made about upbringing and child care?

5. *Relationship with children*. What alliances are made with the children? For what purposes? Are particular children identified as belonging more to one parent than the other?

6. *Family myths*. Do the partners collaborate in the maintenance of myths? Do they strive to present a certain image of their marriage, their family, themselves?

7. *Money*. Who makes how much? How are expenditures controlled? Who does the bookkeeping? Is money viewed as power, as love?

8. *Sex*. Attitudes may differ on such fundamental considerations as frequency of sexual relations, who initiates sex, alternative sex objects (homosexual, heterosexual, bisexual, fetishistic, or group sex), means of achieving or heightening gratification (fantasy, playing out of fantasy), and fidelity. How do feelings of love and consideration interrelate with the sex drive and its fulfillment?

9. *Values*. Is there general agreement on priorities, such as money, culture, school, home, clothes, personal moral code, religion, politics, other relationships? Values are reflected in most of the other areas listed here but they also merit specific consideration.

10. *Friends*. What is the attitude of each toward his mate's friends? What does each partner seek from friends? Can the partners share friends and each have his or her own as well? What ground rules apply to developing friends at work, personal friends, opposite-sex friends? Can both spouses understand that each cannot (and should not) try to fulfill all of the other's emotional and recreational needs?

11. *Roles*. What tasks and responsibilities are expected of each partner? Who will do the housework, cooking, shopping? Who will take responsibility for child care, vacation and recreation plans, entertainment, financial matters? Are roles narrowly gender determined, or shared, or flexible in accordance with time and proclivities?

12. *Interests*. When interested in an activity, do spouses insist that their mates share the interest? Are differences in interests respected or resented? Interests related to both work and leisure should be examined here, and their relationship to the closeness-distance parameter of category 2 should be considered. Which interest is an expression of individuality and which an expression of a need for distance, or, conversely, for clinging and dependence?

This is of necessity a partial listing. Every couple, like every individual, has problems specific to the particular relationship. For example, differences in race, religion, or social class are relevant parameters for some couples but not for others. The list is, however, complete enough to provide both patients and professionals with an awareness of the most common areas of difficulty encountered in marital therapy. Others may be added as specific situations indicate.

SOURCES OF CONTRACTUAL DIFFICULTIES

The sources of contractual difficulties vary. The marital partners may be operating under two very different incongruent contracts. A classic source of such incongruence is the culturally derived difference in the role expectations of men and women. If one partner has intrapsychic conflicts about his own needs and wishes, the terms of the contract he is trying to implement on the level of dual integration will reflect these conflicts and contradictions. Obviously the "deal" can't work under those circumstances, and disappointment is inevitable.

I treated a couple in which the woman partner typifies many contemporary women. She was trained from birth to be "feminine"; her role was to become a wife and mother. After she married and had children she experienced a need (of which she was not fully aware) to be more independent and to use her intellectual capacities in productive work. On the one hand, she was fairly independent, and, on the other, she had an overpowering need to be taken care of by a strong, effective, parental man. She was appropriately ambitious and unusually competent in her avocation and wanted to work full-time. At the same time she felt that only she could attend properly to her children's needs. Without fully airing her conflict, as she was not totally aware of her seemingly mutually exclusive drives or of her fear of losing the love of her "parental" husband, she unconsciously changed her original contract with her husband, which had provided that she would have major responsibility for daily child care. She then proceeded to act on the assumption that her husband had agreed to take some time from his work activities to be with the children. On occasions when he refused her request to do so, she was angry with him because she believed he was holding her back in her own development. When he did agree to her requests, she was fearful that he would see her as too competitive and would stop loving her. She was also competitive with him for the children's affection, fearing they would love him more than they loved her if he gave them "too much" time. Her conflicts were reflected in her unilateral contract revision and the resulting disruption in the family. It was the husband in this case who insisted that they seek therapy.

Frequently one partner frustrates the expectations of the other in a specific area because some aspect of the transaction arouses a great deal of anxiety. However, there are some relationships in which a sadistic partner enjoys the sense of power he or she derives from frustrating the other. Some marriages are destined to fail because one or both spouses' contracts are based on unrealistic expectations; although one spouse fulfills his obligations, his own needs remain unfulfilled because his partner simply does not have the capacity to gratify them. This may happen, for example, when one partner is significantly less intelligent than the other or when one suffers from serious psychopathology. Finally, some expectations are doomed to disappointment because they are based on fantasies that no relationship can fulfill in reality.

AWARENESS OF THE CONTRACT

For clinical purposes it is useful to consider each partner's awareness of the individual marriage contract on three levels:

Level 1. Conscious, Verbalized

This would include what each partner tells the mate about his or her expectations in clearly understandable language. Although a spouse may express himself clearly to the other, the second may shut out the communication and not hear or allow to register what has been stated. This may occur because the latter has a different expectation or mind set. In communication, receiving is as important as broadcasting. Thus, it is necessary that mates listen to each other as well as express themselves openly and honestly. As we noted earlier, the reciprocal aspects of the stated expectations are not usually verbalized or recognized. The statement is usually made as a wish, desire, or loosely defined plan, but not in terms of "what I expect you to do for me in exchange."

Level 2. Conscious But Not Verbalized

This refers to each partner's expectations, plans, beliefs, and fantasies, which differ from the content at level 1 only in that *they are not verbalized to the mate*, usually because of fear of anger, rejection, or shame at their disclosure. Uncertainties about entering a fuller relationship, incipient conflicts, and disappointments may enter awareness but are not discussed and aired openly. Occasionally willful deception for manipulative or narrow self-gain purposes may be involved. This is more rare than might be anticipated when the couple is considering marriage or living together. It is more common in brief-encounter relationships.

Level 3. Beyond Awareness

This third level comprises desires or needs, often contradictory and unrealistic, of which the contractor has no awareness. They may be similar to or in conflict with the needs and expectations that are operative at levels 1 and 2, depending on how well integrated the individual is. Some of the contractual clauses in the third level may be preconscious and close to the surface; others may be further from awareness. This is the area of power and control needs, closeness-distance, contradictory active-passive impulses, child-adult conflicts, gender identity conflicts, and so on. In many respects this is the most significant contractual level, because the forces involved, the defenses against them, and the effects the defenses produce determine so many of the subtleties of behavior and relating.

The manifestations of severe mental illness, schizophrenia, primary affective disorders or organic psychosis may very well make it impossible to maintain a reasonably fulfilling relationship.

The aspects of individual marriage contracts that are not accessible to conscious awareness may be regarded for clinical purposes as working hypotheses inferred from the behavior, fantasies, and other productions of each spouse. Contracts on this level may have the irrational, contradictory, and primitive characteristics that are attributed to "the unconscious" in accordance with psychoanalytic theory. As a rule, these terms of the contract cannot be fulfilled because of their mutually contradictory and unrealistic aspects, and marital discord arises from the spouse's inability to fulfill them. Nonfulfillment of unconscious expectations tends to evoke intense emotional reactions that are puzzling and disturbing to both spouses. The affect may be displaced so that the reaction appears to be inappropriate to the reality of the immediate stimulus.

Contracts on any or all levels are dynamic and may change at any point in the marital relationship. As might be expected, such changes frequently take place when there is a significant modification of needs, expectations, or role demands of one or both partners, or when a new force enters the marital system. Thus, there are several points in the family life cycle at which one might find the nature of the marriage contract of particular interest: during courtship, at the end of the first year of marriage, after the birth of children, during and after a dislocating experience, when the children leave home, when either spouse has a significant illness, and so on. For purposes of therapy, the nature of the contract at the time of the clinical examination would, of course, be the most important. For premarital counseling the contracts during courtship and the couple's projections for the future would be paramount.

Congruence of contracts on the first level of awareness may well lead the couple to the altar; disparity on the second level leads to difficulty early in the marital relationship, often by the end of the first year; and incongruence on the third level, when nonambivalent complementarity does not exist to a reasonable degree, contributes significantly to neurotic object choices and lies at the root of the problems one encounters most frequently after the first few years of marriage. Problems that originate in contractual incongruence at the third level of awareness are often overtly expressed in petty differences in the couple's daily operations, which usually mask the true dynamics at work within the dyad.

As a general rule we are able to elicit "contractual terms" at awareness levels 1 and 2—the conscious, verbalized aspects of the contract, and those that are conscious but not verbalized—directly from the partners themselves. By the time couples come for therapy they are usually prepared to verbalize what they had feared to previously and have little trouble with what had previously been conscious but not verbalized. For the contractual content that lies beyond awareness (level 3) we depend in part on the therapist's interpretation of material that he selects from his patients' productions. The conclusions the therapist arrives at with respect to the contractual dynamics at level 3 will, of course, reflect his particular theoretical bias and must be regarded in this light. Interestingly, spouses are often more aware of their partner's third-level needs than of their own. They can be helpful in shedding light on each other's terms. A wife will not infrequently say, "I know he likes to act so strong and possessive, but I also realize how dependent he is on me and how like a little boy he is in so many ways." On the other hand, a husband may say, "She is in such conflict—she really wants to be independent and to do her own thing, and at the same time she wants me to be Big Daddy and take care of her."

Having set up the basic areas of the individual marriage contract —expectations of marriage, intrapsychic and biological needs, and external foci of the two areas—and having perceived that all contract clauses are exercised at three levels of awareness, we are ready to examine the third unwritten document that underlies all marital arrangements: the operational or interactional contract through which the marriage functions.

3

The Interactional Contract

IN THE PREVIOUS CHAPTER the areas and levels of awareness of individual contracts were detailed. We shall now try to understand how two individuals become a marital system and how the two separate contracts find their operational expression in the couple's interactional contract.

THE MARITAL SYSTEM

When two individuals marry they become parts of a new social unit, a "marital system." This system is different from its component parts; it is not merely the sum of two personalities with individual hopes and needs but a new and qualitatively different entity.

Psychiatry only recently has conceptualized the individual as a system that functions as a subsystem in numerous multiperson systems. Each system affects and helps to determine the individual's behavior while he is functioning as part of that system. Each may influence the individual's behavior not only while he is in that system, but also when he steps out of it to function in another. In daily life we generally define a person in terms of how he or she functions in different systems: "She is a marvelous mother and an excellent teacher but a poor friend." "He is a considerate and loving

23

husband and a topnotch tennis player but not a very good father." Increasingly, the individual is being studied in relation to the larger systems of which he is a part. Even before Von Bertalanffy provided the theoretical conceptualization of general systems theory and applied it to living beings, psychiatric clinicians and theoreticians had moved intuitively toward a systems approach to marriage and the family. "General Systems Theory," Von Bertalanffy (1952) wrote, "is a new discipline whose subject matter is the formulation and derivation of those principles which are valid for systems in general," and he defined a system as sets of elements standing in interaction (1956).

When two people begin to interact and establish a continuing relationship, they communicate with each other verbally and nonverbally. They either follow courting rules or violate them in a predictable fashion in accordance with some variation of counterculture behavior. They establish ground rules for their conduct and methods of communication together, including stereotyped or shorthand messages and responses. They gradually but continually move toward becoming a system. If they marry or make a serious commitment to one another, each has a set of expectations of the relationship and of the other person.

In marriage, a man and a woman come together with their individual contracts and create a new system with a contract of its own. This contract may be comprised largely of features of both contracts, or it may be quite different from what either spouse had bargained for. Since many people are unaware of what they most deeply want, it is not unusual for them to feel that the third contract is "autonomous." Marital systems often serve purposes of which neither partner is aware.

Goals and purposes of the marital system can change from those that were first developed. For example, a couple may appear to agree as an essential of their married life that each is to pursue a career and that having children is very low among their priorities. Soon after marriage, however, both may feel pressure from within themselves and from other people to have children. The fact that they are married has led to the development of a *new goal* or *purpose* for the relationship.

The newly created system usually continues to take on additional purposes and functions, while earlier ones may be discarded. It may become invested in these functions to the detriment of its original functions as conceived by the individuals involved. The new functions may differ from, if not conflict with, the contract of one or both partners, or with the original implicit or explicit contract for their union. An example might be the husband who becomes so preoccupied with making money for his family and maintaining a high standard of living for them that he virtually cuts himself off emotionally from his wife and children. Here one function of the union has superseded other functions, frustrating the fulfillment of needs that his wife may have for companionship and affectionate exchange with him.

The new dyadic system becomes an autonomous "third party" whose purposes may complement or conflict with the marital goals (contractual parameters) of either the husband or the wife. Further, the effects of the marital system on either partner may deeply affect his or her functioning in other systems. The husband who feels pressured to provide a better standard of living for his family may become more assertive and/or effective at work; he may change from a relatively noncompetitive person to a competitive one. If he is not ambivalent he may be highly successful in the commercial world, but if he is ambivalent about his business competitiveness, he may ultimately lose out in his commercial system as well as in his family system.

The goals and functions of the marriage need to be continually redefined and clarified, since they can greatly modify the system. The tasks that must be carried out to achieve a goal—to make money, as in the example above—alter the system. The idea that *the task changes the system* is of great pertinence and has far-ranging implications for treatment (see Chapter 9).

The evolving marital system exists within an environment that affects it in various ways. Each spouse may operate independently a good part of the time, but a major part of his actions may still be influenced by the marital system even when he is not actually in the presence of his mate. The degree to which this is so varies from system to system, and even between individuals in the same system.

Indeed, the influence of the marital system on the same individual may vary greatly at different times.

In recent years the "style" of marital systems has been shifting from that of two closely intertwined persons with clearly designated, gender-determined roles to that of two "free" and independent people, each very much his or her own person. This is a trend, not a fait accompli. To the extent that it occurs the marital system tends to become more a system to which both spouses have a part-time commitment, similar to each partner's work system, school system, club system, or family of origin system. This concept of marriage as one of several systems for both spouses makes more understandable many of the changes now taking place in husband-wife relationships. Men have commonly had other sources of fulfillment and self-definition, whereas significant numbers of women are only now beginning to develop such extramarital and extrafamilial sources. For the person who has other significant areas that involve her or him creatively and emotionally, the marital system need not now represent survival importance; *it need not become the sole or major potential source of fulfillment or definition of self for the individual.*

The marital system comes into existence under the following conditions: when each individual makes an investment in the system consonant with his or her understanding of his marriage contract and his or her willingness and ability to give and to receive; when goals and purposes of the new system (marriage) are more or less defined on various levels of awareness and may be constantly reexamined and reaffirmed or changed; when roles, tasks, responsibilities, and functions for each person are assigned or assumed, in order to achieve the new goals and purposes; and when some method of communication is developed so that intelligence can be transmitted. Rules of the system are set up according to a single or double standard, in terms of each partner's *Zeitgeist* (his global as well as immediate environment—friends, family, colleagues, mass media, literature, nationalism and so on), and of each partner's marriage contract. It is best when all parameters of the relationship are negotiated in some way. This need not necessarily be done in advance but as the need arises.

The marital system most frequently causes antagonism and disappointment when a partner feels he could not have participated in building this monster which does not follow his specifications (his individual contract). When a single joint contract is arrived at in which goals, tasks, and purposes have been clearly stated, discussed, and accepted on all levels, the relationship is likely to improve, provided love and the will to move toward a harmonious existence together are present. Such a contract will probably not dispel all the unconscious or even conscious ambivalence of the spouses but such ambivalence need not destroy the system if it can be made available for further discussion. Developing the single contract is an ongoing process; since it describes a dynamic system, it is constantly changing and evolving. In the new single contract the quid pro quos are explicit and clear, so that each partner knows what he or she is expected to give and what to expect in return; only then can there be a basis for rational living. This does not imply any exclusion of the pleasures of mystery and serendipity that two people share as they go on discovering in each other.

The systems approach, once elucidated, offers the therapist a number of ways to treat marital dysfunction. The problem of the individual versus the systems approach is a false one, although it remains with us and continues to be marked by such questions as "How can a woman (man) marry and still be her (his) own self?" Entering a closely or loosely bonded relationship (system) does change the individual. The point is that it can be either a restrictive experience or one that opens up new vistas for growth.

The following section will elaborate on some of the factors that determine the essence of the marital system in action.

THE INTERACTIONAL CONTRACT

Although their individual marriage contracts form the basis for a couple's specific styles of interacting, other determinants contribute to the uniqueness of their interactions and the quality of their relationship.

In addition to each partner's own marriage contract, every couple has a common, single, largely nonverbalized *interactional contract*. This third contract is not at all the same as the single contract that evolves therapeutically as the disparate terms of the two individual contracts are resolved. That single contract deals with desires, what one is willing to give, the goals and purposes of the relationship for each person and for the marital system itself. The interactional contract is the operational one in which the two mates are trying to achieve the needs expressed in their separate contracts. It is the set of conventions and rules of behavior, of maneuvers, strategy, and tactics that have developed in their dealings with each other. It may have positive and negative elements.

In this interactional contract the two partners collaborate to establish and maintain a method of achieving sufficient gratification of their biological needs and both their adult and remaining infantile wishes. To remain viable, the marital system must accomplish this without arousing enough defensive anxiety or aggression to destroy the marriage as a unit capable of fulfilling its goals and purposes. The interactional contract deals with how a couple tries together to fulfill their separate goals and purposes. It is the *how*, not the *what*.

The individual contract of each spouse is very real for him or her, but, because it is not a static entity, it is not usually an accurate portrayal of all expectations or factors that determine behavior. The individual marriage contract is modified by interaction with the partner and often new clauses are added to "correct" the behavior of the mate or to provide a way of adapting to the relationship. Individual contracts help the therapist understand the individual ingredients that contribute to the couple's interactional system. The couple and the therapist may then be able to visualize the interactional contract that is in operation. In their interaction both partners are usually unaware of the nonverbal cues, as well as the verbal expressions, that contribute to the quality of their interaction. *This interactive contract provides the operational field in which each struggles with the other to achieve fulfillment of his own individual contract, including all the realistic, unrealistic, and ambivalent clauses that it contains*. It is the place where each partner tries to achieve his own objectives and force the other to behave in accordance with his design of the marriage.

The couple's interaction and interactional patterning *are* the structure of their relationship.

The interactional contract is unique for each couple because it evolves from the most basic wishes and strivings, as well as the defensive maneuvers, of each partner. Each spouse stimulates defensive maneuvers in the other that may or may not be characteristic of that partner in another relationship.

Each partner's behavioral style in the relationship can be assessed by means of the clinician's observations of the parameters of the three categories of contractual terms of the marriage contracts. These parameters may all be viewed in terms of what role the particular area plays *at this time* in the relationship. The most significant of the areas that determine behavior in intimate relationships are the 13 biological and intrapsychic parameters of category 2 (see pp. 13-16). Evaluating the emotional charge of each of these areas and the behavior that ensues as a result of their motivating forces and the defense mechanisms employed, we can then use a shorthand term in the form of a designative behavioral profile to describe the significant attitude of each partner in the interactional system (see Chapter 6). These profiles are a summary of the basic quality, flavor, and methodology of each mate's interaction with the other. Behavioral profiles are not absolute; they can be modified as the relationship continues. Each mate has many other behavioral characteristics, but for the profile I prefer to choose the main thrust of the current mode of interacting with the partner. In the course of an interaction, partners may exchange roles with each other or switch to another role as the interactional cycle or sequence proceeds.

Much of therapy consists of making the interactional contract and the partners' behavior in it more conscious, and of using this consciousness to work toward a new single contract that provides the basis for healthier interactions, interactions that will fulfill reasonable objectives and purposes and provide as full a measure as possible of adult goals for each individual and for the couple. Since the goals of the marriage are determined by the couple, the clauses of each individual contract come into the foreground and have to be dealt with. I try to make clear the salient positive and negative aspects of the separate contracts, so that each partner can bring his own more into line with necessity by resolving conflicting and ambivalent clauses within it. Awareness is not necessarily a prerequisite for change, but willingness to make the effort to change is necessary.

To complete this précis of a couple's interactional dynamics we must describe briefly the two kinds of bonding, expose our ignorance about love, and discuss some factors involved in mate selection. We will also discuss some of the categories of threats to the marital system and the system's reaction to these—its assertion toward fulfillment and its defensive reactions to threats from within and from outside the system.

Bonding

Tiger and Fox (1971) hypothesize that the bonding forces for human societies are the same as for other primate societies—the male control of females for sex and dominance (which leads to short-term bonding as I use the term) and the female use of the males for impregnation and protection. The parenting and family protective role of the male, *as structured by society*, then establishes the need for long-term bonding, which they believe is not necessarily biologically determined. Tiger and Fox suggest that we in effect talk ourselves into accepting long-term bonding (marriage) because society forces it upon the male. To make it palatable, the couple try to recapture the excitement and specialness of the early days of their love—usually without success. The authors sharply separate the mating bond and the parenting bond for the males. The former bond is biological; the latter culturally determined.

Whether it is biological and/or culturally determined, almost all late adolescents and adults of both genders have a need to bond. This need, although it is often influenced by hangovers of infantile wishes, as well as transferential factors in mate choice, also exists as a mature need. It involves feelings of love, sexual desire, a wish to be with one's mate a good measure of time, and the goal of functioning with the mate as a unit in the economic, child-bearing and rearing, and planning aspects of life. It means sharing hopes and expectations as well as present daily life, and involves a considerable community of interests. For most people it now includes allowance for each partner to participate in activities and relationships of various sorts with other persons.

There appear to be two types of bonding. The short-term is most often characterized by intense sexual and loving feelings, with anguish when separated, and from my observations usually lasts from a week up to three years. The second type is long-term bonding. Short-term bonding may turn into long-term, but the long-term variety may develop without necessarily going through the intensity of short-term bonding. The long-term type is, at its best, characterized by a deep acceptance of the other and of oneself, along with each person's limitations. Both partners assume that they will pass together through the various phases of their own life cycle and the marital cycle. There is loyalty, devotion to each other, and communality. Some partners sustain the intensity of short-term bonding passion for several decades; others settle into a less passionate but no less meaningful relationship. Strife, conflict, and a more or a less good resolution of important contractual differences may be part of the picture. Some long-term relationships are beautiful. Some are ugly—but something holds these couples together; at times the glue may be fear of aloneness, or hostility, or anger; other negative reasons for remaining bonded are inertia, fear of developing a new relationship, and questions concerning financial and other kinds of security.

Mate Choice

We will deal with just a few of the factors involved in mate choice that relate to the quality of a couple's interaction. The complexity of the object relations involved in marriage has been described by Dicks, who indicates that some regressive behavior in marriage is normal and necessary to the human dialogue (1963, 1967). He has further hypothesized, using Fairbairn's object relations concepts as applied to couples, that parts of the parent that were introjected as a child are later projected onto one's object choice. According to Dicks, one tends to choose a mate who, one unconsciously hopes, will play the game of accepting the projection. In other terminology we might say that one unconsciously seeks a mate who will fit into one's transferential needs and will respond with the appropriate countertransferential behavior. We see in the individual marriage contracts how people set themselves and their mates up for this. Even if the object choice were to behave as the transference or projection demands there would be difficulty, since there is usually ambivalence and conflict between the introject and the projection. These kinds of data become clear as we examine the individual contracts along with the interactional contract.

The extensive sociological literature on mate selection tends to substantiate the hypothesis that persons of similar racial, cultural, geographic, religious, and socioeconomic backgrounds are more likely to continue their marriages than those of dissimilar backgrounds. In our rapidly changing, relatively rootless society this may not continue to be so.

Love is a prime factor in mate selection and in determining the quality of couple relationships. However, we remain baffled by that common yet esoteric phenomenon called love and its role in human relationships. We can describe the behavior of "being in love," the fact that people can "fall in" or "fall out of" love, but we are unable to explain *why* a person is in love, what causes him to love or to stop loving. We know love by the evidence of its presence, but we do not know what it is. It is a polymorphous syndrome, but we do not know the etiological agent. We have many hypotheses, but we have not been able to isolate the variables that would allow us to predict. Is it a sickness, a transferential or regressive phenomenon, a figment of one's imagination and wishes, as when one says "Beauty is in the eye of the beholder"? Is it an instinctual need that one must gratify to get the greatest rewards and/or suffering in life? Why can love or its absence kill some people, whereas others are not moved much by love or by their apparent inability to achieve the love of someone whom they desire? Is it just that some people are "well defended" against their feelings while others "overreact"? Perhaps love is closely related to reproduction and the possibility for procreation must be a prerequisite. Yet this would not hold for homosexual couples who love each other, or for couples who are past child-bearing age. Some animals are at least as monogamous as we, if not more so. Love is not the same as monogamy; although many who love are monogamous, others are not.

Our various hypotheses seem only to reveal our ignorance. Perhaps we can only say that a phenomenon called love does exist, that it is a very important and strong force whose presence or absence is significant in determining the quality of dyadic relationships. When one partner of a couple is no longer in love, the process can rarely be reversed and love restored, even when both partners wish it. It is understandable why magic love potions and spells are still in demand.

Despite our ignorance about love, we are forced to appreciate the full force of its power. We cannot deny or ignore its existence any more than we can deny the existence of wind because we cannot see it. Love is an extremely important ingredient in the equation of a couple's interaction, although it remains an unknown number in that equation.

Mate choice is determined as much by feelings as by facts, as much by unconscious as conscious determinants. Both mates know that they desire the kinds of support and gratification that they can get only in consort with another person over a period of time. Yet, as their marital system develops its own rules, customs, and interactional style, which *are* their relationship, many couples find that the longed-for happiness and gratification do not ensue, or are only marginal. Spouses frequently appear to be a source of more unhappiness and frustration for each other than of happiness and gratification.

Unconscious determinants, as they play their role in mate selection, are no more infallible than conscious ones. Although the expressed primary objectives of marriage are greater pleasure, fulfillment, realization of biological, psychological, and culturally determined goals, the partnership more often than not does not sufficiently fulfill these positive goals. As clinicians and behavioral scientists, we have to discover, and if possible change, the factors that produce the negative interactions or question the validity of such goals. Is it possible to fulfill them?

Many people choose a mate whom they consider inferior—a compromise choice—as a result of their own anxiety about having the "superior" person they really would prefer but don't dare aspire to. Unless there is acceptance of one's mate and oneself, the marriage is in jeopardy. Other persons may choose a partner whose qualities they feel or sense will be complementary. For example, a person who is sexually shy and inhibited may select (or allow himself or herself to be selected by) a partner who is sexually open, uninhibited, and enjoys sex. Depending on their interaction, the shy partner may flower sexually and become more like the mate in this respect. Contrariwise, his own defenses or the style of the mate may increase anxiety over sexual fulfillment and he may withdraw sexually or become critical of the mate's sexual openness (this is what was wanted and perhaps is still wanted, but its enjoyment is not allowed). A sexually shy person may criticize the mate for his or her former sexual experiences and cause him to feel bestial. The mate, in turn, after a period of trying to overcome the spouse's anxiety and win trust, may become angry or threatened and react with defensive aggression or be injured and withdraw. The defensive interaction is then established between them and will continue either on a downhill course or on one of ups and downs to maintain the "just right" level of sexuality that keeps one mate's anxiety at an acceptable (to him) level at which he can function moderately well, and the other's just below the level that would cause this spouse to seek a resolution with someone else. Such a compromise is usually unstable and both partners are likely to have major distress reactions to relatively small stimuli from other sources.

Assertive and Defensive Marital Patterns

Assertive (or striving for fulfillment) and *defensive maneuvers are functions of the couple's individual and collaborative desires as expressed in the three marriage contracts as well as defenses set up to cope with the anxiety generated by approaching either fulfillment or frustration.* The defenses are also responsive to outside-the-system attacks and interference with achievement of the system's goals and purposes. The individual may react to stimuli both individually and as part of the couple system.

Assertion-defense reactions facilitate fulfillment of *all* clauses of *all* marriage contracts—the common marital goals of both spouses and the separate goals of both mates. Thus they help to fulfill the goals and purposes that are commonly agreed upon, as well as those in which the two individuals are at cross-purposes and those of each contract that are internally in conflict or produce ambivalence. When the two partners' objectives are mutually exclusive and not open to verbal negotiation, the assertion-defense patterns are set in motion to attempt to achieve resolution within the marital system. Under these conditions they are often a source of negative interaction. For example, each partner has goals designed to produce happiness, gratification, growth, or anything else that may be considered positive. Simultaneously, on other levels of awareness, there may be goals that are negative, destructive, or inhibitory in relationship to the positive ones. It is this inhibitory activity directed against the positive goals that produces much of the ambivalence and conflict within a relationship. The negative goals are not necessarily always unconscious. Assertion-defense reactions may be elicited with as much vigor to further the realization or defense of negative goals as of positive ones. Assertion-defense reactions are elicited by both individuals' conscious and unconscious wishes, needs, and anxieties. Those who have tried to alter a spouse's masochistic behavior in a relationship, for example, appreciate the strong resistance to change of a person's masochistic adaptation. The reactions of each spouse to the other frequently set up a reverberating system and escalations that may be positive or negative in regard to the marital system's goals and purposes. These interactions, including the acts and the feelings associated with them, *are* that couple's relationship.

The *assertion aspects* are efforts to move toward a goal, whether it is a positive or a negative one. The term "assertion" summarizes the forces that have to do with independence, activity, initiative, use of power or authority, control, and reasonably putting off present gratification to work toward a more distant goal—that is, any active measure designed to lead to goal achievement. The goals may be adult, infantile, or "neurotic"; no value judgment is put on them in terms of the factors that elicit the assertion-defense reactions. Conflict arises when the mates' desires to achieve a particular goal are not consonant or complementary or when a satisfactory quid pro quo has not been established on any level of awareness.

The *defense aspects* of the network are activities designed to defend and protect assertion from any threat of interference and from the production of anxiety. These may be positive or negative in respect to marital goal fulfillment and to their effect on the individuals. What is positive for the marriage is not always regarded by either or both spouses as positive for themselves, and what is positive for them may not be so for the marriage. Many of the common mechanisms of defense may have a negative or positive effect on the marital system's fulfillment of its purposes and goals, just as they may for the individual. A defense that works well for an individual but is injurious to the marital system is often elicited when one spouse feels threatened by a sense of growing closeness to the other. For instance, a husband, becoming anxious about being "discovered" as inadequate in some way in a close relationship with his wife, begins to intellectualize and to vitiate his warm and close feelings. The wife is hurt by his emotional withdrawal and unsuccessfully tries to maintain the closeness. If she is unsuccessful in reversing his distancing maneuvers, she then becomes upset and reacts by expressing anger, which is displaced onto inconsequential matters. The husband, experiencing his wife's apparently inappropriate anger, then feels confirmed in the correctness of his having withdrawn before "this unpredictable woman" could reject him. In this instance the husband defended himself from anxiety by insulating himself and putting distance between himself and his wife so that he would not be discovered as inadequate. The wife defended herself from her resulting anxiety by not dealing with its source—the threat of abandonment— as her husband withdrew emotionally. Instead, she expressed anger and irritation over minor facets of their daily life. Both partners had a basic fear of abandonment; neither could deal openly with it. Yet, paradoxically, it was just this fear that caused them to practice brinkmanship with a cardinal purpose of their mariage—the assurance that each would never be abandoned. Their individual defenses had produced interactions that ran counter to the marital system's purpose.

The defense part of the assertion-defense network may respond to threats from three major sources: 1) either spouse's intrapsychic operations; 2) the system apart from the intrapsychic dynamics of either partner—their interaction, the goals and purposes of the system or the methods chosen to accomplish these goals, and so on; and 3) objective reality threats outside the marital system. Whatever the source that evokes the defensive maneuvers, the reaction by either spouse affects the entire marital system.

The defense arm of assertion-defense reactions can use the defense mechanisms of either subsystem or of the marital system itself. When the subsystems work together, the defense is considered good marital unity and teamwork if it is appropriate to the outside reality. If not appropriate, it may be considered a *folie à deux*. The marital system or either partner may also respond with assertion, or by becoming demoralized. In other couples or under different circumstances the system may respond by shifting the focus of its activities—such as "let's take a vacation" or "let's have another child"—to save itself. That is, the marital system may deflect its energies from dealing with the causes to less anxiety-provoking attempts at solution. A *folie à deux* may be regarded as a system-defensive maneuver in which the two partners act or perceive in unison. Even if this is not consonant with reality, and further removes the couple from others, it tends to preserve the integrity of the system and its own inner "reality"

MECHANISMS OF DEFENSE

The defense mechanisms discussed here often defend the marital system, transcending individual ego and/or id defense maneuvers—although they also serve to defend the individual's ego in the marital relationship, and to control impulses and their related affects. Individual defense mechanisms are readily elicited within the marital relationship, as might be anticipated, because of the interdependence and the transferential and regressed behavior that the contracts reflect, and also because of the actual potential for fulfillment and disappointment of one's adult and childish wishes that exists in a committed relationship. This potential for fulfillment and/or frustration makes bonding the intensely affective relationship that it is and accounts for the low threshold at which each partner's defense mechanisms are likely to be triggered.

Manifestations of the defense mechanisms are a major part of what mates show to each other in their transactions and therefore are very often what each reacts to within the relationship. Hence the defense mechanisms are one of the three major determinants of marital system interaction (along with categories 1 and 2 of the individual contracts).

To summarize, the mechanisms of defense that are manifested by one or both mates in their interaction are the same that may be observed in the individual ego's defense systems against impulses and their related affects. The forces that activate the defense mechanisms can be within the individual (intrapsychic), within the marital system, or within objective reality outside the marital system. Overall, these mechanisms can have a positive effect toward fulfillment of the common and/or individual goals of the partners or a negative effect by interfering with that fulfillment. They influence a significant number of the partners' transactions and contribute to the quality, style, and expressed rules of their marital system. Frequently partners collude in the use of mechanisms. One type of collusion, for example, results in a kind of *folie à deux* in which both defend themselves against exposure of the fallacy of a marital myth, such as "we are a loving couple who never argue or fight," or against admission of marital difficulties by placing the blame for their problems on other persons or events.

The following defense mechanisms are especially important in working with couples. Definitions of the mechanisms (see Freud, 1966, and Fenichel, 1945) are not included except where I use them in a particular way.

1. *Sublimation* is a defense that often goes with acceptance of a reality limitation within the relationship for either or both spouses. Sometimes there may be a common or "system" sublimation; for example, a couple who both wanted children but were unable to conceive founded a children's summer camp where they were called "Mother Connie" and "Daddy Chick" by 90 children.

2. *Altruistic surrender* of one's own yearnings and desires is most obviously and commonly observed when a wife supports her husband's fulfillment while eschewing her own, except as secondary to his. Former generations of women were trained from birth to do this.

3. *Regression* is one of the most popular mechanisms used in marriage. Almost invariably the therapist observes regressed behavior on the part of one or both spouses in the first session. The transferential components in marriage and mate selection appear to make this defense an inevitable choice for many couples. One spouse, male or female, may assume a "permanent" regressed stance with the other or both may be regressed.

Yet such spouses may relate with people other than the mate in a perfectly mature and appropriate manner.

4. *Repression* is a common defense used to cope with impulses and affects generated in the marital system that produce anxiety.

5. *Reaction formation* is very commonly used in the marital system, especially to obviate aggressive and hostile feelings. For instance, one wife who had already unconsciously made a decision to leave her husband suddenly felt compelled to give him expensive gifts. Reaction formation may also be used as a defense against warm, loving, and/or sexual feelings. The source of such anxiety in the adult is commonly related to the fear of becoming vulnerable to rejection or of being controlled by the threat of loss of someone loved. Hence the adult may not allow himself to feel the loved one's full importance to him. This defense is not as frequently initiated by an infantile source of anxiety due to fear of libidinal feelings as one might expect.

6. *Denial* of those manifestations of the feelings or behavior of one's spouse or oneself that would disturb the marital system's basic assumptions and both its modus vivendi and modus operandi is a common defense. The *perceptual defense*, a particularly important type of denial mechanism in marital relationships, is an active, unconscious process of avoiding perception of the true significance of what the senses take in. To perceive the true significance would be too anxiety-provoking, or the response demanded by the true perception of the situation would be too anxiety-laden. For example, a wife may fail to allow herself to perceive that her husband frequently makes denigrating remarks to her. She perceives them as appropriately critical and tries to adjust her behavior, failing to see his hostility to her. To perceive his hostility would mean she would have to challenge what he is doing and to do that would be too anxiety-producing.

7. *Inhibition* of impulses includes not only "instinctual" impulses such as the sexual ones, but any impulse to feel, think, act, or say anything which might arouse anxiety or cause the mate's disapproval or cause him or her to think less of the mate. For example, a woman inhibited her taste and desire for the cuisine of her native country and deprecated it when the subject arose in social situations because her husband, who was brought up in Paris, had once thoughtlessly referred to her country's fare as peasant food. Inhibition of sexual feelings is common in marriage and is a frequent presenting complaint. In diagnosis it is difficult to differentiate inhibition of sexual response to a

desirable person from lack of desire for someone who is not seen as sexually attractive.

8. *Introjection, incorporation, and identification* with one's spouse contribute negatively and, occasionally, positively to the unity of the marital system. They can be most destructive when used as a means of submitting to a partner and losing one's own individuality. Introjection—swallowing—is an attempt to regain the omnipotence previously projected onto adults. Incorporation, although an expression of "love," objectively destroys the object as an independent person in the external world. Incorporation may be an expression of hostility, and may also be a way of identifying with and coping with a hostile object.

9. *Reversal*, or turning against oneself, is very common among couples and is often manifested by one partner's becoming transiently or chronically depressed by the fear of acting to remedy a disturbing trend in the relationship. The anger that is generated is turned against oneself.

10. *Displacement* of strong feelings from the actual cause to a less emotionally laden issue is almost universal. It is so generally understood that it is often used as a comedy gambit in family television shows. In real life it may be humorous or unimportant, but it can also be extremely destructive.

11. *Projection* is a common mechanism through which one endows the spouse with one's own feelings or impulses.

12. *Intellectualization* can be very obtrusive and irritating to a mate who seeks greater closeness with the intellectualizing one. People often marry with the idea that love will shortly melt away this defense. In other instances the need to intellectualize and to vitiate affective responses does not emerge until after marriage, when the couple operates closer together. Love and closeness sometimes overcome intellectualization; more often they elicit it in the prone individual as a defense against exposure and closeness.

13. *Undoing* (magical), a primitive mechanism, is not an effective interactional defense because the compulsion to repeat the same act is often so irritating that it elicits intolerance and hostility. Symptoms that represent expiation belong in the undoing category, because the idea of expiation is an expression of belief in the possibility of magical undoing.

14. *Fantasy* can be used defensively as well as for pleasure gratification. When it is a defense, fantasy reverses the real situation so that denial is sustained and a threat to the system is blocked, or at least postponed, by sweeping feelings about the source of disturbance under the carpet.

Defenses are important determinants of the couple's interactional contract. They can be effective in facilitating normal goal achievements, and can relieve stress on the marital system; they can also lead to dissension and abrasiveness in a marriage as the couple use their defenses in interaction. Defensive maneuvers can be anxiety-producing to the mate, cause distancing, be threatening, excluding, and often evoke negative reactions. The partners will then react, usually in some predictable fashion within the rules of the couple system, and so the conflict escalates. The therapist needs to identify the defense mechanisms used by each spouse and to deal with them as he thinks best in line with his therapeutic approach.

When anxiety is reduced by the interplay of defensive and assertive maneuvers, the couple may well have completed a cycle or seesaw of changing or reversing behavioral profiles with one another that is their characteristic adaptive dance. If all has gone well in this process they then return to their steady state of existence together, poised and ready for the next cycle (this cycle is illustrated in the Smith case in Chapter 5).

SOME SPECIAL MARITAL SYSTEM DYNAMICS

A few aspects of marital dynamics that have been given insufficient attention in the marital and family therapy literature require closer examination. These dynamics, which play an important role in many marital systems, are singled out here to illustrate the variety of important material that we can readily discover within the activity of the marital dyad and to illustrate an approach to a couple's interaction. An understanding of the dynamics of the marital system is ready to be mined. It lies like ore in an open pit; we do not even have to go down deep before reaching a vein that has a high yield.

The dynamics that will be described are: the double bind as manifested in marriage; the double parental transference; mates' susceptibility to similar sources of anxiety although their mechanisms of defense may differ greatly; and the concept of the uneven development of different parameters of the marital system.

Double Bind

Don and Jane Washington, married four years, both work. Don cannot dispel the anger, resentment, disappointment, or fear he feels toward Jane, because of his intrapsychic conflict. Hence much of what he does in relation to Jane ends up in a wrangle. For example, Don wants Jane to share decision-making power but he also fears that Jane will then dominate their relationship. Don offers to give power to Jane and then struggles against the domination he believes he will suffer because Jane will then have control. Many people believe there is just so much power in a couple system, and if one partner has some power, it is often felt that it must have been taken away from the other. Jane is therefore caught in a double bind. She has been told that her sharing of power with Don will be welcomed. Power is thrust upon her, but when she exercises it she feels Don's displeasure and tension. She cannot please either way.

Originally described in terms of parent-child relationships (Bateson *et al.*, 1956), the double bind is an equally important mechanism in the marital system. In this instance there is no problem of communication because the message received does accurately reflect the sender's (Don's) conflict and ambivalence. The receiver (Jane) has interpreted correctly when she recognizes that no matter how she responds she cannot possibly please Don in this transaction. Because Jane must deal with Don, she cannot escape from the transactional field. She reacts with depression as she feels powerless (reversal, as a defense) and her assertion-defense reactions feed back into the couple's system. Her message, conveyed by her depression, then activates the potentially negative reactions of Don, who can't tolerate her affect and in turn becomes overtly angry with her. His anger releases hers and they are off and escalating until they reach a crescendo, become distant and slowly simmer down—but with no resolution of the real problem. The transaction was inevitably destined to make trouble because of Don's conflict over his own mutually exclusive ambivalent impulses.

This example of the marital double bind highlights the need to be aware of both intrapsychic and system-interactional factors. To deal adequately with a situation of this nature requires staying with the here-and-now interaction and the feelings involved, as well as being aware of the intrapsychic forces. The therapist must also develop methods of bypassing or resolving, and thus neutralizing, the conflict in the partner who sends the double message. This can be accomplished in a variety of ways, including confrontation to force recognition that Don sends double-bind messages, or insight into what the conflict is that spawns the message with the "no win" payoff. The ambivalence, even if not completely resolved, can often be defused of its negative potential when both partners are aware of its presence. Parenthetically, the description of the Washingtons also illustrates an important aspect of their interactional contract, their collusion to remain distant from one another. Distance is maintained when Don's anger releases Jane's and their fighting escalates, closing off what closeness had been developing when Don gave his double-bind message.

Double Parental Transference

The transferential determinants that play so important a role in mate selection and later are the source of so much marital system malfunctioning are well known. Less known is the *simultaneous* mother and father transference to the mate. We are accustomed to considering the usual transference to one's mate that has its origin in the person's adaptation to the parent of the opposite gender, and we also see transference reactions that are based on early feelings toward the parent of the same gender. In subtle aspects of the marriage contract we may also find that patients have significant simultaneous mother and father transferences that determine the projection of what they want or expect onto their mate, to whom they ascribe fictitious attributes, ideals, or behavior. This double transference may become an important determinant of double-binding messages that express the sender's conflict and become a source of disturbance in the relationship. Double transference is frequently seen in marital therapy and is evident in many contracts. It will be clearly illustrated at length in the Smith case (see Chapter 5).

Similar Anxieties, Different Defenses

How mates deal with each other's anxiety and defense mechanisms is one of the most crucial determinants of the quality of a marriage.

Ideally, one of the important services partners can perform for each other is to react in a positive way to allay each other's anxiety. A common disservice—yet an inevitable aspect of many spouses' interactions—is to compound the partner's anxiety by reacting with one's own anxiety. For example, a husband needed to maintain his image of his wife as a strong person who could handle all adversity. He was distressed when she would, at times, become anxious and ask for help or reassurance. The husband's need not to perceive her as "weak" caused him to use a perceptual defense, so that he did not "hear" her call for help. Instead he would become impatient and angry with her about something trivial or would withdraw when she most needed him. She would then feel there was no one for her to turn to. Over the years her expectations that her husband would be there when needed were repeatedly disappointed. His failure to respond to her need caused her to lose her respect and love for him.

Much of the behavior that closes off communication and intimacy and increases distance and anger is a result of the operation of defense mechanisms. The intent is not necessarily to injure one's partner or the relationship, but all too often the defense does just that.

It is common for two spouses to be sensitive to the same underlying source of anxiety. In the example that follows, it is the fear of abandonment, a very common source of anxiety. This deep fear is usually obscure to both spouses because they see only each other's defenses, not the source of the anxiety. For example, Carol reacts to her fear of abandonment by demanding reassurance. To her, love is expressed in terms of being taken care of materially. When anxious she demands gifts and attention, despite her own ability to give love emotionally. Walter, her husband, has a counterphobic reaction to his fear of abandonment and continually surrounds himself with friends and sycophants. These two spouses were often hurt, depressed, or angry because of the effects each one's defenses had on the other. Carol's demands pushed Walter further away because they caused him to consider her exploitive and jealous. On the other hand, if Walter had understood and acted in a way to reassure Carol, the couple need not have had many of their negative transactions. Conversely, Walter's need for constant company was akin to overlighting the house when one has a neurotic fear of the dark.

It made Carol feel that he was not satisfied with her, that she could not fulfill his needs for meaningful love and friendship. She feared he would abandon her; her fears increased her need for material reaffirmation of his love. From there on their feelings escalated as each exchange appeared to prove the worst fears of each. If Carol had understood and supported Walter's need for friends and had not felt threatened, fights need not have ensued. (However, it is not my intent to convey that this would be the best or only solution.)

Mates often unrealistically hope that the other can handle for them the situations, real or imagined, that make them anxious. The similarity of the anxiety-trigger for both spouses usually becomes clear as the individual marriage contracts are reviewed. This is why the shy person who fears abandonment will often marry the extroverted, seemingly socially at ease person who also fears abandonment. They each look for a negative complementarity that appears to be there and is, but only on the surface. It cannot supply the desired support. The first recognition of their underlying similarity may produce anger and frustration and even a sense of having been deceived or cheated, but usually, when both spouses understand that they are sensitive to the same anxiety-provoking stimuli, it is easier for them to develop a new positive complementarity. Openness usually leads them to find satisfactory means of supporting each other as each one needs it.

An awareness of the mechanisms of defense, and of how each mate's defenses may make the other angry, depressed, or anxious, is important to the therapist searching for basic causes of marital discontent. The negative manifestations of the spouse's defenses are often what are seized upon to prove one's worst fears (transference, the projection of introjects) about one's mate. The defenses should be included in the terms of the contracts, at least as developed by the therapist if they are beyond the couple's awareness—for example, "When I see you anxious, I will deny it. I want you to be strong."

Uneven Development

Just as individuals and nations do not develop all their potential resources evenly and simultaneously, so the marriage contracts make clear that there is uneven development in the parameters of the marital system. We may consider a parameter healthy or functioning well when it fulfills its purpose for the individual or the marriage. Some parameters do not function well, or are "under" or "over" developed. They may interfere with or frustrate the realization of their goal or purpose.

In treatment, as we work with the "over" and "under" developed and conflictual parameters in the two contracts, we often find that we give one area a push, another a shake there, and gradually (or sometimes suddenly) the picture changes so that an area that had lagged behind suddenly shoots forward.

Working back and forth among parameters or contractual terms is a common and necessary strategy of treatment. Not all areas need be dealt with directly in the course of therapy. A shift in one often changes others. Two important concepts emerge that are of concern to us at this point. The first is that relationships, and the people involved, usually exist at varying levels of maturity or competence and the development of maturity of their various parameters is uneven. The second is that effecting a change in some parameters often produces shifts that create further changes elsewhere in the system and its subsystems.

Therapy is a little like tuning a stringed instrument. A string is tightened here, another there, and then one is attended to a few notes up or down the scale. Each tightening or loosening changes the tension of the entire instrument, including the frame to which the strings are secured. This first round then necessitates a second, and perhaps additional rounds of tightening and loosening. In this step-by-step process a state of fine tuning is finally achieved in which the frame and the strings are a harmonious entity, a well-functioning system ready to carry out the purposes it was created for. Some instruments—like some marriages—are more susceptible to getting out of tune than others.

These four examples of marital dynamics do not begin to exhaust the list of phenomena that we find as we try to understand the complexities of the committed dyadic interactional system. They are but a few among many illustrations of interactional dynamics. They do indicate an approach to thinking about how the couple's system may affect behavior and demonstrate the challenges to the therapist's will to help, as well as to his curiosity and skill.

4

Use of the Contracts in Therapy

How THE CONTRACTS ARE TO BE used will affect the way the data are gathered and processed or assessed.

FOR WHOSE INFORMATION AND USE ARE THE DATA?

Data obtained by structuring the hitherto amorphous, largely un-expressed and unconscious marriage contracts are for the use of both the couple and the therapist. When husband and wife struggle to put their individual contracts on paper, the resulting information often clarifies their thoughts about their marriage and themselves and mo-bilizes the first efforts toward constructive action. (A reminder list of the contractual areas appears in Appendix 1.) The couple's written contracts, if they are asked to prepare them, have to be supple-mented with information gathered by the therapist. The contracts may be used after the first session or later in the treatment process, depending on the couple's readiness and willingness to tackle and work on basic problems together.

The contract areas are also intended as a checklist for the thera-pist's use. He may choose what he wishes to use and may add items as needed. The contracts are not meant to be a "test" of the patients; rather they are a notation of each partner's feelings and needs at this point in their relationship.

47

From the first, treatment can be centered on the two separate contracts, enabling the therapist to pinpoint sources of malfunction within the marital system rather quickly and to begin working out a schematic model of the couple's probable interactional contract. He can thus avoid becoming enmeshed in an indecipherable welter of complaints and countercomplaints that often spiral to the point of leaving both spouses exhausted on the battlefield and the therapist feeling as helpless as a U.N. peacekeeping observer.

Only once in my experience has serious disruption resulted from a couple's writing out their contracts. In this instance the wife in a 28-year marriage read her husband's contract without his consent and found a reference to an extramarital affair. They both focused their anger on me for "causing" this incident to be brought to light, and withdrew from therapy. The experience of uniting against me— the enemy who threatened their system and who became a convenient scapegoat—may have been therapeutic, since it was one of the few times they had pulled together in many years, but, of course, it would have been better if they had stayed in treatment and tried to work through their problems. It is doubtful whether this would have occurred in any case, because the wife found conjoint therapy too threatening to the status quo of the marriage. For her, it was safer to maintain the marriage with all its malfunctions than to relinquish her control of the marital system. The husband, after having engineered his hostile shot at his wife by leaving his contract where she was sure to see and read it, retired to his usual acquiescent style. His compliance in the withdrawal from therapy was another manifestation of his masochistic collusion with his wife to maintain their status quo.

The marriage contract is a dyadic and individual phenomenon as well as a therapeutic and educational concept that tries to spell out the vague and intuitive. It penetrates to the core of any significant dyadic relationship and rapidly unmasks what makes the relationship good, poor, or impossible. The individual contracts are the products of the two patients and are real; they have existed in reality even if they have not been fully verbalized before. Unlike a complicated x-ray scan, the two contracts are not only intelligible to the trained professional, but they can also be easily "read" and understood by the spouses themselves. The therapist can, however, elicit additional unconscious contractual terms and use these, too, in the couple's behalf during treatment.

How Are the Data Collected?

There need not be, nor can there be, a rigid method of collecting the necessary information. Data on the first (conscious, verbalized) and second (conscious, not verbalized) levels of awareness can be supplied by the couple during the sessions as well as by their responses to the therapist's request that they each write out their contracts. Explaining the concept of the two contracts and giving them a reminder list of topics often facilitates the couple's understanding of what is expected of them, and at the same time lessens some of the fear of putting their thoughts into writing. I have found that the reminder list is usually well received by couples in all socioeconomic and cultural groups. The contracts need not necessarily be written out by the patients, but my experience demonstrates that as I have become less anxious about asking couples to write their contracts, the positive response to doing so has increased.

The therapist can use the reminder list as a guide to himself in obtaining contractual information verbally. This is an effective means but somewhat time consuming, and it may tend to infantilize the couple. For these reasons—and because each spouse may be a little more forthright when alone—my preference is to use what the patients can produce on their own at home as well as material elicited during sessions.

A request that the couple write out the contracts is contraindicated if 1) the partners see their problem as confined to one specific area and will not consider further exploration at this time; 2) one mate has a secret of major proportions, whose maintenance would negate the entire process; or 3) one mate is so paranoid and/or destructive that the technique would be counterproductive. Some couples are never asked to write out their contracts because I surmise that they will be resistant and find it impossible to look within themselves. Others would be unable to talk to each other without using the information in a hostile way.

When couples come with the intent of separating or divorcing, I may ask them to write out their contracts as best they can reconstruct them as of the time they married and to note where they feel they or the mate have not fulfilled the terms. I may also ask them what their ideal contract would be today. I do this because some couples do not want to separate and on one level are asking to be stopped from doing so and this may give them time, as well as a face-saving excuse to try once more to resolve their differences. In any case, two people who have been seriously involved owe it to themselves to take their time in separating and to learn from the experience of their relationship.

Sometimes only one partner is willing to write out a contract. Most often it is the one who is less motivated to maintain the relationship who fails to do so. Nevertheless, failure to bring in a contract should not by itself be taken as evidence of a desire to withdraw from or to sabotage improvement of the marital system. Although writing out one's contract seems like a formidable task, all who have done so (with the possible exception of the couple referred to earlier) felt well rewarded. The resistance to doing so is understandable. Many are reluctant to examine their most important adult relationship. It is threatening for most people to assay their own role and that of their mate—whether their marriage does give them what they want or not. Further, some therapists, reluctant to examine their own situation, may sometimes support a couple's resistance or reluctance to do so.

As treatment proceeds further data are gathered during individual or conjoint sessions with the therapist. Questions along the lines of "what do you wish, want, need, expect, or fantasy would be ideal," with regard to various aspects of the relationship are addressed to each partner. Reversing the question and asking one spouse what the other wants or expects is also fruitful because it elicits cross-discussion and corroboration or disagreement as well as exposing misconceptions.

Data on the third level, the terms of the contract that are beyond awareness, are naturally the most difficult to obtain and are more controversial since often they depend on theoretical constructs or suppositions. The first step is to take a brief history of each spouse and attempt to reconstruct latent content from conscious interactions. Dream material may also be requested and examined, and the individual's understanding of his own parents' relationship and his guesses about his own parents' contracts are helpful pieces of information.

In the short run the greatest aid in getting to unconscious material is each spouse's understanding of the other's deepest needs. The extent to which spouses are sensitive to each other's psychological needs and conflicts is both astonishing and understandable. The written contracts often reveal great understanding of each other's needs, even among patients who have not previously had any type of therapy, and the conjoint interview is extremely helpful in getting beyond the conscious material included in the written contracts. Human beings know more about themselves and those close to them than they admit *until pressed to do so*. Seemingly unsophisticated people can reveal insight into their own and their partners' deep conflicts over gender identity, power, dependency, passivity versus activity and so on. Clues are the thoughts, fears, misgivings they have hitherto pushed away.

I frequently offer tentative hypotheses about the third level of the couple's contracts, which may then be confirmed or negated by the reactions of the spouses. These hypotheses are often interpretations, and, although exploratory and diagnostic, they are also part of the therapeutic work. For example, in a conjoint session I said to a woman who was very ascerbic and defensive, "I am sitting here trying to imagine how you must have been hurt for you to be so sharp with David and to hold him off at such a distance. You are afraid to let him see the parts of you he will like." This combination of hypothesis, observation, and interpretation released a flood of feelings that allowed her to be more open and less defensive.

In the first session the contracts may begin to emerge from the material of the session. The therapist can then proceed to organize this information. Ordering of the data can begin immediately, with the three classifications of contractual terms as reference points: 1) terms dealing with the expectations of what each partner wants from and will give to the marriage and what goals and purposes the marital system has evolved; 2) those terms that are based on biological and intrapsychic determinants, as well as each individual's characteristic mechanisms of defense; and 3) the terms that are the secondary manifestation of categories 1 and 2, and emerge as the complaints the mates have about each other. As the two individual contracts emerge, so too does the interactional contract—the rules, strategies, and tactics of the relationship.

Wife and husband are regarded as an open system of two interdependent persons. I begin immediately to speculate to myself about each partner's contract and how congruent, complementary, or mutually exclusive different parts of the two contracts may be. The data are tentatively organized as they surface. I am ready to reorder information quickly as the picture continues to develop. I try not to have an investment in maintaining my early hypothesis. I *do not* put top priority in the first session on gathering a specific amount of contract information. What has brought the couple to treatment and what they urgently want to deal with or communicate to each other and to me comes first. The history unfolds dynamically, as does contractual information. The leads I follow come from the couple's necessities.

After the pressure of the couple's urgency is reduced, I begin to flesh out the picture by determining how loving and considerate they are to each other, the extent of the investment they have in staying together, background material, observation of their interactive, communicative, and cognitive styles, their values, respect for each other, the reality stresses in their lives, effects of other family members, and so on. I regard as significant the factors and incidents that arouse feelings of conflict, disharmony, non-caring, and pain, as well as those that fulfill the purpose of the marital system and/or expressions of love, concern, caring, and tenderness. Structuring of the individual and interactional contracts can be developed from the couple's interaction—what they say and how they say it, their body language, and my hypotheses deduced from the totality of their productions. Additional clues come from the history of their parents' marriages, and how each related as a child and relates now to parents and siblings. Each spouse's view of the mate's current relationship with his own parents is often illuminating. I inquire further into what each spouse expected of the marriage and of the partner and what each wished to give in return at the time of courtship, and how these expectations have worked out since.

Although the main modality of therapy is the conjoint session, it is important in the first session or very soon thereafter to see each spouse alone for at least a short time. Mates are entitled to areas of privacy, and important parts of the aware-but-not-verbalized (to the partner) terms of the contract may be expressed to the therapist at these times.

Exactly when to introduce the concept of the marriage contract to patients cannot be rigidly determined. First of all, the therapist must be convinced of its value if he is to employ it effectively. Second, no questionnaires or forms should be used on a routine basis. Whether the reminder list is responded to at home or worked out in conjoint sessions with the therapist, the contracts should not be introduced routinely on the first, second, or any other visit. The proper timing for them is when the pressure of immediate complaints is alleviated and when it is determined that both spouses wish to work on changing the relationship.

I often introduce the concept by discussing with the couple the fact they are two closely interdependent persons but that the dreams, hopes, and expectations that each had of the other, of himself, and of the marriage have somehow turned into something that was not anticipated. I then elaborate on the contracts, extracting from what they have already expressed some of their contractual understandings and misunderstandings. I try to illustrate to them the sources of some of their feelings of disappointment, anger, depression, or self-pity. If the evidence is present in the data, I show them how each feels cheated because he believes he has kept his part of the bargain but his mate has not fulfilled some terms of a contract that was never agreed upon. The need to point the finger at who violated "The Contract" first is almost universal; self-righteousness and self-justification are often the first hurdle to be overcome in treatment.

At this point I may give the couple the reminder list of the contractual parameters to help them clarify their present contract. Some couples may have already touched some of the salient points during the session and have already begun to develop their individual contracts.

Later in therapy I may ask the couple to begin to write out together sections of a single contract that both can subscribe to. By then we have usually moved far along in this direction, although sometimes we are not aware of just how far until the more formal work together on a new joint contract begins. A couple's attempt to work on a single contract often stimulates an exchange that is a valuable new experience for them. The therapist must keep in mind that the contract is a tool that, to be useful, must be employed with great flexibility, particularly as the most significant aspects are often pre- or unconscious.

One couple, after two months of stormy therapy during which they separated and moved back together twice, wrote out their individual contracts. When they returned with them they said they had now decided to separate. The process of writing on paper what each wanted made each independently know he did not want to be married anymore and that the marriage had been a mismatch from the start. In this case the result was positive—it had been clear to me for several weeks that divorce was inevitable for this couple. I had asked them to write out their contracts in the hope that each would arrive independently at the same conclusion. In many similar cases using the contracts as a confrontation technique has been very useful. (See Chapter 11 for a series of couple's contracts that had a variety of outcomes.)

The interactional contract is determined by observing how the couple interact together in the conjoint session, by their own reportage of their transactions, and by the way they carry out their duties and responsibilities of being a couple. Videotaping or audiotaping of sessions is an excellent way to observe interactional patterns at work, and the instant playback confronts the couple directly with how they deal with each other. With these techniques we can help patients turn more quickly to making less injurious transactions.

How the Data Are Assessed

The assessment process begins with the couple's and the therapist's noting where the partners' contracts agree or complement each other and where they conflict. (For further discussion of congruence, complementarity, and conflict, see Chapter 8.) The connections among complaints, interactions, and contract terms have to be made by the therapist in his assessment. If one spouse has given considerable weight to an issue not mentioned by the other, the therapist can ask about the point and note the response. I frequently start arbitration or negotiation of several difficult areas at once, to test the give-and-take potential and motivation of each spouse. Areas that resist simple quid pro quo solutions often derive from significant intrapsychic factors and a basic distrust of self and/or the other. These become the basis for multifaceted therapeutic work. When the partners have written out their contracts it is a simple task to mark off with a colored pencil the problem areas of each contract, as well as where there are meaningful differences between the two partners. A nonresponse to a particular subject can often be indicative of a troublesome area.

Once areas of congruence, complementarity, and conflict have been identified, the therapist helps the couple evaluate the emotional needs underlying their behavioral patterns. Obviously, behavior that places the most stress on the marital system receives the most attention. For example, a man may have a deep psychological need to have his wife be parental to him. If his wife has a complementary need to be parental, no conflict need arise. But if the wife's conscious or unconscious recognition of her husband's need produces anxiety in her, she may put pressure on him to "be a man" and take care of himself. He may react to this "lack of giving" or "understanding" by withdrawing, and the problem becomes exaggerated without either spouse knowing why they have become so dissatisfied and unhappy with each other.

The therapist can use this classification of contractual terms to help organize the data he seeks and receives from couples. Whether expressed in these particular terms or not, the essence of most marital therapy, by whatever means it is practiced, educates the partners to the need for a single, mutually acceptable contract and works with them toward that end. Removing the blocks in the way of achieving a workable single contract, along with setting up mechanisms for review of it when necessary, constitutes the process of therapy and in itself becomes a goal of treatment. Consequently it is necessary for the therapist to possess a knowledge of dyadic dynamics, systems theory, individual psychology and psychodynamics, and a wide range of techniques deriving from behavior therapy, transactional analysis, Gestalt therapy, psychoanalysis, and marital therapy. Anything that will help to produce planned and desired change, and that will give the couple the necessary insight and equipment to function together *as a system* and *as individuals* can and must be called into play by the therapist.

Ideally, the contract approach becomes a lifelong project, initiated with the help of the therapist and sustained by the couple themselves. It is not an end in itself but is designed to help the couple achieve their goals and purposes. Contracts do exist operationally for all couples. Our job as therapists is to try to call them forth into full consciousness and to use them constructively.

5

The Smiths: A Marriage in Transition

"After seven years it's like the cycle of marriage has had a beginning, a middle and an end—it's a cycle or like a spiral. At the end of seven years we were in the death throes of that phase of it. Now it's taking off on its second spiral. There's a lot to be said about sticking with something, because if you would give up at the seven there is a death, but there is a resurrection coming if you can just stick with it. In this resurrection everything now has a double entendre, a richer meaning, it's more interesting."

SUSAN SMITH

THE CASE OF THE SMITHS not only demonstrates how marriage contracts can be used in therapy, but also illustrates the particular multifaceted, flexible, eclectic approach that I try to use. The Smiths, their contracts, and their therapy will serve as a clinical reference point for the concepts discussed in subsequent chapters.

My prime interest in this presentation is to illustrate the use of the marriage contracts as a conceptual and operational tool. Any number of treatment approaches, theories, or techniques could have been used instead of the ones described here. In fact, as the reader follows the case, I am sure he or she will see many instances where particular transactions could have been handled differently, or he may disagree with the entire theoretical and technical approach. The point here is to judge how the marriage contracts may be used conceptually and as guidelines to therapeutic intervention within the framework of the reader's own convictions.

The contract concept can be useful and valuable within the framework of almost any theoretical or technique system that allows for the interplay and validity of both transactional and intrapsychic aspects as determinants of the quality of a marriage. It provides a means of understanding these dual determinants and a way of using them therapeutically.

In practice a case may not be detailed to this extent, but here, for demonstration and didactic purposes, I want to share the process with the reader as fully as possible.

Susan Smith, aged 30, and Jonathan, 32, had been married seven years and had a son of five and a daughter of two when they came for treatment. The husband voiced their complaints first in the conjoint session: "Too much bitterness, not enough satisfaction, we fight about unimportant things." From Mrs. Smith: "I wanted a strong husband but not too strong or I would not be free. Once more it would be like it was and still is between me and my mother. Jon isn't free enough with me and often he's more stubborn than strong. I can't play with him, he doesn't imagine enough. Sex is poor. It's not frequent and I don't have orgasms anymore. We don't have sex unless I start it."

Jon, an engineer, took a position a year ago at about two-thirds of his former salary. He enjoys his new job because it allows him to be directly in command of a large number of employees in the field, rather than mostly doing paper work, as in his previous job. Susan favored his taking this position because he would enjoy the work. She doesn't care if her husband doesn't wish to climb to the top of his profession, but she is concerned because they are committed to a high standard of living which necessitates that they once again accept money from her mother. Her mother, in turn, is insistent that Susan join her in her business. Susan does not want to do so because her mother has a tough and domineering stance with her, especially at work: "You are not my daughter then—just another employee." Susan is a folk-song writer and singer of moderate success who has also worked successfully and creatively in her mother's business. Her rage toward Jon was apparent as she looked at him and pointedly said that she did not mind accepting money from her mother but she would not accept her mother's control.

Jon had agreed to come to see me with his wife after they read a professional article (Sager *et al.*, 1971) on marriage contracts that a friend had showed them. Therefore, when they came in they were already prepared to work on their contracts. I did not deal formally with the contracts at this first session because of the great pressure of their frustration and pain, but I partly did so when I elected to center first on their sexual relationship, which they had brought up as epitomizing much that was wrong in their marriage both as cause and as effect. My decision to enter and to intervene in their system at this point was determined by the sharp difference in the terms of the sexual part of their contracts and by their agreement that improvement in this area was a high-priority goal. Each wanted a definite style of sex from the other, each thought it had been promised, and now both were disappointed and angry because each felt the other had not fulfilled his part of the contract. From my point of view, the sexual parameter epitomized their poor communication and misunderstandings about each other, and therefore could provide an excellent field on which to begin work toward a single contract. I decided that in this case sex could lead us rapidly to the center of their differences.

Susan was a woman who had been uninhibited and assertive sexually; she had had sexual relationships with several men before her marriage. Her husband liked to hear stories from her of the details of these experiences and would become excited by them. Susan now felt that she wanted to be sexually desired by her husband and wanted him to excite her and not vice versa. This desire was consistent with her romantic image of having spontaneous sexual love in a forest glade, where she would feel one with all nature and with her mate. She felt that sex should not begin in bed but was part of a total loving, warm, and supportive relationship. Jon, who had also had considerable sexual experience before marrying, wanted to be sexually passive and expected her to be seductive and wanton and to initiate passionate sex with him. His wife felt guilty and repentent about her promiscuous past and felt she should be loved as a woman and mother, not just as a sex object.

Susan presented herself in the session as a sort of flower child, yet also very much in touch with reality. She had a beautiful, fluid way of moving in and out of her ego boundaries. Jon was more pragmatic; he was set about his likes and dislikes and clearly passively aggressive in his adaptations. He had an honesty and bluntness that was very refreshing and was obviously devoted to his wife. He said that he wanted to be more giving to her but did not know how to do it her way. She wanted "to open him up more and then I will be more open," and as she said this her smile made clear the intent of her double meaning.

He talked readily about his depressed, "morbid" moods and his preoccupation with violence. He was currently in charge of developing and overseeing the installation of the security aspects of a new prison. In this first session he was able to talk about his sadistic fantasies, the pleasure he received from the idea that "his" prison would really be secure and keep the male inmates separated from society (and women) because they had injured innocent people. Susan, on the other hand, expressed love for all mankind. She wanted to be true to herself and to be one spirit with the sky, sea, and earth. Their opposing views on crime and violence and his need to sequester "criminal forces" constituted the fodder for a running battle between them. He stated at one point that he enjoyed reading about violence and fantasized doing violence to those who hurt others. He recognized that this was his way of controlling his own inner violence and felt he was in good control of these feelings. The 1971 Attica prison revolt and its aftermath had left them at each other's throats as he sided with "law and order" and she with the inmates as victims of the social ills that had spawned their crimes. As he put it, "I am more concerned for the victims of violence and she for the perpetrators."*

---

* The reader can see how easy it can be for one's own value system to make the therapist a partisan in this type of exchange or to color the therapist's attitude and sympathies to either spouse.

I commented on their seemingly opposite views and feelings about violence and how they might be closer than they suspected, depending on whether they looked at their positions as points on an almost closed circle or as the extreme poles of a straight line. I did this not because I thought they would accept this almost-closed-circle idea but to illustrate how even the most apparently divergent viewpoints may be closer to achieving reconciliation than the protagonists realize, both philosophically and practically. He seemed to be in better touch with his primitive anger and the threat to his omnipotence than she. He sublimated his in his work and fantasies about violence freely, whereas she used reaction formation as a major defense against her murderous impulses. Actually, each was coping differently with underlying feelings of infantile rage.

When I suggested the sexual area for initial work, I instructed them to take turns at home playing out each other's sexual desires. *In this way neither would be capitulating to the other,* an important issue to them. To avoid an argument over whose fantasy would be acted upon first, I asked him to approach her the first time. In view of her more stubborn feelings of injury, it seemed that it would be easier for him to make the first move. She could then reciprocate more easily. This was the beginning of teaching the possibility of quid pro quo solutions to impasses.

Susan had fantasied how sensual and gratifying it would be for them to make love in a wooded area near their home. My task assignments to them were that within the next two days he should initiate and make love to her in the woods. Within two days after that she would initiate sex in the style he had fantasied, with her taking the initiative and being "wanton" and passionate while he remained passive. They both agreed and seemed delighted with these instructions. It was as if they had been waiting for someone to cut the Gordian knot of their power struggle. The tasks were designed to see if they could accept what they claimed they wanted, and if they could give to each other. I was not concerned about their sexual functioning since it was clear there were no sexual dysfunctions here. But how would they react to the opportunity to have what they claimed they wanted?

I saw them again a week later. They had made love several times, taking turns playing out fantasies, and *both* had enjoyed *all* the experiences. It had been their most peaceful week in a long time. However, all was not well, as was indicated by Susan's dream the night before the second session. She had dreamed that her pubic hair was growing very long and that Jon stuffed it into her vagina so that her vagina was completely filled and blocked. She felt somewhat depressed in the dream because she could not have sex, though these feelings were not strong. Jon reported no dreams.

When asked about his reaction to her dream, Jon said he thought it showed that she believed he wanted her not to have sex. He said, "I don't want her to make love to other men but I certainly want her to with me. Perhaps she thought stuffing the hair was like I was putting a chastity belt on her—we have kiddingly talked about that once or twice." Susan said there was something in what he said but she felt that he, or maybe she herself, wanted to turn off her sexuality. That idea bothered her because she had enjoyed it this week. I pointed out that it was her dream. She had had her husband stuff her vagina. Perhaps she wanted to blame him if she turned off sexually. Was she upset in any way about enjoying sex this week? She said she felt better when they had sex in the woods, rather than when he was passive. She enjoyed his activity more. I suggested that in view of all they had been expressing about control and violence it was understandable that she might be on guard against trusting herself with her husband; yet she seemed to prefer him to be assertive.

They both appeared to agree with my statement but it made Jon somewhat defensive. He responded by stating that she had known how he was and she had seduced him by telling him about the other men she had been with and how sexually active she had been. They both knew that he was jealous but tried to control it. She said that she had been seductive at the start of their relationship but she had changed and now, years later, she no longer wanted to talk about her previous sexual affairs, even when he pushed her to do so. She wanted their hearts to be open to one another and when that happened sex would follow naturally and easily. He interpreted this to mean that she wanted to close up her vagina to him unless she had her way. At this point he reacted with mixed feelings while she expressed adamantly that loving feelings and openness had to be evident for sex or she felt as if her vagina were closing up—"I can't even lubricate." I reviewed with them how good sex had been and suggested that the dream had brought to the surface her feelings of anxiety at their sexual success and that these feelings possibly reflected his anxiety as well. I told them they need not agree fully but they should look at how much each had enjoyed implementing the other's fantasy.

Feeling that to pursue sex further at the moment would be counterproductive, I then drew them out about their expectations of each other's feelings toward their two children, the role assignments of the children, parenting responsibilities, and so on, thus getting more contractual material without trying to push them in sensitive areas. It was apparent that Susan enjoyed mothering but wanted greater participation with the children from her husband. She included the children as central in their unit. Jon kept them somewhat at a distance, to some extent resenting their existing as an intrusion into the marital system.

We then discussed the basic ideas of the marriage contract, using the concepts of the article they had read, which described the three levels of awareness: verbalized, conscious but not verbalized, and beyond awareness. This was done with emphasis on the exchange quality: I do for you and expect you to do for me in return.* I asked them to write out their contracts separately at home, using the article as a model, and not to discuss them together until both had finished. If they wished to read or discuss the two contracts after that, it would be fine. If they made any changes or additions, they should leave in the original terms and clearly note any changes that had been added as a result of the discussion. Thus, I asked this couple during the second session to write out their contracts at home and bring them in for the third session. I believed they were ready to do so and would use the opportunity constructively.

The Smiths left the second session with two sets of instructions: to write out their separate marriage contracts, and to continue to take turns initiating sex and playing out one another's fantasies. The initiator would play out his or her own fantasy. I knew that genuine

---

* The reminder list had not yet been developed for patient use but was beginning to be used by staff. I used the published article as a model for patients, giving them a reprint and verbal instructions.

progress toward a single sexual contract would be achieved when each also used part of the other's fantasy on his own initiative, so that the leadership went back and forth in the same sexual encounter without thoughts of "What is for me and what is for him?"

At the beginning of the third session they reported that the first week's improvement in sexual activity and pleasure had not been sustained. Susan felt that her husband was merely following my instructions and did not feel the proper love for her because he acted lovingly only when he wanted sex. She saw me as her mother pulling the marionette strings and her husband as her weak father. I used this to point out that many matters in their relationship had to be reevaluated, but that good sex and love were ready for them when they both felt willing to give as well as receive and that was not up to me or for me. I interpreted her transferential designation of me as strong mother and showed her how self-defeating that was for her in this situation. Sex would have to wait for further attention or would eventually take care of itself when suspiciousness, hostility, and the use of sex in their power struggle were no longer necessary.

The early focus on sex had illustrated the essence of their problems to them and indicated that remedy and satisfaction were possible if they wanted it, but that their sex problem was a symptom, not a cause, of their more general marital difficulties.

I suggested that we look at the marriage contracts together. They had not had time to discuss them together before the session but in response to my question said they did not mind the other's learning the contents now.

SUSAN SMITH'S CONTRACT

This is my summarizing miniscript:

If you make it possible for me to be independent and need no one you provide me with stability and security. When responsibilities overwhelm me i stop giving love and sex. I will not give love if you do not provide status and security. In return I will be a loving wife. Hestian.

My obligations
to be faithful
to enjoy giving pleasure
(injunction from husband "Don't
be close" interferes with my fulfilling my obligations)
HESTIAN—I will care for hearth
and children.

My benefits
to have children
to receive pleasure from husband
and children
POWER—I will have power to do
my own work and pursue my
way of life.

The More Detailed Contract:

1. *Verbalized*

Expectations
He will give me financial and
emotional security—to be a sane
balance wheel for me.
He will share my interests.

Receive
I will get deep satisfaction from
our relationship—I will feel safe
and protected.
We will work toward a common
end (we're after the same
rainbow's end, my huckleberry
friend).

2. *Conscious But Not Verbalized*

Give
I want to be completely at his
mercy, his victim. He will make
me feel. Weak women feel.
Strong women don't feel. I will
put myself completely at his
mercy. I will be his concubine,
slave, victim.

Receive—in exchange
He is powerful male.
Womanly deep feelings—it is
good to be dependent on this
strong man; it is my realization
of my deepest being as a woman.
A strong man. So I will receive
protection on an earthly level.

3. *Beyond Awareness*

YOU ARE A STRONG MALE unlike my father.
I fear your strength and I want to destroy it.
I will not encourage your strengths because you may destroy me.
I need to be the strong and independent one.
I want you dependent and weak.

JONATHAN SMITH'S CONTRACT

Conscious Verbalized

Give

1. Support you monetarily to the best of my ability.
2. Be your companion and escort socially.
3. Be faithful sexually.
4. Assist you in solving day-to-day problems.
5. Do work around the house which is heavy or unusual and which I am capable of doing.
6. Be a father figure for the children.
7. Share verbally and emotionally in shareable experiences.
8. Accommodate to your personal hang-ups and prejudices.

Take in exchange

1. You will be a good wife and mother; carry the household.
2. You will be my companion and escort socially.
3. Be sexually faithful.
4. Share shareable experiences.
5. Help relax and ease tensions after the day of work.
6. Be understanding of personal hang-ups and prejudices.

Conscious Not Verbalized

Give

1. Will allow you to engage in activities which I personally dislike—religious, spiritual, etc.
2. Tolerate your moodiness.
3. Will not impose on you sexually but will be available sexually on your demand.
4. Prepared to admit I do not earn enough to properly support you.

Take in exchange

1. Allow me to engage in activities you don't like.
2. Want you to be passionate and demanding of me sexually.
3. Bear with my negative personality traits.
4. Make do with my income without complaint.

Sub- or Unconscious

Give

1. Prepared to "forgive and forget" past sexual experiences al-

Take in exchange

1. Want a wild, passionate and whore-like bedmate who will be

though I am jealous and feel insecure in comparison to [your] former sex partners.
2. Prepared to forego demand that you don't take money from your mother because I realize it's absolutely necessary.
3. Prepared not to pursue other women though attracted to the idea.

verbal in lovemaking and accommodate to my sexual fantasies.
2. Want an adoring and verbally complimentary female who will be ego-massaging to me as both person and male.
3. Want you to be attractive and teasing to other men but never to be available to them.

These "contracts" are quite revealing, even in the way each mate headed the columns. Susan used "expectations" and "receive" while Jon used "give" and "take." Both sets of terms are valid but her terms suggest her more gentle approach, as compared to his bluntness. However, in reality she is just as firm about what she wants as is he, if not more so.

The ability to be in touch with strong contradictory desires on a deep, "beyond awareness" level is not unusual, though, of course, if these terms were fully beyond awareness there could be no response. The existence of the category and the areas suggested in it cause many people to get in touch with vague feelings they often have not dared to examine or think about openly before. This level of awareness is therefore significant and consciousness expanding for both spouses. Usually it leads to greater understanding for both.

Susan indicated great conflict over control, wanting to be in charge and also wanting to be enslaved, and not being able to trust. She apparently related this ambivalence to her feelings toward her mother. Her desires to be a mother and a wife and to do her own work were clear and seemed to be consistent with her actual behavior. She was in good contact with her "unconscious" need to be strong and in charge. This was the cause of internal conflict for her and also between them, although she also enjoyed and accepted her strength. Jon drew sharper limits and definitions about what he would and would not do.

When we first discussed the two contracts I thought the differences were sharper and more rigid than they actually proved to be later. Jon's need for distance became clearer as time went on, but clues existed in his "share shareable experiences" and "allow me to engage in activities you do not like." The desire and determination to make their relationship work were stronger motivating forces than appeared on the surface of the contracts, and understanding and compassion for each other were greater than apparent.

The major problems seemed to be in their different life and cognitive styles, in his difficulty in openly showing love and being close, in her ambivalence about control and power and his about closeness-distance, and in his passivity at home. Each wanted independent activity and appeared to be willing to allow it to the other—a good quid pro quo if this were to stand up in practice. His sexual desires were not antithetical to her, provided he also gave love and sex on her terms, which involved his being less passive and making her feel more desired. The money issue and his supporting her economically and physically with the children remained important points of difference. Increasing his willingness to include them in the family (marriage) would be a crucial factor here.

Each lacked security in adult femininity and masculinity, and each required strong reassurance and affirmations from the other. She wanted to feel his strength, to have him master her while loving and protecting her. She wanted to see him as a strong, loving father—not a weak father or a strong mother. She was angry, partly because she felt he had the ability to give her what she wanted but was not living up to his potential to do so.

Addressing themselves to writing out their own contracts had begun to clarify their understanding of themselves and each other. In the therapeutic process both had spontaneously begun to see how damaging their feelings of injury and anger were when each believed that he/she had delivered on his part of the contract but the other spouse had not done his/her part as specified in the unilateral contract.

Just the first paragraph of Susan's contract opened up an entire area that fit in with Jonathan's failure to fulfill her contract as she stipulated the terms. In the "minicontract" at the top (this was her idea) she wrote, *"If you make it possible for me to be independent and need no one you provide me with stability and security. When responsibilities overwhelm me i stop giving love and sex. I will not give love if you do not provide status and security. In return I will be a loving wife. Hestian.*" She felt that Jonathan did not give her sufficient emotional support at home with housework and the children, and that she therefore would not give him love and sex.

Jonathan thought he gave his wife the strength, security, and freedom from material concern she wanted: "I do give her all that— it's just the damn money—not that I don't want to become fully responsible financially but I will not maintain our standard of living by doing work I do not want to do. Either we change our standard or accept money from her mother or Sue will have to work." She understood his position and claimed no anger at that, but she did want emotional support and "togetherness" from him—he should not act as if the children were hers alone. Emotionally she felt that a man who did not make enough money for his family and expected his wife to do so was weak, like her father. She knew that if she worked for her mother she would be successful and would eventually take over the business. She would then be wealthy but would have no respect for her husband; further she would not be doing the work she wanted to do (music). Intellectually and ideologically she believed otherwise, but she could not alter her feelings.

Dialogue on this basic question continued. The position of each was founded on deep psychological needs. The money issue, like sex, was a symptom, not the real problem. Susan's problem arose from her ambivalence (weak women feel; strong women like her mother do not feel) between wishing to be strong and to be weak and taken care of. The roots of Jonathan's difficulty lay in his need to maintain the illusion of infantile omnipotence through his manipulation of Susan as doting mother image. At work he now felt competent as an adult, since his new job gave him power over others, although it did not allow him much room to be creative.

Ambivalent feelings Susan had expressed in her contract were pointed out to her—she knew her husband was indeed a strong man, unlike her father, and she had to be the strong one because she feared his strength. I asked her if she also perceived him at times as she did her strong, controlling mother toward whom she had such ambivalent feelings—at once wanting to be her slave (and thus to glean some privileges by serving her well) and at the same time rebelling to be free. She loved and hated her mother simultaneously. Because of what she could write in her contract, plus the feelings she expressed and her good ego strength, I felt that I could safely restate back to her what she had said in other ways. They both agreed and each gave a supporting anecdote. Jonathan then added ruefully, "Neither of us can win that way, can we?"

The crux of their struggle was clear. He needed reassurance, support, the love of an adoring woman, sexually teasing to and desired by other men, but letting the world know she belonged to him. If she did not behave so as to reassure him and quell his anxiety he would withdraw punitively and not give her what she wanted. Her contract demanded that he be strong and weak at the same time, which presented him with an impossible double bind. Actually her sexual withdrawal and refusal to move toward him sexually gave her a potent weapon in her struggle for power. He could not satisfy her for long because of her contradictory needs: He was to be strong and she his slave, but on the other hand to be enslaved was to be controlled by mother and required rebellion. She could be independent only if he were weak and her slave (as her father was her mother's), but if this happened she would despise him as she did her father. She had endowed Jonathan with real and fantasied qualities of both parents. (This is an example of a spouse being endowed by the beholder with both mother and father transferential reactions at the same time, which is discussed in Chapter 3.) By using the marriage contracts in marital therapy we are often in a better position to observe this phenomenon than we might be otherwise. Thus with her husband's unwitting collaboration Susan found it easy to evoke countertransferential (parataxic) reactions from her husband that readily supported her own distortions and negative expectations.

Each was acting the role of a childlike partner in their interactional contract. I classified them as childlike-childlike partners, or two children in search of a parent. This is in contradistinction to the childlike partnerships where the spouses are playmates, the "sandbox marriage."

Mr. Smith was not as close to his unconscious as his wife was

to hers and to his, but for a man who considered himself a prag-
matist he was surprisingly ready to cooperate in the therapeutic
venture, with its demands for openness, exposure, and change. Ap-
preciating how much more difficult the therapeutic process was for
him, I found myself feeling increasingly warm and supportive to him.

From the data gathered in the first three therapeutic sessions I
began to develop the Smiths' individual contracts more fully while
the treatment continued. The marriage contracts as I formulated
them more elaborately were developed after the fifth session, with
the use of all the information available to me, including the contracts
the couple had written; my evaluation of their productions, including the initial history; the dream material; their statements about each
other and their parents. How they interacted in sessions, reacted to
and treated each other as they reported other events, how they
carried out tasks, as well as their reactions to these, all contributed
additional interactional information. The contracts as formulated at
this point were working hypotheses constantly subject to change.
They were to be a guide toward the goal of one commonly agreed
upon single contract. Compromises would have to be made between
the two individuals and within each person in regard to his own
conflicts and ambivalence. Some new contract terms would have to
be created. Compromise with acceptance is one method of arriving
at a common contract, while using newly created contractual terms
or facets that develop during treatment or life experiences is another.

These contracts are formulated in terms of the three major parameters of contractual terms: 1) what is expected from marriage;
2) those terms based on biological and intrapsychic factors; and 3)
the parts of the contract that reflect derivative or externalized foci of
marital problems rooted in the first two areas. In the formulation
presented here the three levels of awareness of the terms of the contract are merged, since it is the therapist's statement. Because these
two contracts are my working hypotheses I find they are more
useful when I pool the partners' information from their three levels
of awareness and from all other sources. What I formulate is done
within the limits of my best awareness and theoretical bias. I am able
then to transmit my hypotheses, observations, and therapeutic maneuvers to the couple so that they can be used constructively to move

toward our common therapeutic goals. Like all psychotherapists, I am subject to blind spots, mistakes, and my own values and countertransferentially determined pronouncements. I try to be aware of these and hold them to a minimum.

PROJECTED CONTRACTS

Susan Smith

Jonathan Smith

1. Parameters Based on Expectations of the Marriage

1. Marriage means that the center of my life and Jon's is with one another and our children. We are a unit, self-sufficient and mutually supportive. My creative career is definitely secondary to the above, yet I must have it too. I should not have to exclude one or the other if Jon will cooperate.

1. Sue and I are central; the children are secondary to us and are often an intrusion. Each of us has our work too, which is also an important center for me. I do not know which is more important to me. If pressed I might choose my work over Sue and the children.

2. We are the family unit—Jon, me, and the children—not his original family or mine.

2. Same as Susan but the children are secondary. The less we have to do with our original families the better.

3. I want him to be gentle and understanding as well as firm as a father. He should be concerned and participate in caring for the children.

3. I will be a father image to my children. They must see me as strong, wise, and just. I do not want to be too close or involved in daily problems with them.

4. Family life will be run democratically and decisions about what, when, and how we do things will be joint. I prefer that Jon make decisions about money and support—I don't want to know about these, just that it is all OK.

4. I will take care of money and my work decisions; Sue will be in charge of family and social matters as long as I can depend on her to do what I want.

5. Roles will be traditional. That approach makes me feel right and

5. Same as Susan. But she should not expect me to bail her out or

Susan Smith

content. I will care for home and children; he will earn money and be my protector against outside forces I can't cope with.

6. In marriage two people should like the same things, think similarly, share their feelings and thoughts. I feel uneasy and troubled when Jon won't accept what to me is so important (nature, spiritualism, the concept of the essential goodness of mankind, etc.). If he can't do this I don't know if I want to try to meet him on what he wants.

7. In marriage we should be sexually available to each other. If he gives me security and love I will then be a model wife to him. He must want me sexually and reassure me of my desirability if I am to give him what he wants.

8. I do not want to be controlled in my marriage as I was at home by my mother. If I am secure with my husband I can flower and grow like a plant that gets the right nutrient, water, and sun. I can then be free to be creative. My husband will be richly rewarded for this—I want to and will take care of the house and children (with his help) and give to him sexually and make life exciting for him with my rich fantasy and imagination.

Jonathan Smith

fight her battles with some of her far-out friends.

6. I am a private person, I share only what I want to. My likes and dislikes can differ from Sue's and do. I am a separate person and must remain so. Sue wants me to merge with her—I won't and can't. That is definite!

7. I expect my wife to always want me sexually and to show it. My wife will be my refuge, my supporter. She will cater to my ego needs and will demonstrate how much she loves me and how sexual a man I am by her making passionate love to me while verbalizing how wonderful I am and how I turn her on.

8. My wife must understand my needs—I am special and should be catered to because I am a man and because I am me. I must control our life. I will allow her some freedom to pursue her silly friends but this threatens me and makes me anxious.

Susan Smith

9. If I do not get what I need I will not give him what he wants. He must be strong enough to give me what I want. I don't want to be allowed to take what I want just because he is weak. I don't want to have to be strong for us both.

10. I will compromise—he does not have to join me in most of my interests if he allows me to pursue them.

11. I do not think much about sexual fidelity. It is not the important issue—being there for another when needed is. I would be upset if my husband could not give to me sexually but could give to someone else.

12. We should be able to let our fantasies go with one another.

Jonathan Smith

9. If I do not get what I want I will not give her what she wants. I must establish my authority so that it is not constantly contested.

10. I will not give her all she wants because she would engulf and change me. If she gives me what I want I will give her as much as I can. I know compromises must be made, like I now agree to accept money from her mother.

11. My wife must be sexually faithful to me—I feel insecure enough about myself as it is.

12. Same as Sue. But our fantasies can be different. I cannot and will not have the same fantasies she has. That is not necessary in marriage. A couple does not have to be the same, but should fit together properly.

Positive: 1. Both want the same general conventional marriage form with similar gender-determined roles. 2. Each may have independent activities, although she wants him to join hers. 3. Each claims to be willing to compromise and make some quid pro quos.

Negative: 1. Inclusion-exclusion of children—ratio differs markedly. 2. Jonathan is more distant and removed and sees this as a desired stance. 3. Susan claims to be more democratic whereas he is autocratic in decision-making, although I suspect that she does not cooperate until she gets her way. 4. Each wants the other to approach sex and love "unself-ishly" and threatens withdrawal and anger if each does not get what he/she wants. There are genuine differences over sex. She wants demon-strations of love—for sex to be more spiritual; he wants concrete reassur-ance of his sexual desirability. 5. Her conflict over weak-strong is the source of much confusion and trouble and is a basic determinant of how their marital system functions. 6. She wants to be left to do her own "thing" (spiritual and humanistic movements and her music), but makes clear she really expects and wants him to approve and participate, which he refuses to do because he fears he will lose his sense of self. She wants him to like what she likes and to think as she thinks, which is antithetical to him. 7. She tries to be guided by a tight definition of "shoulds" and "shouldn'ts" regarding control but she is ambivalent. 8. Both of them state clearly that they will withhold from the other if they do not get what they want. 9. He fears being controlled, even in the fantasy area. 10. He is defensively rigid about his husbandly rights, adhering to a model that is not consistent with the reality of his life today.

At present they live in an uneasy parallel relationship, each going his own way and each very unhappy and puzzled about why they are not joined more harmoniously, since they agree on so many of the superficiali-ties of what they want from marriage. Harmony and growth are not ascendant, as each rigidly insists on having his own way in the particu-lars of living and relating. Ambivalence on the part of both in a struggle for power that each one only half wants is a central negative force.

2. *Parameters Based on Intrapsychic and Biological Determinants*

The therapist does not necessarily need to make as complete a list as is given here for demonstration purposes. In practice one usually selects only those problem areas and strengths that are revealed as crucial ones in the contracts and in the couple's behavior. It is helpful to most couples to point out the positive parts of the contract, and where the contracts are symmetrical or truly complementary, as well as where disagreement or conflict exists.

Since these contracts are my working hypotheses, I include tentative intrapsychic and interactional dynamic formulations. It is not necessary for the readers to agree with my dynamic formulations. Since I can illus-trate but one approach here I have chosen the one I used in this case. The reader may substitute his own formulations based on his own theoretical and clinical approach. In this presentation italics are used to indicate where I have included my hypotheses of intrapsychic and marital system dynamics and comments. These illustrate how the therapist can incorporate the marriage contracts into his own theoretical system.

Susan Smith   *Jonathan Smith*

1. *Independence-Dependence*

She wants to be dependent and independent but in different areas. This generates major conflict that she expects her husband to resolve for her. She wants to be her husband's slave and also to be free. *I do not accept her conscious formulation of this. I believe she wants a strong but loving and benevolent man who will protect and take care of her in return for which she will give him love, sex, children, and a warm family life. In turn he will further provide her with an ambience that permits her to be independent in other areas. Thus there need not be a conflict in what she wants if her husband could give it to her; it is possible and a not uncommon quid pro quo on a more mature level. The master-slave or weak-strong polarization is therefore not an accurate assessment.*

He is clear about his desire to be independent—but this is a false independence. *Basically he requires a giving mother-wife who must fulfill his infantile need in order to make him feel good. In return he will then be a "good boy" at home and help out, share what he wants to share, be sexually faithful. A part of his contract that he cannot yet confront is that the women in his life are expected to give to him the goodies he wants while he lies back passively and is in charge.*

2. *Activity-Passivity*

She is willing to be active to bring about what she wants—active in deed as well as ideationally. In exchange for her ac-

He is more passive than Susan but in a very aggressive way. He states clearly what he will do and that's it. He will compromise

Susan Smith

tive doing she wants his protection and care.

Jonathan Smith

when he realizes he will lose the war if he insists on winning every skirmish, e.g., he agrees not to protest her asking her mother for money rather than cut down on their standard of living. He reacts more than he initiates.

3. *Closeness-Distance*

She claims she wants closeness but her tolerance for closeness is short lived and the closeness must be on her terms. She talks a great deal about closeness but protests too much. Closeness to her is equated with control or being controlled. She tries to bring Jonathan closer, i.e., to make him understand and to accept her style and cognitive approach. *He feels threatened by this and feels his integrity to be violated.* However, he is more able to accept their cognitive style differences than she. *Her attempts to control through taking away his defense—distancing operations—are done in a way that relinquishes her control to him because he is strong enough to refuse to play the game on her terms. She then takes revenge with anger and her own withdrawal.* Her closeness is often within herself—self-awareness in meditation. *On a deep level she does not fully comprehend or empathize with Jonathan.*

He is wary of closeness, is too guarded. *Possibly he is fearful of his violent, infantile, and sadistic impulses.* He will make some gestures of closeness in order to remain distant but draws a line across which he stubbornly will not step. *As Susan said, he gives her the injunction "Don't be close," which frustrates her—robs her of a powerful weapon as well as a source of genuine gratification.*

Susan Smith   *Jonathan Smith*

4. Power

She is clearly conflicted about how much power she wants to have and how much is permissible for her husband in order for her to feel safe—but basically she wants power and control. *She feels she cannot trust him with it. He is too alien and different. She is uneasy about the violence and sadism she senses. Her ambivalence contributes to their disharmony, as it both promises and withholds the mother-wife he wants whom he can control. Their struggle for power is a major preoccupation between them. Both enjoyed it early in their relationship, before it led to a deterioration of their marriage. When she has power she fears it and wants to hand it back to him—but then she can't trust him to take care of her: a terrible dilemma if one sees the alternative only in terms of her syllogism.*

He is not in conflict about power. He wants to have it but wants to delegate the active role to his wife so long as she does what he wants. His is a classical passive-aggressive personality syndrome. *The power and control question is crucial for them. He would want to exercise power as does a little boy who controls his parents. However, this tactic does not always work with Susan and he then becomes upset when he is forced to recognize that his omnipotence is threatened.*

5. Fear of Loneliness or Abandonment

This is a moderately important determinant of her behavior—particularly fear of the loss of the strong-mother fraction of her husband. It does not appear as a prime motivating force; the entire universe is her sisterhood. *Perhaps that is her ultimate de-*

He hides this fear well but he does cave in when Susan really pulls away from him. If she maintains her distant position he capitulates so that he can salvage the remnants of his fantasy of a blindly giving and doting mother-wife. If she threatens to leave

Susan Smith

fense against loneliness and abandonment.

Jonathan Smith

him he threatens that his abandonment of her will be greater,
swifter, and more terrible. *Thus
he controls by stimulating her
anxiety, not allaying it. What
could be an opportunity to move
positively becomes a power
struggle.*

6. Level of Anxiety

Her level is overtly higher than
his. She expresses it openly, is in
touch with it, requests him to do
something to relieve it for her.
When he does not she focuses
her anger on him or punishes
him by not giving him what he
wants. When too anxious she
fears disintegration and protects
herself by withdrawing, getting
in touch with mystical forces
that give her poise, calm, and a
sense of being connected. Therefore, ultimately she feels she can
get along without him if she
has to, but says she wants the
children to have a father.

His anxiety is better defended
against direct awareness and expression. It can most readily be
measured by his sadistic fantasies, authoritarian position, and
dogmatism. Unconsciously he is
fearful of abandonment and Susan senses this and even uses it.
He wants Susan to soothe his
anxiety by ego massage and sexual activity, and in general to
treat him like a beautiful male
infant who is adored blindly.
Without this reassurance he becomes a cold person who knows
he can hurt "mother" by withdrawing. However, this does not
work too well with Susan because he cannot control her this
way and she now perceives him
when he uses this maneuver as
her weak, ineffective father,
whom she despises. At these
times she then assumes the role
of her strong mother—and then
finds with horror that she has
replicated her own parental situation. This is an unstable state

Susan Smith

Jonathan Smith

that she can tolerate only briefly because she then insists that her husband be the strong mother-husband and take charge. His superficial show of being the strong mother-husband for her also does not stand up, as reality comes through to her despite her desire to see him as strong. She then swings back to anger and withdrawal and running away from him to be with her friends in the spiritualist movement. Once again in charge of herself, she returns and they square off for another round. He has learned from experience not to be too anxious about her spiritualism. It provides her with the necessities to stabilize herself and to serve him again for a while. Thus they go back and forth stimulating and relieving each other's anxiety. They are two children in search of a parent. Neither can accept a true parental role for long because they both need to be parented. *Therapy focused on this seesaw very early and the quid pro quo approach was helpful, as was illustrated in the sexual area with the task assignment in the first session.* His chief defense is not to allow her to become involved and to maintain distance from his wife and children.

Susan Smith

Jonathan Smith

7. Consolidation of Gender Identity

Her gender identity is female—but she is confused over whether being female means being like her strong mother. She wants to feel but the strong do not have feelings—that is weak. She still confuses being a "good female" with being Hestian, yet is conflicted by her desire to enjoy a whole gamut of activity independent from her husband. *How can she be Hestian and at the same time be strong, driving, and in charge? This would make her the "male" in the family, like her mother. However, if she is to be independent she must be like her mother and have a weak husband. But she can't carry it off—it frightens her to be strong. To be strong would mean she could challenge her mother and that is a terrifying idea. Besides, she is a child. She sets it up as an either/or situation without full appreciation of the fact that both she and her husband can be strong and accepting at the same time; that a person can care and be cared for, can be weak or strong and can like the spouse taking over in some situations while he himself takes over in others. The possibilities of sharing and of powers shifting back and forth between them are lost in the anxiety generated by the*

His gender identity is male—but a beautiful, loved child, adored merely because he exists, *not* for anything that he gives or does. Ideally he would like to be married to a woman who is a giving "whore in the bedroom" and who adores him, a woman who would use her power and energy solely in his behalf. The idea of his wife working and earning money does not threaten him.

Susan Smith

recognition that one's mate has the same flaws as oneself. The problem of passing control back and forth is one of the more important for them to work out together. It is significant that gender role, control, independence, etc., all become interrelated aspects of the same overall ebb and flow within their marital system. Homosexuality is not an abhorrent idea to her but she prefers a male sex partner. She does not experience erotic feelings toward either weak or strong women.

Jonathan Smith

8. *Characteristics of Sex Partner*

She wants a partner who will be turned on by her and who will make intense spiritual and physical love with her. Unless he instigates it in a loving way she does not want sex. It angers her that her husband does not keep his part of the bargain in the quid pro quo. She feels this is illustrative of what often occurs. Also, she feels she was wanton and "sold herself" sexually before marriage because she felt she had nothing else to offer. She does not feel that way now and resents his demands. Physically he is fine sexually for her and can turn her on when he wants to. There are no sexual dysfunctions. It is his lack of sexual ini-

His ideal sex partner resembles her picture of herself acting sexually with other men. Physically he finds her face and body beautiful and voluptuous, just what he wants. He is angered at her "refusal" to be wanton with him and to fit into his whore-in-bed fantasy. In exchange for her doing this he would not contemplate other women and would take care of her "to the best of my ability." *Again this is an equivocal and not reassuring statement.* He wants her to accept him sexually; he says he stopped taking the initiative sexually with her because she rejected him. She states that he accepted her "no" much too easi-

Susan Smith

tiative and assertiveness, as well as his not creating a loving ambience, that puts her off and makes her feel undesirable. She stated at one point: "I, too, want to be loved for the person I am, not just a hot cunt." She wants him to be more aggressive and not to be stopped by her rejection of his sexual advances. In exchange she will become sexually giving.

Jonathan Smith

ly and that she wants him to override her objections and take her.

9. *Acceptance of Self and Others*

She basically questions her own worth as a person and as a woman. *Therefore the man who accepts her must be defective too. This produces a perfect stage for the acting-out of problems based on her low self-esteem, particularly as her mate reinforces the negative attitudes she already has about herself and is very parsimonious about offering recognition for her positive contributions and attributes.*

Although he assumes he is an adorable male infant he also fears he is not a match for a "real man" including any of her previous lovers. This lack of acceptance of himself as an adult male contributes greatly to his need to control and structure his world so that he always appears to be in command. *He is strong enough to choose the areas he wants to be "weak" in. These are not necessarily the ones she wants—e.g., she wants him to be strong in making money, in desiring her sexually, in being able to tolerate her going off by herself, in being less passive. He is strong in doing the work he wants to do, and he won his Pyrrhic victory in the sexual area, which precipitated their coming for treatment.*

Susan Smith   *Jonathan Smith*

10. *Cognitive Style, Energy Level, Intensity, Absorption, Enthusiasm*

Susan's cognitive style is open and intuitive. She allows data to flow in and around her and then makes a decision based on her feelings and guts. She writes her lyrics and music and lives this way. This style is markedly different from Jonathan's. She finds it difficult to accept his way and keeps trying to push him into her style. She feels hurt and alone because he won't (can't) join her in her seemingly unstructured approach. Yet, she follows logic and sees to it that the essentials are taken care of for herself and for her husband and children. She has a high energy level, intensity, absorption, and enthusiasm and expects the same from Jonathan, which he does have, but unfortunately not in the same areas as she.

Jonathan's cognitive style is very logical and precise. He, as a proper engineer, surveys all situations, collects information, sifts it through and organizes it into its appropriate categories and weights, and then arrives at a practical decision in accordance with the "facts." He has learned that his wife cannot do the same and will condescendingly tolerate her "escapist, spiritualist, and humanistic activities." This difference in styles makes for communication problems. In addition, each has become impatient with the other's style and thinking. *Because they know they will not change each other's position they tend to cut off communication and are too impatient to listen, each believing that he/she knows what the other will say.* Energy level, intensity, absorption, and enthusiasm are high. He does not care much anymore about the direction of Susan's energies so long as they are not too threatening; ultimately she does what he wants.

3. *Parameters Reflecting Derivative or Externalized Foci of Marital Problems*

These are the complaints that often bring a couple into treatment. They are usually symptoms of something more basic than is conflictual or disappointing in one or both of the other two parameters.

Susan Smith   *Jonathan Smith*

1. *Communication*

Susan appears to be quite open and direct in what she does and does not want, even when these are contradictory. She *appears* to ask for what she wants, but in reality many of her messages are not clear, and often are double binding because of her ambivalence. She is in good contact with her feelings but allows negative ones to pile up and may then explode without adequate thought to the consequences. She can express love and tenderness as well as anger.

However, when she feels disappointed she does not state what she wants but expects Jonathan to know. She will give subtle signs, which are not likely to be understood or even perceived, and then finally blow up with anger when she has accumulated a series of what she considers refusals to respond on Jonathan's part.

In summary, Susan is in touch with her feelings but often does not clearly communicate what she wants.

Jonathan is open in what he wants in terms of events and things but is not in good contact with his feelings and hence cannot express them directly. At times he expects his wife to know and to fulfill his unexpressed wishes. He finds it difficult to express love but can express anger readily. Many of his communications come through in an authoritarian and blunt way that arouses the ire of his wife. Early in their relationship she thought this was an evidence of his strength, but she now sees it as weakness and is angered by it. His hostility is often expressed indirectly and in a subtly sadistic way that only thinly masks his underlying anger.

When Susan gives her minimal signals he does not perceive them or, if he does, usually misreads them. Instead of asking for clarification he "guesses" what she means, usually taking the most negative interpretation available.

In summary, Jonathan, in contrast to Susan, is not in good contact with his feelings but does communicate clearly what he consciously wishes to communicate.

Susan Smith   *Jonathan Smith*

2. Interests

She is an artist and interested in matters of the spirit and in her own work as well as her family life. She had expected him to be concerned with her sphere of interest and to agree with her opinions. She becomes angry and disappointed and feels unloved when he disagrees with or can't comprehend her point of view. She is not especially interested in his work because she has not found a way of seeing how it relates to her basic philosophy of life. Hence she is somewhat suspicious of his work, which makes him angrily defensive.

He is interested in himself essentially. He wants to tell her about his work—but only those aspects that he feels enhance him. He is not interested in what she does but is willing to live and let live. She may pursue her own interests as long as he is not deprived of her wifely services. If he is he retaliates angrily.

3. Life Style

All living matter is one. She wants her life to be free, spontaneous, spent with gentle people, music, singing, dancing, conversation, nature, and without worry about money. She is outgoing. She is willing to compromise, i.e., wants to do all of the above with Jon but will settle for his not punishing her for sharing with others if he will not join her.

He is closed in, ordered, a planner. He likes some people as long as they do not threaten his supremacy. He dislikes being close to nature, prefers motels to camping out. He is very agreeable about spending money if they have it. He goes along with her activities to some extent but is threatened as he comes to realize that the people to whom she is drawn are not like him and he fears he may eventually lose her. He therefore tries to rein her in, which angers and depresses her and makes her pull away.

Susan Smith   *Jonathan Smith*

4. Families of Origin

Her strong mother is a source of problems for her and for them—Sue is very ambivalent about her mother. She uses her mother as the yardstick by which all human qualities are measured, both good and bad. She regards her father as a sweet nonentity. She wants her mother out of her life. Therefore she resents Jon "putting her" in a position of asking her mother for money because she feels that she is the one who must pay for this.

He fears her attachment to her mother and is jealous. He regards her mother as having too much influence in their daily life. But he is partner to perpetuating the situation by not either insisting they live within his income or making more money. He consciously made the choice to accept the situation, rationalizing that he did so for Sue and the children. His family presents no current problems to either except for the effects of his early relationships with his mother and father. At times Sue resents his father's past indulgence of him and his mother's coldness and distance. His father is dead and his mother lives in another state and is not an active force in their lives except historically.

5. Children

They both agree that the children are primarily Susan's responsibility. She gets angry, however, when Jonathan does not carry out his part of the quid pro quo, i.e., to relieve Susan's worry about money and security concerns so that she can do the things she wishes to, such as her music, activities with spiritualist friends, etc. She resents his distant stance with the children, which he considers providing "a proper father image." There are minor conflicts over child-rearing practices but he usually abdicates to her in this area.

6. Money

To her money represents power and freedom, as amply illustrated

Money means the same things to Jonathan but he is not overtly

Susan Smith

above. She becomes anxious as the realization strikes her that money is short. Rather than cut down she takes the easy way of accepting money and therefore control from her mother.

Jonathan Smith

concerned about material matters and feels confident that financial needs will be met one way or another.

7. *Values*

There is nothing to add here to what has been covered above. There are many areas of agreement in addition to some profound differences.

8. *Friends*

Friends represent independence to her. She claims she would like to share but she did choose a husband who can't share her most significant friendships.

He has few friends of his own. He is willing to share those he does have with her but she finds his choices dull or obnoxious. It is all right for her to have her own if they do not threaten his sexual possession of her.

9. *Roles*

She is willing to follow traditional gender-determined roles if she gets what she wants in return. She resents his not fully accepting responsibilities of his role as money maker.

In his honesty and bluntness he at times appears as an exaggeration of the dominating and yet ultimately complying husband. Roles are clearly gender-determined for him ("I will help with the heavy work at home, if I can") but he wants to define his responsibilities and brooks no discussion about them. His intransigence is frustrating to her.

It is clear that the derivative factors were perceived by me as well as by the couple as secondary to the intrapsychic and interactional. Hence in therapy we were soon able to deal directly with the latter factors. In the communication area the clue was that Jonathan had difficulty in comprehending Susan's more idealized concept of giving and love. This may or may not have been due to the fact that his only warm and giving parent was his father. Susan needed to become more competent in helping him see what she meant and in communicating directly. Therapy could be helpful in this. Because some aspects of my value system were closer to hers than to his, I had to be alert not to make myself his competitor or to be patronizing, but rather to be an ally to both partners. Susan almost refused to respect Jonathan in his work area because of what she considered her humanistic values, but their values were more similar than they realized. Jonathan felt threatened because he felt he couldn't be the spiritual man she wanted and struck back out of fear of losing her. He was puzzled by and attracted to her capacity to experience joy and her artistic qualities, which fascinated him, confounded him, and made him feel defensively inadequate.

TOWARD THE SINGLE CONTRACT

After I had formulated the preceding contracts, with their dynamic hypotheses, the Smiths and I began in earnest to work toward a single contract. Most of the next session was spent reviewing the marriage contracts they had written out earlier, along with my additions and comments. One would read a section of his contract, starting with the verbalized part; the other would then read the corresponding section; then we would discuss similarities, differences, and sources of problems. I elaborated on conflict or cut through to common denominators, explaining to them the differences in their cognitive styles and the significance of the disparities.

Both of the Smiths wanted to work directly on their sexual problem. I had thought earlier that we could use sex as an entry to their change system, but we were now at a temporary impasse and would not be able to go further in that area until we had dealt with some other anxiety-producing parameters. Because sex was so laden with significance and meanings that related to all these parameters, to pursue their sexual avoidance syndrome directly as a means of changing the total relationship could not work. At this time I thought they should postpone attempts to improve the quality and quantity of their sexual expression for the sake of improving the overall marital relationship. I explained my reasoning to them.

Before again focusing on sexual expression we would first have to soften the defensiveness and anxiety produced by other parameters. In the future, if it were necessary to do so, sex might be used in this way again or as an end in itself. Because of the uneven development of different areas in their marital system, we would need to move back and forth between different areas.

Proceeding on the basis of this concept of uneven development, the Smiths and I agreed that the major areas of difficulty for them were dependence-independence, passivity-activity, inclusion-exclusion, closeness-distance, power, acceptance of self, differences in cognitive styles, and communication. With their agreement I chose the areas of cognitive style and communication as the next ones to work with directly.

I had already begun by pointing out the difference between their cognitive styles—he assembling data, sorting out, examining, and arriving at a "rational choice," she more "intuitive" and dependent on feelings for making her choices. Examples were given of the differences in the way they approached problems, including those with each other, and of how this, too, affected their communication and made them impatient with each other. They each believed that just a few words would cue them to what the other thought about any issue, and that because neither could influence the other's thinking it was useless to say more. Long ago they had arrived at a communication impasse. It was important that they accept their differences in style and try to understand each other's cognitive approach, as these were givens and could not change. Both styles were perfectly valid, but different. I told them I thought they complemented each other very neatly, and gave them the task of finding ways to use their differences to their common advantage. A related task dealt with passive-active aspects, since they were to discuss together all plans that affected them and the children, to make clear to each other how they felt, what they wanted, and why they wanted what they wanted. They were told to question each other carefully if they did not fully understand the different points of view. Emphasis was put on communicating clearly and simply with each other, understanding and listening to each other, and then trying to arrive at a compromise or a quid pro quo agreement without either's feeling defeated in the process. This task, along with the one of using their different cognitive styles, might accomplish changes in their relationship expeditiously if it did not cause too much anxiety and consequent sabotage.

In the next session they reported having talked more openly and freely for a few days but having then begun a mutual withdrawal and distancing. Neither had made sexual overtures during the week. Jonathan stated he felt upset by a lack of sex. I urged him to assert himself and make his desires known. When I asked Susan how she would like him to approach her so that she would be most likely to respond warmly, her answer was definite but vague in the particulars. "I want it to come from the heart as well as the penis—you make me feel as if it's just your penis that wants me." I asked him if he knew how to translate what she said into feelings and actions. He did not. I turned to her and told her to tell him more definitely what she wanted. She now became more explicit and he was able to comprehend and to begin to appreciate the kind of loving relationship she had in mind. For the first time he was able to hear her and she could appreciate his difficulty in not having understood her previous figures of speech.

After that session we did not meet for two weeks, because Susan had impulsively gone on a weekend retreat with her spiritualist friends. On the night of the day she returned Jonathan had the following dream:

> There is fucking in the dream. Sue and I return from a dance with B and A [a couple]. We pass a house and Sue says, "Many a fuck have I fucked there." We go someplace, probably home. B and A are still with us. I angrily ask Sue, "How many times did you fuck there?" She answers, "I'm not going to tell you." We go back and forth like that a few times and then I hit her a few hard punches in the face. Blood comes from her mouth and she says, "No tell." She's in pain, and the blood is oozing out and she then says, "I'll tell you. Forty or fifty times." B and A disappear. I say, "See, you wasted all your cunt juice there and now there's nothing left." I then added, "The girl who will eventually take me from you won't even have to be pretty; all she'll have to do is fuck.

Jonathan's controlling passivity was demonstrated by his having told the dream to Susan for her to write down. She read it to me. In this indirect way he let her know his anger over her leaving him for three days, which he had not expressed to her before she left or afterward.

The dream provided the opportunity to go into Jon's feelings of sexual rejection by Sue, his fear of her desertion aroused by her having gone to the retreat, and his anguish, desperation and passivity about direct expression of his anger. Her going off at a time when they were working together and with me and its provocative effect were dealt with too, and Sue came to realize that she had been anxious about their growing closeness and had physically, as well as emotionally, distanced herself.

Her action in going to the retreat, along with his dream, made it possible to confront both Jon and Sue with their sense of inadequacy and their need for distance so as to avoid discovery as inadequate persons. His violent reaction in the dream was what she felt to be smoldering within him. It frightened and fascinated her as she toyed with provoking him enough so that he would be violent. Violence would be an impotent defeat for him—but, on the other hand, did she really want him to be effective? That was one of her dilemmas that he complemented so well with his aggressive passivity. He behaved as she (neurotically) wanted, despite its frustration for her.

Jonathan's dream provided a wealth of material that could have been interpreted in a number of ways. I elected to take from it the aspects that I thought pertained to the direction of our work at the moment. To get into other aspects, including the other couple's significance, would have diverted us from the immediate task, so we used what was necessary to continue work toward the immediate goal. After this there was a deeper appreciation of the valid and genuine difference between their cognitive styles, of their sense of worth to each other, and of the fact that they could communicate better *if they wished to*—for example, if she had stopped to feel her anxiety about closeness, instead of running away, and had talked about her feelings with him.

Gradually, over the next six weeks, we worked toward agreement on significant aspects of the single contract. Jonathan became more sensitive to himself and to Susan but had further to go. She became better able to accept her own strength as well as her interdependence with her husband. He accepted the children much more, particularly after Sue stopped using them to increase his feelings of exclusion by insisting he do more with them. Her insistence had made him distance himself from them; left to his own resources he began to include them. Consulted now in the process of making decisions that affected the children, rather than just carrying out Susan's decisions, Jon showed evidence of taking the initiative in developing his own relationship with each child.

When Sue showed an increasing readiness to have Jon take over more family power, he became more active in assuming it. They continued to have sharp disagreements but were now able to discuss them more effectively and arrive at a resolution, rather than invariably withdrawing or abdicating in anger.

They agreed to accept their differences on numerous issues and types of problems and worked out several quid pro quos with me present as well as on their own. I was concerned with teaching them the process of discovering and elucidating sore spots and then arriving at their own acceptable solution.

It was important for them to learn in their sessions that both wanted similar things—love, security, independence while being cared for too; that each could give to the other if assured he/she would not be taken over; that each wanted power to make sure their world held together, but was also fearful of having power and was only too glad to hand it over to the other if assured he would not be hurt. Some tasks were designed to break their impasses by developing trust, to overcome the watchful waiting and suspicious assessing and weighing of the "who-did-what-for-whom-last" approach. A very useful task—one that helped with the passive-active area as well as power and trust—was instructing each to be in charge for three days at a time. The strong feelings engendered by this task were then discussed in the next session. With some ups and downs, trust began to improve. Jon became more active on his three days, and then became dependent and asked Susan what to do or sometimes planned activities he knew she would not like. She reciprocated in kind in her turn. But they were beginning to change their interactions with each other.

Therapy had to be terminated (ten sessions had been planned for) before some of the changes hoped for could be realized. Treatment was stopped with the knowledge that all was far from perfect but that they had turned a corner and were now better equipped to identify and work on the problem areas of their contracts.

FOLLOW-UP INTERVIEW

At my initiative I saw the Smiths nine months later in a lengthy follow-up interview. I was struck at once by their changed appearance. Sue had lost considerable weight and her face was composed and beautiful. She looked as if she had a new pride in her own being. Jon had lost his air of dogged defensiveness and had an ease and self-assurance he had lacked the year before. He seemed much more in charge of himself.

They had had some difficult times but had continued to review their contracts. Jon was now more accepting of her spiritualist friends and no longer so threatened by them; he realized that he had a solid relationship with his wife. They discussed some of their feelings and ideas together these days. At one time during the meeting I misunderstood something Jon had said and Sue quickly informed me of my mistake, which had conveyed a negative connotation about Jon.

A few months ago Sue had considered divorce, faced the alternatives, and decided that life with Jonathan offered her most of what she really wanted. She now spoke lovingly about him and with understanding for him, including his position about law and order. Although she disagreed with many points, she now respected his opinions and saw validity in much of what he said. They sounded as if they had been listening to each other with increased respect. Jon also spoke lovingly of Sue and indicated a true sense of understanding and affection for her. He said that he now realized and accepted the fact that she has periods when she must withdraw emotionally. When she reassures him that it is not his fault he can accept this and be there for her when she is ready to come back.

Recently Sue had lunched with her mother, who had told her she now realized her daughter was an artist, respected her for it, and could understand her need to be true to herself. She would no longer try to make her daughter a business person. Apparently Sue's changes also affected her relationship with her mother, from whom she now elicited a very different response.

Sex was excellent when they had it, but some of the old problem of lack of assertion on Jonathan's part persisted. His tendency to be rigid and literal surfaced in unexpected ways, despite a general change in regard to understanding Sue and her style. Her style and her messages certainly were difficult to understand at times. For example, now that it was summer she wanted to sleep on the ground out of doors. She had compromised by sleeping on the floor next to their bed but had not told Jon why she had left their bed. He took her sleeping on the floor as a rejection, as she was not in bed with him. He did not wish to follow her to sleep on the floor if she had "moved out." Therefore they had not had sex for ten days. He was surprised when I asked Sue why she was on the floor and she said it was a compromise because she wanted to sleep outside but she knew Jon would not so she met him halfway by sleeping on the floor in their bedroom. She had hoped that he would come to the floor and make love with her there and then get back into bed or not as he wished. Sue thought she had made an advance to him by what she had done. Sue had not told Jon why she was on the floor, and he had not asked her. Both felt hurt and abused by the other.

In this case Sue's moving onto the floor of the bedroom was her offer to compromise—she just wanted Jon to visit her there on the floor. His not understanding what she had done and what she wanted in return made her feel cheated and rejected. She, too, wanted and missed love and sex. Her sleeping on the floor without explanation was taken by Jon to mean she was refusing to have sex with him. On his part he never thought to act or even to discuss her actions but assumed that she intended injury. As the truth of this situation unfolded during the session it drove home to them the fact that they could not count on subliminal messages and had to tell, ask, explain openly and clearly to each other. Sue accepted her responsibility in the pas de deux for not having verbalized her intent. Jon accepted his for not having questioned her and moved toward her.

Later I found myself thinking that after our session, instead of Sue lying on the floor feeling hurt and rejected after she had made such an "obvious" offer of compromise, and he lying in the bed above her angry and feeling controlled, he would now come to the floor and they would make love and enjoy sex. Sometimes he goes back to bed after she falls asleep, I thought, and sometimes he stays on the floor with her all night. And then, too, on some evenings she comes into the bed first and they make love there.

He learns that her being close to nature need not exclude him. Indeed, he likes nature at times—but he never need like it as much as she; he always will remain essentially a bed-sleeper and she essentially a floor-sleeper. Often the presence of the need for touch and closeness will outweigh the need for distance. Each will realize what each now senses—that the essence of what they both want is also feared by each, but to a lesser degree, and that it is there for each of them as they are ready for it.

When I saw the Smiths again, I was to find that my optimistic musings had not fully materialized.

THE SINGLE CONTRACT

Six months after the follow-up visit I telephoned the Smiths to arrange another follow-up session and to ask them to write out together a single contract that would include what they agreed upon as well as their differences. I would send them a reminder list (see Appendix 1) that would serve as a guide. Since they had copies of the individual contracts they had written at the start of treatment, they could refer to these if they wished to. They seemed to welcome the idea, and it was decided that when they had finished their single contract they would mail it to me and call to make an appointment.

Three weeks later, not having heard from them, I called again. They sounded pleased to hear from me. Jonathan had looked at the reminder list, shown it to Susan, and put it in a drawer. They were glad I had called again because my call would help them overcome their inertia. It sounded as if Jonathan were less enthusiastic about

the project than Susan, but within a week I received their single
contract, which had obviously been carefully and thoughtfully
worked on by both of them, and the next day they called and made
an appointment.

THE SMITHS' CONTRACT

The numbers on the left correspond to the item letters of the reminder
list (see Appendix 1). The comments in italics are my discussion and
evaluation when we discussed the contract in the session.

Category 1. Expectations of the Marriage

1. Both expect mate to be loyal, devoted and loving, but not exclusive.
   *In session they said by exclusive they were not referring to sex but
   meant they did not need to be possessive but just to love—could
   allow the other time for him/herself.*
2. Both agreed marriage provided support against the rest of the world.
   *In the session their sense of closeness and being there for each other
   was indicated by several incidents in which they offered support to
   each other.*
3. & 4. Both agreed that they liked solitude and that they did not see
   marriage as a goal in itself.
5. Both agreed marriage helped them in life's struggles but as a tool
   and a support, not a panacea.
6. Both did not believe it was realistic that marriage should last "until
   death do us part."
7. Sex remains a problem area (see category 2).
8, 9 & 10. Children are desired and only they are included in their
   family unit.
11. Home is a refuge from the world. *Husband answered "definitely
    yes," wife a weaker "yes." They explained that home is largely her
    work area, therefore it is not her refuge as much as it is his—she
    must seek a refuge from home at times.*
12. Husband answers "no." *He does not need marriage to give him a
    respected position and status in life.* Wife: "A weaker yes." *She
    wants structure in her life; she was an aimless flower child for several
    years and does not want chaos anymore. This is a key factor that
    came through for the first time—her need for her husband to help
    her maintain order in her life and within herself. She went on to say,
    "I had had lots of sex, a life of free love—it was enough of that."*

13, 14, & 15. They agreed that they were an economic and social unit and that marriage served as an inspiration to work and build, etc., but that marriage was not a cover for their aggressive drives.

17. Susan: "As a lover I have been let down and I am dejected because of this." Jonathan: "Expected more settling by my wife into middle-class life style and higher sexual drive. Result: uncertainty and frustration." Both felt that the answers above served as an adequate summary and had nothing to add.

Category 2. Psychological and Biological Needs

1. *Independence-Dependence.* Jonathan: "Set style and pattern for myself. Feel I am too dependent on my wife physically and materially and not dependent enough spiritually." *In the session he elaborated that he recognizes he is too dependent on Susan to take care of his physical needs at home, such as preparing meals, initiating recreational and cultural activities, etc. By spiritual he meant he has come to recognize and give credence to some of the facets of relating to people and approaching life that she has espoused, even in terms of his developing some interest in music and in the significance of spiritual values.* Susan: "I set the pattern for myself; very often I feel either abandoned—'my God, am I here all alone?' feeling—or else my husband is too dependent on me and I feel put upon. This is a troublesome area." *In the session they talked as if these statements were more from the past; the implication was that although still present such problems had diminished. They cited a variety of incidents to remind each other that there had been a shift, although not yet to the ideal, from the above. Jonathan stated that they were really becoming much more interdependent in a good way, with which Susan concurred.*

2. *Activity-passivity.* Jonathan: "Feel both are too passive and especially me." Susan: "I agree." *In the session much was made by Susan of Jonathan's passivity; it makes her angry with him and turns her off sexually. She does not care how active he may be at work— with her he acts like a passive child. He agreed and felt it was contrary to his nature to be otherwise. However, he said he would accept more responsibility to take the initiative at home.*

3. *Closeness-distance.* Jonathan: "Expected more closeness than I am getting. Am aware of distance between us." Susan: "There is distance between us. When there is closeness it is a noticeable and

pleasant occurrence. Would like it to happen more but can't force this sort of thing." *In the session we went into several incidents in which Susan was responsible for distancing because of her lack of communication to Jon and her projection of her own feelings. For him, on the other hand, closeness meant being the adored child. Actually, they are now closer more often than when first seen. For example, if he wants to watch football on television he often invites Sue to join him, which she sometimes does. She is appreciative of this change from his previous way of just peremptorily picking himself up and leaving her alone. As she has become disappointed in her spiritualist movement she has turned more to him for closeness and support. Most of the time he has been there for her.*

4. & 5. *Power; submission and domination.* There was no response to this subject. *They were not ready to deal directly with all the implications of this area. When asked they said it had been adequately covered in terms of his passivity and that each felt they acted quite independently and therefore shared power. He felt he submitted to her in regard to sex, but not otherwise. Conversely, she felt she was controlled by his sexual passivity and lack of help with home chores. Actually, both still abdicate power in many common areas of their interrelationship and resolve it by an uneasy assignment and assumption of traditional roles and duties. To an extent they remain two children in search of a parent, but with a growing recognition that neither will accept the parental role and that they have to work toward a more mature interdependence with the surrender of more of their childish expectations.*

6. *Abandonment and loneliness fears.* Jonathan: "These fears definitely exist and are an important source of anxiety." *Jon was referring to Sue's withdrawal of affect when she would become more deeply involved with her sect. He knew he could not reach her then. He feels somewhat better since she is no longer as deeply involved, having become disillusioned with her sect's leader, who turned out not to be as strong and loving a father image as she wanted. She now turns more to Jon. He likes this but is also somewhat apprehensive over the expectations and obligations that go with Susan's turning to him more.* Susan: "I feel abandoned when the load falls on me and I feel inadequate." *By "the load" Susan meant the traditional chores of housekeeping and child rearing. She feels that in view of her support to Jon in his accepting a lower paying job that he liked, and their agreement not to accept money from her mother,*

she is entitled to more support in chores and child-care responsibilities when he is home. He agreed but stated that she must tell him what she wants or where she needs help and not assume he should know, because she is not sensitive (resistant?) to these needs. She recognized the need to express her wants as they occur, and not to collect a long series of injuries.

7. *Possession and control of spouse.* This item was not responded to. *Each felt that in category 1, item 1, and under independence-dependence they had been clear that neither wanted to possess, but both recognized in the session that although each "respected" the other's autonomy, autonomy was allowable only in areas of non-concern or nonthreat to the other. Here again there was no answer to a question that is a central problem area. In the session this was called to their attention with humor—a "sure, you don't have to control when you're getting what you want" sort of approach.*

8. *Level of anxiety.* Both responded: "Level of anxiety can get high for each. Triggered by any of the problem areas at any given time. We react to it by withdrawing from each other." *Their recognition of this marks a big advance for them. It was suggested to them in the session that they be more alert to try to deal directly with the anxiety. Not feeling too upset when the other withdrew was fine, but could this entering wedge into helping each other be advanced further?*

9. *Feelings about yourself as a man or woman.* Jonathan: "Often inadequate." *He bases this on the fact that Susan does not stroke his ego and make passionate love to him very often on her own initiative. On the other hand, he recognizes that recently they have had excellent sex several times when he was loving to her; she then responded openly and freely. But he had to be active! He recognizes that he has enjoyed good sex with her, but on her terms. His sense of inadequacy, as well as Susan's, is also based on other aspects that were dealt with in the session. The similarity of their responses was pointed out and the question was left with them of how they could best help each other reevaluate him/herself.* Susan: "I don't feel beautiful or lovable. I cannot abide the feeling that I am desired and loved and I find ways to deny it. For example, I feel that the lover is turning me into an object, or I cannot conceive the meaning of desire without this dimension of mystery, or I use fantasies that cause shame. The feeling of shame is painful so I avoid sex." *Although it had been talked around several times, this was her first*

forthright statement about feeling a lack of lovability. Her avoidance of sex is due, at least in part, to shame for her fantasies and for her past sexual freedom and promiscuity. Jonathan wants her to act with him as she did with others in the past, thus arousing strong shame, anxiety, and antipathy in her. When she is praised for her beauty or for any other reason, she feels it must be false because she knows she is not perfect. From her childhood she has believed that perfection is required of her if she is to be loved. And now her husband loves her for what she considers a most heinous imperfection! This is an apparent contradiction with which she needs additional help. Her rejection of Jon for his passivity in turn increases his feelings of masculine inadequacy which are already so close to the surface.

10. *Physical and personality characteristics of mate that affect your sexual reaction.* Jonathan: "I recognize that my wife is objectively attractive, but her sexual passivity and coldness turn me off. I would like a more active partner who enjoys the activity." Susan: "My husband does not turn me on because he is too absorbed with a male image, being what he thinks is masculine, macho behavior. For example, liking football is a male activity. Also, I feel he is fettered in matter, fettered in his body." *By this last sentence Sue meant that Jon's body is too tight and that he cannot enter sex sufficiently with his spirit as well as his body. Other aspects of their sexuality were covered above; this area is improved but remains a problem that reflects the conflicts within each person as well as between them.*

11. *Ability to love and to accept yourself and your mate.* Jonathan: "Yes." *In view of what he has just stated this monosyllabic answer cannot be taken at face value.* Susan: "No, for above reasons." (See 9 and 10.) *It is quite clear that each can only partly accept himself or the other. There is a growing acceptance of each other that is not based on "I am not much so I am not entitled to more." The latter may have been unconsciously operative for each, but if so it is a diminishing force.*

12. *How do you and your mate approach problems?* Jonathan: "Both make halfhearted attempts to tackle problems, then withdraw." Susan: "Approach problems differently. Gives us something to talk about. I do agree that we make halfhearted attempts and withdraw." *Jonathan often does not state his ideas and feelings—as when he did not question Susan when she was sleeping on the floor—and she*

expects a loving husband-father to divine her needs and feelings. She approaches problems more intuitively, he in an organized "rational" way. Their attempts to resolve problems have remained half-hearted and they are not consistent in pursuing them to resolution; they state a position and then tend to let it rest there, yet over a period of time do change. They seem to be loathe to acknowledge positive changes and backslide somewhat when not in active treatment.

13. Both felt they had covered adequately those areas in which the mate let them down or caused trouble.
15. Both felt no summary was necessary as their wants and wishes to give had been adequately covered among their other responses. *However, both were much clearer about what they wanted than they were about what they would give the other!*

Category 3. Derivative Problems

1. *Communication—sending and receiving.* They agreed they had serious communication problems. *In the session this was a major focus of attention because they, particularly Sue, often do not send clear messages, nor do they always listen to the message that is sent. Sue is too attuned to the latent meaning in Jon's messages; he takes her too literally. I coached them in how to practice open and clear communication.*

2. *Intellectual differences.* They both agreed that these were numerous, and that there are different views of what is important. *Despite this statement, it was clear in the session that they now have much more common ground than they had 20 months ago. They are both highly intelligent people.*

3. *Energy level. Both interpreted this question in terms of active-passive and agreed that Susan's energy level is higher than his and that she wants him to have more energy, more activity. This problem has been discussed earlier.*

4. *Interests, life style.* Jonathan: "Vast differences between us." *He alludes to outdoors, spiritual, cultural, etc., although the activities they had shared most recently were contrary to this flat statement.* Susan: "I love to sing and dance, and we hardly ever do it." *But why she does not arrange for such activities either together or by herself we did not get to in the session.*

5. *Families of origin.* No problems now that peace has been made between Susan and her mother.

6. *Child rearing.* Jonathan: Not a problem area, since husband lets wife do most of it, which she resents, so it is somewhat of a problem area in that respect." *That sums it up neatly. No separate response from Susan, which means they both agree. Like many of the other responses this does not mean that there is an acceptable single contractual arrangement on this issue. It is a statement of what is, and it will require work to either change it or make it acceptable to both by means of quid pro quos or in some other way.*

7. *Children.* Both agree that children are not used in alliances against either parent, nor does either parent identify a particular child with spouse or self.

8. *Family or personal myth.* Both agree that there are none. *I felt that there is a myth about how different they are from each other, which is a false concept in many respects. This idea was not pleasing to either of them—it had the effect of a confrontation.*

9. *Money.* Both agree there is not enough to fight over, but they do have concern about the lack of it. *The strong feelings about money have lessened; they have tightened their belts. I do have some concern because they do not appear to have plans for changing the situation, a somewhat unrealistic position and perhaps somewhat irresponsible. The stress of money shortage is felt more by Susan, who is weighted down by household duties that interfere with her creative work. Therefore this too remains an unresolved contractual area.*

10. *Sex.* Jonathan: "Wife initiates most of the time, mainly because I feel undesired and do not want to impose on her. Very low frequency in sex. No alternative sex partners. Sex is generally not pleasurable or gratifying because of above reasons." Susan: "See category 2. I feel we both want terrific romance in our lives. There is a hardness in my heart that keeps me from feeling or being a good lover. We are opening our hearts a tiny crack toward one another. I feel hopeful, as though the marriage begins again after the first seven years—at a different plateau, with some trust." *As stated earlier, sex has been better than they record here but it is still far from satisfactory. "Hardness" in Susan's heart refers to her alleged disappointment at Jon's passivity, but also to her now revealed judgmental attitude toward herself. Note Jon's complaint and his method of attempting to manipulate Sue into taking the initiative.*

11. *Values.* Jonathan: "I feel wife's values are more spiritual, romantic,

religious, and artistic, while mine are more worldly." Susan: "I feel husband's values are often too male-oriented, or incomprehensible, irreverent, irrelevant. On the other hand, I see his sensitivity for the underdog and the defenseless and would like him to open up more to that side of himself." *Jonathan is somewhat defensively cowed by what he seems to assume to be the "better" values of his wife. Early in therapy I may have countertransferentially helped to increase this feeling, but I believe this is no longer operative. Her response, as well as his, is indicative of their moves toward understanding, even if they do not yet accept one another. In this single contract, as well as in the session, Susan saw many of Jon's positions as being "too male-oriented." Again a single contract is not agreed upon here; the differences are described and Susan outlines how she would like Jonathan to change.*

12. *Friends.* Jonathan: "We share most. I have some of my own, individually. I have no female friends, only acquaintances." Susan: "I have friends of the opposite, as well as the same, gender." *There do not seem to be serious problems in this area anymore. He is much less threatened by her friends now, especially since her disillusionment with her spiritual leader and her turning more to him.*

13. *Gender-determined roles.* Jonathan: "I feel it is husband's duty to work and earn money and wife's responsibility to keep house and rear children." Susan: "When other things are not going well it becomes an irritation and I feel alone in marriage, but if we are strongly together, this sharp division does not actually exist." *As often happens, Jonathan sounds much more rigid and heavy-handed than he really is. Susan apparently has come to know this. This was corroborated in the session.*

14. *List those areas where you feel let down.* Jonathan: "Primarily sexual area and common interests area." Susan: "I feel let down on Jon's energy level, our lack of communications, that our interests are so different, and I am disappointed in sex life. But I don't dwell on it." *This is their common refrain—except for her last sentence. Note that whenever both write different responses, Jonathan is always first. I forgot to ask why.*

15. *How do you react when you have been let down?* Jonathan: "I withdraw." Susan: "I feel anger and withdraw."

16. *Other areas not mentioned.* No responses.

17. *Summary statement.* Jonathan: "See my summary at end of category 1." *Actually he had not summarized, and he did not elaborate*

further except in our discussion. Susan: "I want high energy with a lot of verbal and love give-and-take between my Beloved and myself. In turn I will give high energy level and verbal give-and-take and love give-and-take between Beloved and myself. I now see my husband giving more with the children. I'd like him to initiate more activities. There are some beginnings here that I want to encourage. I want an outdoors man. In turn I will play cards."

Susan continued:

I will give:

I want to give receptive devotion. I want to be a nurturing adult to my children and an uplifting force to my husband and home. I want to see the possibility of my divine self, what is creative and loving in me, expressing itself.

In return I will get:

I want to get a partner with fire in his spirit whose spirituality, good thoughts, and sage advice give a fatherly life-giving character to our family. I visualize a mature father, radiating his creative power of love and warmth toward our children and affectionate caring for them. *Does she ask for more than she has a right to expect from Jonathan? Can she make compromises without being bitter? Can he insist upon open communication from her and that they accept one another on a more realistic level? I believe they have moved some in this direction. I also believe they want to continue to do so. The decisions will, of course, have to be theirs.*

DISCUSSION

The single contract indicated that each knew himself better now and had fewer illusions about the other. They were very clear about where and what their problems were. They saw themselves as a couple and had made some advances in trusting each other, but sex, although better in general, still suffered from each one's being set in his own fantasy of what he/she wanted to receive before giving.

They no longer accepted money from her mother, so that financially they were in a crunch, but they felt united and pleased with themselves. However, Susan showed her resentment over the pressure on her (a large house, no help, and caring for and chauffering children, etc.) with what she felt was too little help from Jon. She resented what she described as his macho position. They agreed they had many ideological and taste differences.

When they came in for the follow-up interview I felt much better about them than when I had read their single contract. They looked well and happy and treated each other with affection and respect. I asked them how they felt about the single contract. They said it had been difficult for them to write out because it had confronted them with themselves and they felt negative when filling it out; however, they went on to say that they had felt much better about themselves since then. They had realized that they had focused on negative things in writing up the contract and there were actually many positive things going on between them.

In working with their written single contract I did not go down the list item by item but stimulated discussion. In advance I had noted areas that needed to be covered or that I wished to interpret or reinforce.

I started by reading Susan's response: "I feel we both want terrific romance in our lives. . . . I feel hopeful, as though the marriage begins again after the first seven years—at a different plateau, with some trust." It was after I read this that Susan responded with the eloquent statement I have placed at the beginning of this chapter.

At one point Sue reminded Jon of several good sexual experiences they had shared recently. He then reminded her of how close they had felt driving together at night through a heavy snowstorm: "We worked together like one person with four eyes." When they got home early that morning they had the best sex they had had in a long time. As the session went on, more and more positive aspects of their behavior came through, not only in what they remembered but in their interaction and tenderness to each other.

Jon pointed out how Susan accumulates frustration and bitterness toward him and then lets it come out all at one time. He made a plea for her to be more open and spontaneous with him. She then responded with the insight about why she gets upset when she is praised or told how attractive she is—not because she fears sex or to be a sex object only, but because as a child she had to be perfect.

She feels imperfect and therefore inadequate. This was a whole new area for Jon; he was surprised because he had felt he was the flawed one.

Susan and Jon have moved closer together. They, with their children, have become more united as a family unit. They are struggling, making headway, and dealing more realistically with each other and their life situation. They are now less like two children in search of a parent and realize that neither will be parent to the other. They still want that, but more as if it has become a pro forma demand—a ritual that no longer has meaning or expectation of fulfillment.

This is not the most dramatically successful case I have treated; yet I am pleased with the results, especially in view of where Sue and Jon were when they began therapy. We have done very well to have reversed a deteriorating process in the marital and family systems and the two individuals. I believe Sue and Jon and their children now have a good chance for a better life together. Their work on themselves will have to continue as they improve their single contract.

In this last session I tried to focus on giving them the tools to continue to work on their own problems by means of the single contract. They are equipped and motivated to continue to try to make changes in their problem areas. We will have another session in six months, or sooner if they request it.

"There's a lot to be said about sticking with something, because if you give up at the seven there *is* a death, but there is a resurrection coming if you can just stick with it."

6

Behavioral Profiles

SOME GENERAL REMARKS made earlier need to be reinforced as we approach the subject of behavioral profiles. Rapidly changing social forces are affecting almost everyone's values these days, and changing values are especially apparent in man-woman relationships. In working with couples it becomes clear that for most of us our ideology is further "advanced" than is our emotional readiness to deal with the effects of our gender-determined training. Money and Ehrhardt (1972) discovered that boy and girl gender assignment has been determined for the child by the age of 18 months and that it is extremely difficult, if not impossible, to reverse gender choice and acceptance much after that time. What we have learned about gender-determined behavior, roles, and expectations is deeply ingrained in all of us. Thus, to some extent we are all the children as well as prisoners of our time. We struggle to change but change is difficult.

The behavioral profiles described in the following pages are presented as I have observed them from as nonjudgmental and unbiased a point of view as possible. Yet I know that bias, including some male supremacist attitudes, must come through because I was brought up as a male in a male-dominated society. As a male I can speak for women with even less authority than I can for men. Further, whatever I say cannot possibly be acceptable to everyone since, of course, strong differences in viewpoint do exist among many people of equally good will.

There are many different roads to the same objective as well as different objectives for different people. It is important for the therapist to keep in mind that other people's values, priorities, and purposes and goals are as valid for them as the therapist's are for him.

In my work with people I make several assumptions that are reflected in this chapter: 1) that most men and women desire, seek, and need a loving and committed relationship with another human being; 2) that love can be and is a potent force in the life of people of all ages and is desired, except by those who were injured at a very young age so that they never learned to love or find it very difficult to do so, and by those who either have loved and been hurt and are fearful of being injured again, or have been seriously hurt by other life experiences.

There is no one paradigm of *how* men and women can or should regard each other, share marital or family tasks and responsibilities, develop attitudes and feelings about a monogamous or a sexually open marriage, and so on. Any two committed persons must find the way that works best for them at that point. For example, the old shibboleth that men are active and women are passive, whether in sex or decision-making, has existed for many centuries, and women as well as men have been taught that they must play out their assigned role or be considered a masculinized woman or a castrated man. Active-passive assumptions, as just one example, have led to much unhappiness and exploitation of both genders through the ages. The belief that passive or active attributes are gender-determined genetically is now changing as the social climate changes. The same can be said for many other factors that affect individual behavior, as well as interactions between men and women.

The subtle attitudes that make it a reality for two people to respect the individuality of each other and to recognize the need to create a matrix for one's partner's growth, as well as one's own, and yet to be joined together as a marital and family unit with joint purpose and goals, are difficult to achieve and to sustain. This is what increasing numbers of women and men want, and have been taught they have a right to expect; yet few are able to achieve and sustain such a relationship over a long period. This chapter explores in greater detail what goes into determining the crucial interactions of two committed persons. At this point in our knowledge we cannot know all the factors that determine a particular transaction, but we can now understand, and therefore influence, such transactions better than we could just a few years ago.

Within committed couples each partner adopts a characteristic way of relating to the other. There may be some fluidity and change in various situations, but for any period of time each has a major mode of relating with the other that is his personality imprint with his mate. With another partner, even one similar to the first, the slight variances that exist can evoke different behavioral patterns for each partner. It is this particular style of the couple that creates the quality of the interaction of their marriage. It is their unique relationship, determined by their unspoken interactional contract.

I have found seven major styles of reacting that individuals have with their mates, which I call behavioral profiles. Each of these partner types describes a way of relating that has broad general characteristics. They are not rigid categories, and most people show some characteristics of different profiles or may shift from one to another in a single day. In working with couples I try to select the profile that is most frequently used in decisive interactions and that best reflects the style and quality of each partner's relationship with the other, but I also try to be alert to the variations each individual is bound to encompass.

We have seen in previous chapters how each member of a couple has his own contract, of which he is partly conscious, and how the couple also has a single, probably unexpressed, collusive interactional contract, some components of which may be in their two individual contracts. The interactional contract contains the essence of how they deal with each other, including the games they play together.

Any related couple is a system with its own rules, conventions, customs, dos and don'ts, and style of doing or not doing things. These may be similar to, or different from, what either or both mates individually believe or the way in which either or both would act with other people. They comprise a system which is determined in part by the total life experiences and heredity of each; nevertheless, it is separate and different from all other dyads because their combination is as different as each person's fingerprints. We can classify relationships in broad categories with the realization that, unlike fingerprints, dyadic interactions and patternings change, though often with great resistance.

When the name of a particular profile is used for each of the mates, the combination of the two names—as, for example, romantic-childlike partners—provides a simple rough typography of the marriage which can be very helpful in therapy. For example, two other sketches are the parallel partner and the equal partner profiles. Together they would then be a parallel-equal partner couple. The determinants of these behavioral profiles are multicausal, but at this point in our knowledge their causality cannot be explained any more successfully than one can explain why one person is obsessive, a second has hysteria, or a third has a low anxiety threshold.

Although I cannot say why it is so, those mates who have a particular behavioral patterning also have a somewhat particular patterning of their needs as reflected in the 12 areas of biological and intrapsychic parameters that we look for in the two individual marriage contracts. Each of the couple's needs is rated in relation to each of these areas on a scale from 1 to 9 (see Appendix 2). In the following descriptions of the profiles these 12 areas of needs and expectations are referred to in summarizing the characteristics of each behavioral profile. On a simple observational and evaluative level, this approach to typifying each partner's behavior and consequent transactions with the other appears to have merit and clinical applicability. Adequate refinement of methodology for testing these hypotheses lies ahead.

Clinical observation suggests that each partner acts with the other in the relationship as a certain "type," in accordance with one of the seven behavioral profiles. In considering these profiles, three important points should be borne in mind. First, the seven behavioral profiles do not comprise all the possible types, although other identifiable qualities could probably be subsumed under one of the seven descriptions. Second, an individual's choice of mate may have been guided by his perception of that mate as a particular type, but his perception may not be accurate; it may be colored by his own realistic or neurotic needs, including the need to deny positive or negative attributes in terms of his own value system and unconscious needs and fears. What evolves is often quite different from what each mate may have anticipated or is currently aware of. Third, as experiences and circumstances alter the dynamics of each partner and of the marital system, each spouse may suddenly or gradually behave as a different type from what he was at another time in the relationship.

The profiles described here typify the normal as well as the mildly-to-moderately psychopathological. They could be described as the dyadic interactional pathology of everyday life, to paraphrase Freud. Although I do not attempt to describe the most pathological or bizarre forms of dyadic interrelationships, any of the profiles, extrapolated to its extreme, could make for an extremely pathological relationship.

Each profile is defined, in part, in terms of a complementary type of partner. This clarifies the full interactional dimensions and quality of the partner type. The seven partner profiles to be discussed in detail are the *equal, romantic, parental, childlike, rational, companionate,* and *parallel* partner.

Equal Partner

The possibility of being an equal partner in marriage is an optimum toward which many (not all) people in all classes of today's society seem to be striving. It reflects the emergent philosophy of our time regarding individualism, maintenance of one's self within a relationship of sharing, and equality between men and women. An intellectual ideal for the middle-class intellectual of yesteryear, this philosophy began to become a reality for the working-class woman during World War II, when her participation in the work force became an important part of the nation's and her family's economy.

The person who acts as an equal partner in his interactions seeks a relationship on equal terms for himself and his spouse (whether or not the partner wants equality). The equal partner expects that both will have the same rights, privileges, and obligations, without any overt or covert double-standard clauses. The equal partner expects each to be a complete person in his or her own right, largely self-activating, with his own work and friends, but responsive to the needs of the mate and emotionally interdependent with him or her. Consequently, each would respect the individuality, including weaknesses and fallibilities, of the mate.

An attempt to summarize the "ideal" relationship of the 1960s was made by Frederick S. Perls in his often-quoted poem:

> I do my thing, and you do your thing.
> I am not in this world to live up to your expectations.
> And you are not in this world to live up to mine.
> You are you and I am I,
> And if by chance we find each other,
> it's beautiful.

At first reading these lines seemed just right to me. Then gradually I realized that there was no reference to "our thing." The lines conveyed no sense of commitment or determination to try to keep something beautiful alive. It seemed to be a reaction formation to the negative aspects of centuries of no-divorce, loveless marriage. A couple I know who were living together had a framed poster with the poem and a lovely picture of a couple holding one another in the long grass of a field. Early on they kept the poster in their bedroom. A year later they moved to a larger apartment with a study-guest room and hung it there. Then they moved to a house, got a dog, bought a boat together, and a year later decided to become married. When I last visited them I noticed the poster again. It was now resting on a shelf off the staircase on the way to the basement. When I brought the poster upstairs to copy the poem, both asked me if I would like to keep it. I smiled, said no, and we talked about how our ideas and values change. They felt that they now lived as equal partners and no longer had to talk about it very often. A few months later they told me that the husband's 13-year-old daughter had noticed the poster. She asked if she might have it for her bedroom and they gladly gave it to her! Apparently, as the couple's commitment to each other deepened the poem was moved further away. The youth saved it from oblivion and started it on another cycle. Perhaps the poem beautifully expresses the ideal for a brief encounter, or short-term bonding, but is not appropriate for the long-term bonded commitment most people seem to seek. For a long-term relationship, the equal-partner idea needs to be tempered with more commitment to each other and to the relationship.

The equal partner must be reasonably able to welcome and tolerate a mature peer relationship, to be relatively noncompetitive with the spouse, and to understand and respect gender differences so that these are not used to the disadvantage of either mate. The equal partner must be relatively free of urgency to have infantile needs fulfilled, and aware that his own lovability cannot be dependent on how effectively he fulfills the infantile needs of his mate. Yet, at the same time, there is a capacity to sometimes be the child and be taken care of, or to be parental to one's partner when that is needed.

In the 12 areas of the biological and intrapsychic determinants of the marriage contract (the thirteenth, dominance-submission, is subsumed under power), the equal partner tends to have the following characteristics. *These reveal a trend or tendency;* they are the more common findings but are not absolute or exclusive of others.

1. *Independence-dependence.* Tends to be more on the independent side; is not defensively independent but is cooperative and emotionally interdependent with his mate.
2. *Active-passive.* Tends generally to be more active than passive and is generally self-actuating; can accept being passive when it is appropriate for his mate to be more active.
3. *Closeness-distance.* Tends to be capable of close, sustained intimacy without clinging. A positive characteristic of this type is the ability to be appropriately close without incorporating or being swallowed oneself by the mate. There is minimal need for defenses against closeness.
4. *Power.* Is able to share, to accept areas of greater decision-making responsibility and to allow the mate to do the same; is around the midpoint, being neither submissive nor dominating. Competitiveness with mate is not destructive if it is present.
5. *Fear of abandonment.* Is at the most only mild-to-moderate, or an equal partner could not function as such; would be

shaken and pained, but not broken, by abandonment. It is *not* a major influence on his behavior.

6. *Possess and control spouse.* Wants neither to possess nor to be possessed, but does give and expect commitment.
7. *Anxiety level.* Very low-to-moderate. Rarely is it high for very long.
8. *Defense mechanisms.* May utilize any of the mechanisms of defense against anxiety. The defenses used commonly, but not exclusively, are likely to be repression, projection, intellectualization, sublimation, perceptual defense, and identification.
9. *Gender identity.* Usually no significant problem.
10. *Sexual response to mate.* Can vary all the way from most exciting to only moderately sexually responsive.
11. *Capacity to love self and mate.* Excellent to moderate.
12. *Cognitive style.* a) Respects own mate's style; acutely aware of own and mate's. b) May have any cognitive style. The style the equal partner has is usually well developed and defined.

ROMANTIC PARTNER

Just as the equal partner is the wave of today, the romantic is the wave of the most recent past. The romantic partner concept still prevails widely, even among many of those who now aspire to be equal partners. The exciting and polymorphous element of love is paramount for the romantic partner.

The romantic partner behaves as such interactionally even if he does not have a romantic ideology. He acts as if he wants and expects his partner to be his soul mate and as if together they will be one entity. Such a person acts as if he were incomplete—only with his partner can he become whole.

Since the romantic believes he can function at his best and be happy only when in a relationship with another romantic, he becomes vulnerable when his partner refuses to play the romantic with him. Again and again he tries to make his partner into a romantic. This frequently becomes the major game they play together: the romantic pushing and testing, the partner pulling back but encouraging just enough to keep the game going. The game also becomes the vehicle for their complaints about one another—the romantic complaining, "He (she) is not sensitive, loving, etc."; the partner, about the romantic, "He (she) is always clinging and demanding, always wants me to prove my love, always to be with me."

The security some couples find as a romantic dyad appears to release abilities in either or both that cannot be self-activated without the love of the other. The romantic seeks fulfillment of his childhood aspiration to be the sole object of the love, adoration, and support of his mother or father. His need is frequently rooted in the oedipal situation and the desire for exclusive rights to the services and loving affect of the parent of the opposite sex. Consequently the romantic is often insatiable and cannot receive enough proof of love. When reasonably secure in a romantic relationship, that individual can then flower and exploit his potential more fully. Because of the romantic's great overvaluation of his partner and lack of sense of completion without his mate, he tends to be very jealous and protective of their relationship. Love and sexual passion are usually very important and intensity of passion is often used as litmus paper to test the current quality of the relationship. Interdependence is usually pervasive, playing a role in many parameters of functioning.

Most romantics become anxious when they believe their partner may discover something about them that will not fit into the partner's romantic image. They also fear discovering something in the partner that will not concur with their own image of the idealized partner. They want to believe! Hence they will rationalize perceived deviations from their idealized Gestalt (individual contract) or will use a perceptual defense to shut out the sound of internal warning bells that would cue them to a trait that could be inconsistent with the perception of the mate.

The tendency of the romantic to use perceptual defenses and denial makes understandable the great sense of betrayal that is experienced when the romantic can no longer deny behavior in his partner that makes the latter appear to have changed or to have duped him, although no significant change in his partner's actions or affective state may actually have occurred. Yet, the impossibility of getting his partner to behave as a romantic, too, would have been apparent to any perceptive outsider, who could readily see that the mate could not deliver, and had not agreed to deliver, what his spouse expected of him.

Romantics tend to place great significance on sentimental symbols, possibly as a method of concretizing their uniqueness to one another and of holding onto or recapturing the passion of their early bonding period. Thus anniversaries become important to them (date of the first time they met, kissed, had sex together, the sharing of songs that are especially meaningful to them, and so on). This is similar to the magical thinking of the adult who tries to recapture memories and symbols of positive childhood experiences to make the past alive in the present.

In the 12 areas the romantic partner tends to have the following characteristics:

1. *Independence-dependence.* Is dependent on his mate, although he may or may not initiate or set the style.
2. *Active-passive.* May be anywhere along the line from extremely active to quite passive.
3. *Closeness-distance.* Very close emotionally.
4. *Power.* Anywhere from submissive to equal to dominating. Because the romantic partner expects and wants his mate to want, feel, and experience as he does, there may be pseudo domination, submission, or equality. Varying degrees of competitiveness with partner may be present.
5. *Fear of abandonment.* A high and a significant motivating factor in determining behavior.
6. *Possess and control spouse.* Is very possessive and controlling, even when appearing to be submissive to his spouse.
7. *Anxiety level.* Tends to be on the high side. The need for a partner who will complete the sense of self often indicates a deeply felt sense of incompleteness and inability to cope with a hostile world.
8. *Defense mechanisms.* Most likely to be used are repression, regression, reaction formation, projection, introjection and identification, denial, perceptual defense, sublimation, fantasy, altruistic surrender, and reversal. As might be anticipated, commonly requires the use of many defenses.
9. *Gender identity.* Some mild gender identity problems may exist. These may be manifested in an apparent overidentification with one's spouse and with contra-gender concepts, sensitivities, and so on, that are not accepted by the romantic on a deep level.

10. *Sexual response to mate.* Usually very intense.
11. *Love of self and mate.* May be high or the romantic may feel empty and need the mate desperately. Love and fear often become confused. Sometimes this may not be the true love it appears to be; there may be a narcissistic quality in which identification with one's mate as part of oneself is so marked that loving one's mate is loving oneself.
12. *Cognitive style.* a) Usually wants or feels impelled to respect his mate's style and may use the complementarity between the two very effectively. b) Style may range from intuitive to moderately well organized.

PARENTAL PARTNER

The parental partner may be considered a master, which is essentially a controlling and authoritarian parent extrapolated to an extreme. Intermediate between the parent and the master are the schoolmaster or schoolmistress and the teacher who relates to his mate as if the latter were a child. Many possible variations and modifications along the good-parent-to-master continuum occur to accommodate to individual needs. The "rescuer" represents a particular and often transient form of parental partner.

The prototype of the parent or master is Torvold, Nora's husband in Ibsen's *A Doll's House.* The parental partner exercises governing and caretaking control over his mate and infantilizes him or her. He or she may do so from his own proclivities, or be maneuvered into being parental by the mate, or through a combination of both. The parental partner's role may be a benign and loving one that fosters, within limits, the "child's" need for growth and independence. The script requires that the child continue to feel either sufficiently insecure to accept being "bought off," seduced and overpowered, or masochistic enough to give up individualism or freedom. On the other hand, rather than assume the role of the protective parent, the parental partner may behave as a punitive, authoritarian parent and seek to elicit from his mate the counterpart role of the obedient child held in psychological bondage. When the childlike partner threatens to disturb the status quo, the parental partner often becomes more demanding in an effort not to lose the child. A more mature and less pathological parental partner who loves his childlike partner might consider what is best for the latter and help the child prepare for a new relationship or collaborate in establishing a new and more equal modus vivendi for the two of them.

The essence of the dynamics of the parental partner is that the parent needs to shore up his sense of adult self by being parent to an obedient child-spouse. The parent's word is law and an important cornerstone of this type of dyad. Transgressions may be tolerated so long as these are the actions of a mildly rebellious or foolish child whose irresponsible foibles may be forgiven by the understanding, benevolent, patronizing parent. The parent's underlying lack of self-esteem is defended against by a rigid structure designed to prove that he is adult, competent, lovable, just, and kind. Closeness may exist, but it must be on the parent's terms.

The parent has no time to listen to his mate talk about growing up and making decisions for himself. He may encourage the mate to open a boutique or to take a course or even to matriculate for a bachelor's or advanced degree, but these activities are regarded as akin to opening a lemonade stand on the side of a quiet road in summer. When the "child" reaches for serious work or study, there may be subtle sabotage, if not outright fear and rage, as the threat to the status quo becomes apparent to the partner. The child may also be needed to enable the parental partner to express those aspects of herself/himself that are psychologically prohibited to the parent. As would be expected, the parent in the couple's interaction emerges as the more assertive and active style setter of the couple.

Rescuer Subtype

The rescuer, a subtype of parental partner that warrants particular attention, usually forms a complementary relationship with a "save-me" type. This is often a relatively transient and unstable contractual arrangement. When the crisis is over, a new contractual agreement is reached, or the relationship dissolves, or a new crisis emerges that again requires a rescue operation. There are some who strive, with their mate's collaboration, to maintain their rescuer role.

The rescuer needs to be, or is, manipulated and accepts his mate as someone who requires saving from a difficult life situation; he is prepared and eager to take responsibility for the rescued person. Mutual rescue is not uncommon. Two romantics may start their relationship as a mutual rescue from their respective "nonromantic" spouses. In general, however, the rescuer usually has to feel superior to the person rescued, who may then be patronized for his weakness, childishness, lack of worldliness, etc.

The rescuer's basic contract is premised on an effort to be one-up in the relationship—not merely to help someone who is loved, but to indenture some "helpless" person to himself by saving that person from a bad situation (parents' home, bad marriage, poverty, alcoholism, drug abuse, poor health). He will continue to protect his mate as long as the saved person will remain loyal to him and accept his "save me" position. The rescuer who does his job well may slide into becoming a parental partner.

The rescuer may be kindly and well motivated; he is not scheming or evil. He simply may have a need to rescue, based on his own sense of inadequacy about his ability to be loved.

In the 12 areas the parental partner tends to have these characteristics:

1. *Independence-dependence.* Tends to be more on the independent side. However, he may be very dependent on the childlike partner to stay in that role and may go to great lengths to keep his mate there, reflecting his own deep dependency.
2. *Active-passive.* Tends to be more active.
3. *Closeness-distance.* May be anywhere along the continuum from closeness to great distance.
4. *Power.* Has a need to experience and use power and to dominate his mate; is competitive and must constantly demonstrate his superior competence.
5. *Fear of abandonment.* An important behavioral determinant. He cannot afford to lose his mate.
6. *Possess and control mate.* Need to do so is great, although the childlike mate often has greater control ultimately.
7. *Anxiety level.* Ranges from almost absent to extremely high.
8. *Defense mechanisms.* Most commonly used mechanisms of defense are likely to be repression, reaction formation, intellectualization, displacement, perceptual defense, and fantasy to sustain denial.

9. *Gender identity.* Usually no marked problems, although sometimes his stance may be a defense against a deep gender insecurity.
10. *Sexual response to mate.* May be anywhere along the scale from great responsiveness to virtually unresponsive; generally tends to be more on the responsive side.
11. *Love of self and others.* May be anywhere in the continuum from none to extremely positive.
12. *Cognitive style.* a) Tends to deprecate or be patronizing about his mate's cognitive style. b) His style tends to be well organized and to lead to prompt problem solving.

CHILDLIKE PARTNER

The childlike partner is the counterpart of the parental partner. In the extreme and most pathological form, the "child" will become "slave" to the "master" partner. The childlike partner has a predisposition to interact as a child and reacts unbecomingly if his partner desires to be a child himself, and may maneuver his mate into the parental role. In the interaction he aims to be cared for, protected, disciplined, and guided. In exchange for being taken care of, the child offers the parental partner the right to feel more adult, to be needed and to have his defense system supported. Additionally, the "child" may bring joy and gladness to his "parent" in many ways.

As in some actual parent-child relationships, the childlike partner often becomes the true wielder of power. His power derives from the parent's overwhelming need to keep the child in a childlike role so that he can define his own sense of self as an adult. Most child partners sense their power and are able to exploit the situation by threatening to leave. Although often present in heterosexual dyads, the child's power is most clearly seen in homosexual dyads, in which the parental homosexual frequently lives in fear of losing his controlling child partner.

Most men and women retain aspects of childhood dependence regardless of what realistic competence they have achieved. It is the ability to bring forth the creative child in oneself that adds to the charm of many partners. However, the creative and playful child in everyone is not to be confused with the person who utilizes childlike dependence and pseudo-innocence as a major adaptation with his mate. The demanding or helpless child can put a strain on any relationship.

Save-Me Partner Subtype

This common subtype of the childlike partner is the complementary partner of the rescuer discussed under the parental contract.

The save-me partner feels threatened and overpowered by a hostile world he cannot cope with alone. A parental person (good parent or rescuer) is required to take over—to protect, to act in the "child's" behalf, to resolve conflicts and cut through ambivalence that retards action. In return, the save-me partner offers loyalty and love (gratitude). Generally the save-me partner is a very complex person who has childlike fears and holds onto salient qualities of his childhood, yet at the same time is highly competent and mature in many parameters.

The save-me partner may be a conscious or unconscious manipulator who uses the rescuer to escape from a difficult situation and who then either leaves, precipitates a new crisis, or works toward a new relationship with his partner. In any case, after the rescue the relationship will probably change drastically as different external necessities impinge on the system. Once external stress is removed, the couple may find that they now lack essential qualities between them that would allow them to live together happily, even though they were perfect for each other during the rescue operation.

In the 12 areas the childlike partner tends to have these characteristics:

1. *Independence-dependence.* Tends to be on the dependent side of the continuum.
2. *Active-passive.* Tends to be on the more passive end of the polarization.
3. *Closeness-distance.* May be anywhere along the continuum.
4. *Power.* Tends not to exercise much power and to seek to submit to his partner. However, in some instances he may control and use power to dominate when he knows that his mate is emotionally dependent on him. Competitiveness may be minimal to great.
5. *Fear of abandonment.* High; motivates much of his behavior.

6. *Possess and control.* Usually submits to being possessed and controlled by spouse, but see 4 above for reversal of this pattern.
7. *Anxiety level.* Usually on the high side of the continuum.
8. *Defense mechanisms.* Most commonly used are likely to be repression, regression, reaction formation, magical undoing, projection, displacement, identification, perceptual defense, fantasy to sustain denial, altruistic surrender and reversal. As might be anticipated, commonly requires use of many defenses, particularly more primitive ones.
9. *Gender identity.* The possibility of gender identity problems exists, but they are rare. Problems are often in child-adult identity, which should not be confused with gender identity problems.
10. *Sexual response to mate.* Usually on the positive to enthusiastic side of the spectrum.
11. *Love of self and mate.* Can be anywhere on the continuum. Narcissistic inability truly to love self or others is present with fair frequency.
12. *Cognitive style.* a) Is often spurious and ridiculing of his partner's more organized style, although he deeply appreciates the fruits of the partner's cognitive abilities. b) Tends to be somewhat on the chaotic and intuitive side of the spectrum when it comes to his own style.

RATIONAL PARTNER

The rational partner, as the appellation implies, defends himself against admitting that emotions may influence his or her behavior. He tries to establish a reasoned, logical, well-ordered relationship with his mate. Duties and responsibilities between mates are clearly delineated by the rational partner. He fulfills his responsibilities and cannot comprehend why his mate does not do likewise. The mate's failure to carry out a task or a responsibility may be followed by patient, logical explanation of the necessities. If the mate's ways are not corrected, he may go on to exasperation. His implacable logic often confounds his mate and triggers sharp reactions to him. Although the rational partner often does not demonstrate much overt affection or passion, he is capable of deep feelings of love and can experience a great sense of pain and emptiness if he loses the person he loves. He tends to be "economic" in his approach to matters having to do with life with his partner. He is pragmatic, down-to-earth, understands the rules of the system, and inherently tends to play the game of life according to the rules. Rarely does he create new rules or change the given ones. On matters of a factual nature he assumes he is correct; on matters of taste, style, and culture he will often defer to his mate.

It is easy to see that a rational partner will arouse hostility in some mates, even when the rational one is responding to the mate's own demand that limits be set for him. The rational partner is then blamed for being "so damned rational," for not being more of a free spirit, at the same time he is being maneuvered (willingly) into taking over and being extremely responsible. The rational partner often has social grace, kindness, and consideration and is usually there when needed, even if he does not appear to be sensitive to all the nuances of his mate's feelings. He is not to be confused with a narcissistic person who is essentially incapable of object-love. The rational partner may, if the dynamics are right between mates, slip over into a parental partner. This latter type of behavior is likely to be elicited when his mate plays out a helpless child-partner role, that of a person who cannot deal with all the complexities of life because his behavior is so largely determined by his childlike feelings and dependency.

Once he is committed the rational mate tends to be loyal and to devote himself to making the relationship work. Often it is his apparent lack of sensitivity to his partner's feelings and emotional needs that contributes to disharmony in their interaction.

The rational partner is to be differentiated from the parallel partner, who lives without close emotional touch with his mate. Often the rational partner has a close and intimate partner relationship. Whether he does or not, the essence of his behavior is the cool logic by which decisions appear to be made, the balance sheet always being automatically updated. Unless he loses his partner, he and his intimates may never fully realize the truly interdependent roles that the rational partner and his spouse play out with one another.

In the areas of the biological and intrapsychic category of the marriage contract the rational partner tends to have these characteristics:

1. *Independence-dependence.* Is often more dependent than he appears to be at first sight. He forms close and emotionally dependent mate relationships in which his emotional needs are hidden by his being in charge of the practical administrative operations of the couple's relationship.

2. *Active-passive.* Will be very active in practical matters and leave to his spouse the aspects of their common existence that have greater emotional content. Therefore he works out a quid pro quo division of responsibilities with his mate which may or may not be satisfactory.

3. *Closeness-distance.* Can be quite close, although he tends to stay clear of deep, continued expressions of motivations and analysis of feelings; may actually be distant and removed.

4. *Power.* Tends to assume and use power and to appear as dominant but in many instances the mate often has ultimate power while he has the position and appearance of the one in charge. There can be great variation in range, from being submissive to completely dominant. Usually he is not competitive with his partner.

5. *Fear of abandonment.* This can have a wide range, from deep-seated pervasive fear to practically none. He is well defended in this area.

6. *Possess and control spouse.* Same as for power—appears to control and often in many respects does control spouse.

7. *Anxiety level.* Usually on the low side—from average to low.

8. *Defense mechanisms.* Most likely ones to be emphasized are repression, reaction formation, intellectualization, perceptual defenses and denial, displacement and inhibition of impulse and affect.

9. *Gender identity.* No particular predilection for problems in this area.

10. *Sexual response to mate.* There can be a wide variation from needing a spouse to meet particular acceptable standards of appearance and sexual behavior to unimportant. If there is any trend, it is in the direction of adhering to conventional concepts. It is not unusual to want a mate who expresses the openness and impulsiveness one fears in oneself.

11. *Love of self and mate.* Generally feels a deep and lasting love relationship.

12. *Cognitive style.* a) Is not likely to accept a different style from his own, except in a condescending or patronizing

way. b) His style is to be organized, collect all data, and arrive at a "correct," logical conclusion. Expects others to conform to his conclusions because he feels they are obviously correct.

COMPANIONATE PARTNER

The companionate partner's operations are designed primarily to ward off aloneness. He or she can usually accept closeness. The companionate partner does not expect love but does seek thoughtfulness and kindness, for which he believes he is willing to give the same in return, perhaps in conjunction with economic security. Essentially, the companionate partner wants a companion with whom to share daily living; he does not aspire to romantic love (although this may be a deep desire) and readily accepts the quid pro quo necessities of conjugal living. Some companionate partners could be described as "burned out" romantics.

The companionate partner's arrangement can be very gratifying when it fulfills the major needs of persons who are no longer uncompromising about their ideals. It is seen increasingly among older couples who live together in or out of marriage. (Sometimes the latter is chosen because marriage would result in loss of alimony payment, trust fund income, widow's pension, or social security.) The companionate partner considers his relationship to be a realistic arrangement between people who no longer have illusions, who know their needs and what they are willing to give in exchange for having those needs fulfilled.

The companionate partner's style, as he interrelates, is based on genuine deep needs, plus consciously made reality compromises that are acceptable to him on all levels of awareness. The companionate partner is not to be confused with other partner behavioral types who may enter a relationship for fear of being alone or unloved, where the wish is still for romantic love, rather than for companionship.

In the 12 areas the companionate tends to have these characteristics:

1. *Independence-dependence.* Often is a mixture of dependence and independence without swinging to either extreme pole.

2. *Active-passive.* Tends to be somewhat more active than passive, but may cover a wide spectrum.
3. *Closeness-distance.* Tends to avoid either extreme.
4. *Power.* Exercises power but does not usually have to be at either extreme; usually not competitive.
5. *Fear of abandonment.* Not a major motivating force. He prefers a life with a partner, but not at any price.
6. *Possess and control mate.* Same as power. Does not need to possess or be possessed.
7. *Anxiety level.* Generally moderate to low.
8. *Defense mechanisms.* Most commonly used include sublimation, repression, reaction formation, intellectualization, fantasy and perceptual defense.
9. *Gender identity.* Usually not a significant factor.
10. *Sexual reaction to mate.* Can vary from very positive and constant to not especially significant.
11. *Love of self and mate.* If we change love to acceptance, then this is important. Love in the usual sense of including passion need not be present, but acceptance, need, commitment and kindness are.
12. *Cognitive style.* a) Can accept spouse's style if it does not change markedly from his original perception of it. b) Style tends to be well ordered and rational.

Parallel Partner

The parallel partner interacts so as to avoid an intimate sharing relationship. Despite any protests to the contrary, he or she wants the partner to respect his emotional distance and independence. In the dyadic relationship he may be responding to his mate's unconscious attempts to elicit this distant response from him when a predisposition exists, or he may have his own imperative need to remain emotionally removed, or there may be a combination of both factors. A parallel partner desires the conventional appurtenances of marriage, including home, children, dog, slippers, and washing machine, but does not wish to be intimate. He prefers separate beds or bedrooms and sometimes even separate residences. Figuratively speaking, he prefers fingertip touch to a full embrace. He will "share" children, attendance at community and family functions, and so on; he and his spouse appear together but are not intimate together.

For the parallel partner it is of paramount importance to maneuver his mate so that the two keep their distance and do not move closer than the perigee that keeps him comfortable. The contract of the parallel partner is predicated on a fear of losing his integrity as a person and being controlled. He struggles against being merged in any way. The defensive system of parallel partners is emphatically demonstrated by their emotional distance; they appear as cool and guarded people but may be extremely charming.

The parallel partner's need for distance is often a reaction formation to a great dependency need that is inadmissible for him to acknowledge with awareness. Such a person is often reactively ultra-independent. If successfully penetrated—and perhaps this is why he maintains his defense so well—he may melt into a romantic with a need for a partner with whom to complete himself. This would leave him extremely vulnerable to his mate. The struggle of the paralleler is never to allow himself to care enough emotionally for his mate to become aware of his own vulnerability.

In the 12 areas the parallel partner tends to show these characteristics:

1. *Independence-dependence.* Tends to be more on the independent side of the spectrum, but does not desire that his mate be dependent. In fact, he prefers his mate not to be, but in either case the mate must respect his basic ground rule of emotional distance.

2. *Active-passive.* Generally tends to be on the more active side of the spectrum and is self-activating.

3. *Closeness-distance.* Is definitely on the distant end of the continuum.

4. *Power.* Tends to be in charge of himself and of setting the basic style of the relationship. Otherwise prefers that his mate have his own power in his designated areas of functioning and his own work. Competition is usually not high.

5. *Fear of abandonment.* Well defended against by his basic defense. The strength of the defense is indicative of the intensity of the anxiety.

6. *Possess and control mate.* On one level does not desire to possess or be possessed, but on another he has the need to exercise extreme control to the extent that his spouse must adhere to the basic ground rules.

7. *Anxiety level.* Tends to be on the low side and is well defended against. See 5 above.

8. *Defense mechanisms.* Strongly operative. The most commonly used are repression, reaction formation, intellectualization, sublimation, inhibition of impulses, and displacement.
9. *Gender identity.* Usually not significant but in rare instances there may be problems or uncertainty on a deep level.
10. *Sexual response to mate.* May be anywhere along the continuum. When strong it is often on a straight physical level with few emotional (or admittedly such) components. This can make the parallel partner a technically competent but emotionally ungiving partner.
11. *Love of self and mate.* On the low end of the spectrum, as love must be inhibited. Narcissism is common.
12. *Cognitive style.* a) May or may not respect mate's style; is rarely able to use the positive aspects of his mate's style to complement his own because that might require closeness. b) Tends usually to be at the better organized end of the spectrum; rigid style.

SEXUALITY IN PARTNER PROFILES

In my early thinking about the behavioral profiles I included as a separate category a sexual partner profile, with two subtypes. On further observation and study I realized that these did not stand up as profiles in their own right, that the characteristics of the sexual partner may be subsumed within any of the other profiles. And yet the two sexual subtypes can be seen clearly enough to warrant special mention. (I shall deal with the more general considerations of sex in marriage and the sex-related terms of the contracts in Chapter 10.)

The first subtype is composed of those who seem to confuse a strong sexual need with love. The role of sex becomes overvalued within the context of the total relationship. The second subtype includes those who seek sexual fulfillment with the desperation and all-consuming passion that a heroin addict seeks his fix. These two types are on a continuum. No sharp line divides them. Essentially they are quantitatively different, yet somewhere along the continuum a qualitative change takes place that makes the need for sexual contact the predominant determinant of a person's actions.

Some of the elements of these two subtypes may be present in the behavior of mates who share a more complex relationship without being necessarily at the pathological extreme of the sexual continuum.

The first subgroup, those who appear to overemphasize the role of sex in their relationship, may use their urgent and strong sex need as a means of affirming themselves. Since they often confuse sex with love, sex may become the major determinant of their concept of self and of their choice of mate. It is frequently a driving, ego-reinforcing adventure. It may produce a sense of joy, an experience in the here-and-now that leaves one with an afterglow that colors the perceptions of the mate with warm colors and denies the perception of negative aspects of the interaction. The sexual part of the relationship comes to be regarded as the whole.

Many young people with a strong sex drive may seek a mate so that sex is readily available to them without the rigors and anxiety of repeated courting procedures and rejection. The need for sexual gratification predominates in their choice of mate; other factors are of negligible consideration. The dynamics of this type of sexual partner need not be very complex. Usually a younger man, but now, with increasing frequency, it may be a woman, desires a safe and frequent source of sexual gratification. He or she may be too shy for wide experimentation, or, having fallen in with a suitable sex partner, may have confused this important parameter with love and therefore prematurely entered into a pseudoromantic coupling. This type of relationship goes on to marriage less frequently today because more people are free to live together without marriage. Living together obviates the need for premature marriage and provides an opportunity for the individuals to learn about total relating as well as the role of sex in a more inclusive relationship.

Large numbers of relationships exist between older and younger persons. When sex is the major factor in determining object choice, the basic interactional ambience may be that of a parental-childlike partnership, as one might expect. On the other hand, although the younger spouse may try to force the older into a parental role, the basic ingredient for the male to enter the relationship is more likely to derive from the woman's sexual desire for him. In such instances his sense of masculinity and lovability is reinforced by the woman's receptive attitude. The same often holds true when the older mate is a woman and the younger is a man, a combination which appears to be on the increase. The younger person in such a partnership often expects (contractually) the older partner to be strong and to take care of him or her, despite his or her own real abilities and accomplishments.

The second type of sexual partner's life is one fraught with a more imperative sexual urgency. Life centers around his or her sexual experiences. In extreme cases all other considerations—work, children, reputation—are secondary. This group of men and women experience the urgency of sex as so great that they pursue sexual fulfillment as if they were addicted. Sexual gratification not only makes them feel good but solves all problems and provides all spiritual and interpersonal sustenance. For this "addict" type, sex is not an ego trip, or just the normal intense adolescent sex drive. It is a matter of survival and a force that allays anxiety. Society has usually condemned this type of intense sexually determined behavior.

The etiology of this type of sexual partner probably varies and is multicausal. Hormonal as well as environmental and intrapsychic determinants may play a significant role. With our present lack of knowledge we can only hypothesize that a person whose sexual desires are so strong and all-gratifying is seeking fulfillment of early love and sexual needs and fantasies. The adult's most exciting and persistent sexual acts and fantasies are often established or have had their Anlagen in childhood. Some needs may be related to feeling tones and anxieties about parental acceptance and rejection. The rapid recurrence of anxiety in these people, with their underlying insecurity, does not take long to necessitate another "fix."

Expensive houses of prostitution and call girls have catered to such drives for respectable men. Women have not been as fortunate in having readily accessible ways of fulfilling their fantasies and desires. The greater sexual freedom of today and the acknowledgment of the existence for women, as well as for men, of sexual needs and fantasies that increase and often add special sexual excitement have made us more aware of the frequency and strength of these desires and the extent of repression and suppression of them by many adults.

If the "addict" can be gratified at home, and his needs integrated into a total relationship, sex may then lend stability to the dyad. This is more likely to be effected when the "addiction" is not used to deprecate or control either party. Many husbands and wives are now open about their desires and fantasies and play them out together within the security of their homes.

This type of sexual partner requires a spouse that accepts him/her on all levels and can respond appropriately. Where significant sadomasochistic elements are involved, the couple must complement each other so that one is not exploited by the other. It is important for the therapist not to interject his own value system, unless the situation is destructive to either partner. As sex is increasingly accepted as not evil,* people with strong sex drives will find it easier to find mates with whom they can safely develop and exercise their other human emotional qualities as well as fulfill their sexual needs.

Our understanding of "normal" regarding sex has been changing rapidly. Just a generation ago many spouses who desired oral sex, for example, had to have this desire fulfilled extramaritally by a person regarded as degraded because both they and their mates believed that fellatio and cunnilingus were sick and disgusting practices. Similarly, many other sexual desires may now be gratified within the marital relationship, although, of course, in the exploration of newfound freedoms not all couples will adhere to the same values as others.

There is a definite, if somewhat elastic, line between the two types of sexually focused partners described here. What they have in common is that each person offers himself to his partner as a sex object and sees the partner similarly. Sex is the primary aspect of the relationship. The first type falls within "normal" limits but does not give adequate consideration to other important aspects of a committed relationship. The second may have edged over into the pathological, although some of its characteristics need not be inconsistent with a good total relationship.

---

* How sex is used may be evil, of course, when it is used to injure, as is any manifestation of man's inhumanity to man.

7
Partnership Combinations

IN CHAPTER 6 SEVEN partner behavioral profiles were described. We will now consider some of the major topological partnership combinations and the reasons why some combinations are more likely to fulfill complex marital contract terms than others. Since there are 28 possible combinations, I shall try to focus on principles which the reader can readily apply to specific clinical situations.

Behavioral profiles change as partners continue to interact and as forces outside their relationship impinge on them. The system is not static and *always* has potential for change. How two partners relate to each other depends on several factors: their individual contracts; their interactional contracts and mechanisms of defense, and how the latter affect their mates; the drive, energy, and purpose they have to win in marital contests; the amount and quality of their love, affection, and consideration for each other; their desire to maintain the relationship and to make it work; their physical health; influences outside the couple, including their family systems; and a host of other variables. Obviously, with our present state of knowledge we cannot accurately predict interactional behavior or explain all that we do observe.

Gratifying and durable relationships exist when partners accept themselves and each other as they currently are. A relationship cannot be sustained for long on the hope or promise that either partner will change. In most good relationships there tends to be compatibility (not necessarily similarity) of style and purpose, or complementarity without ambivalence, and a relative lack of hostility.

The 12 areas of the biological and intrapsychic parameters of the marriage contracts indicate the significant determinants of the quality of the marriage. Only recently have we begun to see more clearly, and therefore become better able to use therapeutically, the significance of each partner's defense mechanisms. We have long been able to discover and describe each individual's defense mechanisms, but we have not seen clearly how much the partners' ego and id defenses determine the quality of their interactions and, thus, the essence of the relationship. The detailed interactions elicit defenses that, in turn, color the interaction further; also, the qualities of a partner and of the particular relationship may elicit defenses that have not been used by a partner since an earlier epoch of his life cycle, or perhaps have never been used before.

Behavior within the couple system is complex and of multiple origins. Each individual brings the genetic and environmental history that has molded his personality, and as his relationship with his mate goes on he changes further. His reactions within their dyadic system are determined by remote factors from earlier periods of his life as well as by immediate and current factors. Other determinants impinge from outside the marital system. When the couple have children, they, too, become additional determinants that can deeply affect the marital system's functioning.

On the levels of interaction that we are concerned with there is no apparent gender-determined behavioral trend. The characteristics of any behavioral profile may be seen in either the woman or the man. The mode or style in which the characteristics are expressed—but not the presence of the factor itself—may be culturally determined. For example, a person of either gender may want power, although the ways in which they go about fulfilling the basic drive for power may differ. It is important to realize that people are people first—then they are male or female. In the following discussion the mate on either side of the hyphenated couple profiles can be either male or female.

The seven behavioral profiles describe the basic behavior of each individual in the particular couple relationship. It is not how he thinks he behaves, or what he professes to be his credo or his image of himself. It is how he actually *is* in interaction with his mate. Clearly no behavioral profile exists in its pure form as described. There are secondary and tertiary subthemes that modify the relationship. These subthemes act to provide gratifications as well as safety valves when the negative pressures become too great.

It is a grave oversimplification to think in terms of blaming one partner for negative interaction. Both may have responsibility, but not necessarily blame, for an unsatisfying or destructive interaction. The innocent-appearing "victim" partner often gives off signals that stimulate his mate to react adversely, much as George, the husband in Edward Albee's play, *Who's Afraid of Virginia Woolf?*, sets up his wife, Martha, to talk about their imaginary child by warning her repeatedly not to mention "the kid," thereby guaranteeing that she will do so and thus allowing the tragedy to run its predestined course. Neither partner ever merely reacts to the other. Both are trying to fulfill their own and the other's ambivalent assertive and defensive needs; both affect and respond to each other in their exquisite unconscious sensitivity. To blame one or the other partner would be an entirely incorrect frame of reference, failing to appreciate the significance of the couple's system. The two mates must similarly develop a "no fault" attitude as they learn how their interaction may work both positively and negatively in their behalf. Both partners are necessary to bring about positive, negative, or any interaction between them.

In the interaction each partner is attempting to achieve fulfillment of his/her individual contract, including ambivalences and self-imposed deterrents to fulfillment. Each wants more from the partner than from anyone else in the world and each is willing to give *something* in exchange for what he wants. And so they play games based on testing, faith, teasing, love, suspicion, coercion, threats, manipulation, and a thousand other ways of attempting to get what each believes he wants, or to see to it that he or his partner does not get what is wanted. Thus partners try to elicit from each other reactions that will fulfill their fondest wishes, as well as prove the truth of their worst fears and suspicions.

Some relationships fulfill the purposes of both mates and those of the system with an accompanying feeling of happiness and pleasure, despite some pain and travail. Others do not fulfill the purposes of the individuals or the system, or fulfill them at the expense of one or both of the partners. There is pain or emptiness, little or no joy; one is sharing his life with an enemy, not a friend.

In his *Transactional Analysis in Psychotherapy* (1961) Eric Berne indicated how a person's "ego state" can rapidly change in a transaction with another individual. Berne defined three ego states: the well-known Parent, Adult, and Child. The behavioral profiles defined here have some of the qualities of Berne's ego states but also include a variety of other characteristics. The two concepts are not mutually exclusive; each describes a part of the dyadic interaction from a different frame of reference.

Some partnership combinations are inherently unstable and, unless adequate and compatible defense mechanisms come into play, will lead to a rapid deterioration of the relationship, with divorce, armed hostility, or chilled distancing as the result. Thus, the types of marriages that follow may be constant, may change, or may lead to separation or varying amounts of unhappiness. The behavioral profile changes that occur may, of course, be motivated by either positive or negative forces.

In years gone by we might have been able to say that some behavioral profiles were displayed predominantly by men, and others by women. This is no longer so.

EQUAL PARTNER COMBINATIONS

When two persons interact as equal partners they may or may not be able to establish and maintain a good relationship. Some seem to fall into this relationship naturally, without much thought, soul searching, or ideological discussions about it; others consciously work very hard at it, trying to overcome the backlog of a lifetime of training devoted to concepts of sharply defined gender roles and differences, as well as defensive posturing.

When an equal partner insists that his/her partner be equal, the couple may be headed for difficulty. Individuals must want their own equality and must participate in trying to accomplish their own changes. A helping and facilitating partner is certainly good, but one who *demands* that his spouse be equal does damage to his spouse and their relationship.

Whether it is expressed consciously as their chosen philosophy or not, two equal partners are functioning in terms of the most popular contemporary model among intellectuals but not necessarily among all socioeconomic groups. The equal-equal partner ideal, although espoused by many, is achieved by few. It is a goal that partners may elect to struggle toward. It cannot be achieved mechanistically but has to come from a deep sense of respect for oneself and one's mate.

When both mates function as equal partners they tend to do well together, but problems are likely to arise when either partner is ambivalent about this equal relationship. A common manifestation of this is the difficulties that arise when one partner cannot accept equality. Relationships founder if either stops loving the other partner, or if one turns to someone else for major emotional and/or sexual gratification or decides not to be committed to anyone at all for a while. Equal partners, with their relatively good self-security, need not act out mechanically in other relationships; they take their commitments seriously and do not lightly terminate a relationship. Conversely, they may also feel relatively secure about leaving a marriage that is no longer productive or loving for them.

Equal-equal partners remain together after the early passion of their relationship has ended presumably because they *want to be together, not because either is afraid not to be.* For most couples an equal relationship is the most difficult to maintain, because it is not as dependent on forces outside the couple themselves, such as social institutions or children, to keep the two people together.

One rare couple I know of this type has remained together for 30 years of marriage not only out of passion but out of a deep sense of contentment and peacefulness with each other. The equal-equal is not a relationship that is dull or necessarily low-key, and it rarely has the flatness that we often see with two compliant or peace-at-any-price mates who are afraid (or just have no desire) to rock the boat.

Equal-equal partners often have an active measure of competitiveness and challenge going on between them. They do not avoid an argument that is necessary to resolve an issue.

In our rapidly changing society individuals are reacting in a variety of ways to the pressure of similar social forces. The differences in what people want in "their" equal relationship are a good example. Many couples who are striving for equal relationships founder on different interpretations of equality, and sometimes the "equality" issue is a smoke screen for other aspects of their individual marriage contracts—possibly a desire to be taken care of, a fear of responsibility, or a sense of inadequacy at the idea of having to compete with others. These anxieties and fears are normal for women and men. We cannot expect ourselves or others to have developed equally and simultaneously in all the various emotional and cognitive parameters. We are "advanced" or "mature" in one area, childlike in another. Yet some spouses point out to their mates that "You can't have it both ways." When said to the husband this may mean, "You can't expect me to work full-time as well as cook, clean, and take care your laundry as your mother did." Said to the wife it may mean, "You can't expect to compete with men and then pull that feminine-wiles stuff." Why *can't* either want it both ways? Most people do. It does not mean we will be able to have it both ways, but the need and desire may be there. These are points for negotiation, considerate handling, and quid pro quo arrangements as the couple work together to establish their own modus vivendi. We are the products of our times, and consequently our struggle against parts of our familial and broader cultural heritage that we wish to change is necessarily an arduous one.

A few of the complexities of trying to be equal partners in a very nonequal world are illustrated by some of the issues that arise among couples that are striving to be equal-equal partners. Discussion of these issues may help to explain why even the best-intentioned couples do not always achieve Nirvana. Add the problem of dynamic change to the 12 biological and intrapsychic parameters and we can understand better how complex the coupled relationship is. However, this is *not* discouraging, because among well-motivated couples a shift in one or two crucial parameters can often change the entire interactional system.

Within the framework of the equal-equal partners' marriage there may be various aspects of the "open marriage," a concept crystallized by the O'Neills (1972). The essence of the "openness" is that every person is an individual and should be free to function as such. One's identification with others is based on one's own activities, not on one's mate's activities or one's designation as someone's spouse. Thus social functioning, stature, and prestige do not depend so greatly on one's marital partner. Spouses do not belong to one another; they do not possess each other as if they were objects. Convention is now beginning to permit not only separate social appearances, but also sexual relationships outside the marriage if that is desired, although this is by no means a necessary pathognomic sign of the equal partner. Each couple develops its own operational rules that reflect not just a philosophical or theoretical position but both mates' deepest emotional needs.

Unfortunately, many attempts at equal partnerships fail because the emotional need of one partner is actually to create distance by using the guise of independence, rather than to achieve equality. The outward manifestation of a partner's need to avoid closeness and interdependence can be strikingly similar to those of the more mature person working toward equality, but the emotional driving force behind each is very different, as is the relationship that ensues.

There are several subtypes of the equal-equal partner combination that reflect diverse philosophies and strivings as well as different intrapsychic needs of the mate whose behavior falls within one particular subtype description.

Gender-Role Interchange

Aficionados of gender-role interchange believe that male and female gender roles are largely determined culturally, not biologically, and reflect varying degrees of exploitative and demeaning attitudes, some of which may have had their sources in economic necessity in the past. They believe that role functions should not perpetuate gender stereotypes, but should be determined by each individual's penchants, as well as by factors of time and place. Some believe that housework, shopping, daily cooking, and aspects of child rearing should be shared equally. Since these were traditionally designated as feminine tasks, the presumably more masculine tasks, such as driving the car when together, making decisions on major expenditures, teaching or playing with children, should also be shared equally. Decisions that affect both spouses or the entire family are not to be made unilaterally.

Gender-Determined Roles

Many people of both genders favor somewhat sharply defined gender-determined role differentiation and yet are equal partners. The equality is based on the beliefs that 1) differentiated female and male roles are necessary for a complete relationship and for the fulfillment of the tasks and purposes of family life; 2) one set of gender-determined tasks is no more demeaning or less creative than the other; and 3) true equality is based on respect of individuality and equality of opportunity. The equal person has the same opportunities as the spouse of the other gender, and participates in choosing those areas for which he will take major responsibility. One is not pressed into a unisex procrustean bed, but makes his own choices and decisions, usually with some quid pro quo reality-based compromise. There are excellent relationships in which roles more or less fit in with conventional notions, yet allow for the continuing growth and development of both partners, in which the equal partner fully respects his mate's opinions, abilities, and needs.

Women's liberation concepts manifestly play a major role in determining the behavior and attitudes of an increasing number of couples. When the couple operates without guilt, provocation, or overgeneralization to reduce male supremacist actions and concepts within the relationship, the results can be constructive. Equal power and authority, to be meaningful, require the assumption of equal responsibility as well. This often creates problems, since an individual's ideology may be ahead of his or her life experiences and he or she may still lack the ability to take the necessary responsibility. Yet this should not be used as a reason for maintaining a characteristic status quo.

Some of the vulgarization of the concepts of women's liberation by mass media reflect the anxiety of men about impending change in the status quo. The most blatant fear is that women will become demanding sexually and the male population will be reduced to impotence. This is quite a reversal of the old shibboleth that mothers (and fathers, as well) taught their daughters—that sexual pleasure was only for the male, and that the "vicious beast" in him would drive a man to any end to achieve his "horrible purpose," without regard for the consequences to the woman.

Economic Equality

Economic equality is considered a necessity by some, if there is to be true equality. I do not know whether this is completely or always true. In the following discussion money is equated to power, although I recognize that money is only one representation of power. There are three major ways for a woman to gain money and "economic security": 1) through her own abilities to work and earn at a rate equivalent to a man's pay for similar work; 2) through marriage to a person who has a good income; 3) through inheritance. One of the most significant effects of the women's liberation movement has been an increase in the effort to provide more opportunities for greater economic equality between men and women. Although the situation for women is better, it is still far from one of equal opportunity and equal pay for the same work. When a woman marries a man who is the sole means of their support, her status depends largely on his accomplishments, not her own. Her sense of self is commonly defined in terms of who her mate is, not who she is. Inheritance as a means of gaining economic security is available to only a few people.

Equal economic opportunity will have to be achieved if there is to be a firm realistic basis for behavioral equality between men and women. At the same time, women who elect to stay home to care for their children and household also can grow, develop, and be creative in ways they wish. There is no one path for all people to follow. Many couples now realize that when the woman does not have a sense of her own worth as a person, ultimate equality is impossible; for some this does require economic equality, for others it may not. Some couples who appreciate the significance of economic liberation for both women and men take measures to allow both partners to develop their own creativity and earning potential. In other situations, where the wife cares for the children and household, the couple makes sure that both partners have equal access to the family funds and an equal say in how they are spent. Although one may earn all the money, it belongs to both. As part of their sharing of conjugal tasks one is assigned to be the wage earner.

Although many women may leave a marriage despite ensuing economic hardship, some others are unwilling or unable to do so. A system that maintains woman's economic dependence on the male is a terrible burden on men as well as women. It severely limits the availability to both spouses of dignified and noncrippling alternatives. Economic self-sufficiency removes one of the fears of terminating a noxious relationship—that of being reduced to a lower standard of living or forced to keep running on a treadmill merely to survive.

Equal-Romantic Partnership

When one mate behaves as an equal partner and the other as a romantic in the interaction, what are some of the dynamic pluses and some of the problem areas of the combination?

This combination often leads to a good relationship, provided neither partner demands that the other change his or her basic interactional profile. In their interaction the romantic who requires a great deal of togetherness may be threatened by his mate's desire for his own space. If his mate remains independent, the romantic may cling, may become more dependent, or may feel angry and betrayed because his partner is not keeping the (unilateral) contract to be a romantic. The equal partner may seek greater equality for his mate and want to thrust egalitarianism upon the romantic, who feels threatened and rejected by this. Simultaneously, the romantic partner, calling on the name of love in vain, demands greater closeness and open communication, which is felt by his mate to be a controlling as well as anachronistic maneuver. The equal partner may feel hemmed in by the demand that he change and hence may react negatively to his romantic partner's pressures. They may then lock themselves in an ongoing struggle that determines the ambience of their interaction, which is in danger of degenerating into a struggle for power.

On the other hand, we should remind ourselves again that no behavioral profile is seen in its pure form in life. Most equal partners also have a strong dash of the romantic, and many romantics subscribe to some aspects of being an equal partner (in fact, they may be quite romantic about the concept of equality). Thus, in the quid pro quos of daily life, if neither partner is a purist, prone to anxiety, or controlled by transferential distortions, the equal-romantic partnership may prosper.

In varying degrees the equal partner can accommodate and be complementary to several other partner profiles—provided his own freedom is not too circumscribed. The equal partner wishes to respect the individuality of his mate and might react adversely to a partner who would be his sycophant or a childlike partner. On the other hand, equality is an elastic concept and the equal partner is often satisfied to have a partner who is a little less equal.

Equal-Rational Partnership

Some equal-rational partnerships begin as an equal-equal relationship, in keeping with the couple's expressed or implied philosophy, but the interaction may change gradually as one partner becomes anxious at the other's independence (which becomes defined as irresponsibility, thoughtlessness, irrationality) and becomes more and more rational in his attempt to control the relationship by keeping his partner's and his own behavior within "reasonable" bounds that ease his anxiety. This partner becomes less free and open as his efforts are increasingly determined by defensive impulses and he becomes excessively logical and reasonable as their interactional contract sucks him into fulfilling the need for "rationality" created by its absence in his partner. He is able to accept equal partnerism intellectually but because of his anxiety he lacks the emotional commitment and ability to follow through. The equal partner in such an interaction often unconsciously presses a little too far in stirring up his mate's anxiety. The latter responds negatively, is then accused by the equal partner of being too restrictive, and they incomprehensibly find themselves in a bitter struggle.

It is difficult for an equal-rational couple to grasp why or where their relationship has gone sour, as they appear to be in agreement and have difficulty delineating important specific complaints about each other. One such couple caused me to flash back to a political debate I had heard years ago in which each of the two candidates was trying to convince the audience that he was a more patriotic American than his opponent while avoiding discussion of any substantive issue. Each spouse presented his argument as the politicians had spoken to the audience, for me to judge which one was the "more equal," at the same time avoiding the significant areas of their differences.

The equal-rational partnership is often a reasonably stable one largely because the rational mate is trying hard to be an equal partner and not to play games that frustrate the positive dyadic potential. *That is, neither of the partners has unconscious needs that require sabotage of the realization of a good relationship between them.*

Equal-Companionate Partnership

The equal-companionate partnership usually works quite well. Although superficially the equal and the companionate may appear to be the same, they are very different. The equal partner believes both mates should have equal status and opportunity and each should be his own person. He usually loves his partner and tries to live out his ideal relationship. The companionate partner makes a realistic compromise and gives up love in exchange for consideration, kindness, devotion. He does not believe mates need be equals; in fact there is often a conventional male-female division of work and responsibilities as well as activities.

Difficulty may arise in the equal-companionate partnership when either mate begins to want more from the other than was originally contracted for and is unable to accept something different. The equal partner may want love or want his mate to be more equal to him, as inequality makes him guilty, interferes with his independent activities, and makes his partner appear less of a person. The companionate person may regard his partner's demand that he be equal or that he love as a cause for anger and exasperation because he did not agree to such a contract and does not feel capable of fulfilling it.

The companionate partner may become anxious as he comes to realize that the equal partner really is his own person and is not dependent on him; or anxiety may develop when the equal partner will not support the companionate partner's dependence.

Equal-Parallel Partnership

This too may work out satisfactorily so long as the equal partner does not make too many demands for intimacy. The distance of the parallel partner is often the carrot in front of the equal partner, who wants greater closeness; the pull-push involved in their interactive process may make for a stormy but lively relationship or may eventually destroy it. The equality may fit in well with the parallel partner's needs as he perceives them. To the extent that each partner can be constructive in the relationship, they may collaborate in living out a kind of pseudo-equal-equal partner combination.

Equal-Parental Partnership

This combination is likely to be an unstable one. The parental-acting partner is driven to try to dominate the equal one. The latter, if sufficiently strong as an individual, need not be pushed into a power struggle, but this is a common sequel. If he is unable to shift the relationship to a more equitable modus vivendi, the equal partner may terminate the relationship; or the parental one, realizing there is a mismatch and needing to appear to be in charge, may force the issue of termination.

Equal-Childlike Partnership

This too is likely to be an unstable equation that must change if the couple is to stay together in harmony. The equal partner in this instance may be a "reformed parent" who feels uneasy as a parent or rescuer. Or the childlike partner of the duo may once have been an equal partner whose dependency needs have become ascendant. The childlike partner may do well with the equal partner for a while, until he fails to meet his own or his partner's expectations of equality in a variety of situations. While he uses every bit of his ingenuity to press the equal into a parental role, the equal mate may come to feel exploited or lose respect for his partner, along with his feelings of excitement and love, because he finds the childlike behavior distasteful and nongratifying.

The childlike partner does not want to be equal. The equal partner does not want responsibility for a child and finds not only that the latter's needs are burdensome but that he does not want a love relationship with someone who is not adult.

Romantic Partner Combinations

Superficially the romantic partner tends to be most complementary with another romantic. The romantic-romantic partnership fits together like two pieces of a jigsaw puzzle, two parts that are incomplete by themselves but together constitute a whole.

However, the "high" of the consummated short-term bonded romantic-romantic partnership with its passion, openness, intimacy, and pervasive interdependence tends to run downhill after a few years. Because the diminution of intensity is often regarded as a loss of love, many couples are unable to make the transition to a satisfactory long-term bonded relationship. Since the change in intensity rarely occurs simultaneously in both partners, the one who still is more passionate often reacts strongly to changes in the partner's subtle and overt behavior. These reactions in turn usually arouse guilt in the partner, or a sense of being fenced in, or a desire to withdraw from an intimacy now regarded as controlling, engulfing, or designed to take away individuality. The former romantic may have changed into an equal, companionate, or parallel partner, or may now wish to establish a new romantic-romantic partnership with someone else in order to experience again the intense high of being romantically in love. The activity and frustration involved in this endeavor can devastate the remaining partner, since the "soul mate" quality of mutual exclusivity and understanding is needed by the romantic partner to provide the security and sense of belonging and passion that he strives for.

When one of the romantic partners senses on some level of awareness that the two are very similar in terms of the underlying sources of their anxiety and that they cannot continue a negative complementarity, as they had thought, he or she tends to become disillusioned with the partner. He feels that he has been deceived, that the partner did not live up to the contract. The similarity of the two on the unconscious level is often masked for a long time, because the partner's defense mechanisms may differ markedly and thus the superficial personality characteristics are considerably different. The two may actually have complemented each other for a time in their methods of defense against anxiety—one may be more depressed and passive, the other more problem-solving and assertive when anxious— but the basic similarity of their underlying sources of anxiety is often their Achilles heel unless they can change the defunct negative relationship into a positive complementarity.

A significant number of romantic mates are so injured and bereft by the loss of their romantic-romantic partnerships that they are unable to allow themselves to love passionately again. They may, after a lengthy reparative period, look for a companionate, non-passionate relationship.

Some romantic partners do not appear to place as great an emphasis on the similarity of values, interests, and togetherness as the soul-mate types do; however, a completion of oneself by uniting with the partner remains an essential prerequisite of the profile. This is often the driving force that negatively affects the couple's interaction as the other mate tries to evade the "captivity" that is the essence of romantic partner bonds. The romantic element of needing the relationship for the romantic partner to function most effectively remains. This type of dependency should not be confused with a mother-child symbiotic relationship, since mutual feeding on one another is not in the forefront. It is closer to a mutual key-lock analogy; the ambience of personal security frees one of anxiety and allows for fuller conflict-free operation and greater exploitation of one's creativity. When the relationship is good, the partners unlock each other's potential. They are inspired by the relationship, as opposed to feeding on one another.

The romantic is rarely able to make himself a true equal partner by following through to differentiate himself from his mate. Not infrequently a romantic, finding his usual methods not effective, may become childlike and attempt to manipulate his partner into a parental behavior pattern. If both are reasonably pleased with this new interactional pattern as childlike-parental partners, or if the gain outweighs the strain, they may continue in a reasonably good complementary relationship. Relationships can change and adapt. It is when a relationship loses its resiliency and edges over into a destructive, nongratifying, or no-growth situation that the existence of that couple system is in serious jeopardy.

Many romantic-romantic partner combinations continue their romantic relationship indefinitely. These are very fortunate couples who are rarely seen in clinical practice. They have usually developed the ability to complement each other well and to shift into supportive or dependent roles in relation to one another as needed. Power may shift back and forth in an appropriate fashion, always with the emphasis on functioning as a unit. Fear of abandonment never emerges as a source of anxiety because each feels secure in the love and continuance of the other. Only death of the mate is feared. Such couples are not free of problems but manage to cope with them and to survive as a unit as they go through the marital cycle.

Some romantics who continue into long-term bonding create their own world, with its secret meanings, that exists only for themselves. Such a couple more likely than not will elect not to have children, or will be unable to include their children in the relationship. Kurt Vonnegut, Jr., in *Cat's Cradle* (1963), beautifully caught the essence of such a couple, the American Ambassador Minton and his wife: "They were lovebirds. They entertained each other endlessly with little gifts: sights worth seeing out the plane window, amusing or instructive bits from things they read, random recollections of things gone by. They were, I think, a flawless example of what Bokonon calls a *duprass,* which is a *karass* composed of only two persons." (A *karass* is only suggestively defined by Bokonon, the fictional prophet, as those persons chosen by God to participate in giving one's life significance.) Vonnegut goes on to say, " 'A true *duprass,*' Bokonon tells us, 'can't be invaded, not even by children born of such a union.' . . . Bokonon tells us, incidentally, that members of a *duprass* always die within a week of each other."

Romantic-Rational Partnership

This is often a difficult relationship because the romantic partner feels the rational one is not close enough, does not express feelings, is too logical, and so on. Nevertheless, many of these endure through a lifetime, often because the relationship has a childlike-parent partnership subtheme that is rewarding to both. There is an unconscious collusion in which the romantic can feel superior as the "more sensitive" partner while he berates his "insensitive" mate and both make-believe that the second theme of the duet does not exist. This unconscious arrangement is usually satisfactory to the rational partner, who indulges his "child" despite the put-downs he is frequently subjected to.

The existence of a secondary theme, of course, is common in dyads and is often the factor that contributes to the relationship's stability. Once mated, most couples bend every effort to try to survive as a unit. The defeat of divorce, the pain of failure, and the end of a dream are hard for most people to accept.

Romantic-Companionate Partnership

This combination is rare in a new relationship, but, it is not unusual in a former romantic-romantic relationship. When one partner's passion has cooled, he may still like or love his mate though he no longer experiences his former intense sexual reactions or need for constant sharing. Often the feeling changes to a sister-brother or parental-childlike relationship. This may be transitional to another form of interaction or to the demise of the marriage. For some couples it ushers in a difficult period during which the companionate partner distances himself in response to the romantic's attempts to reconstitute a romantic-romantic interaction.

Romantic-Parallel Partnership

Much the same pertains here as for the romantic-rational partnership. This combination is even more unstable, however, because the romantic feels the greater impact and rigidity of a more definite need for distance. One reason for the romantic's demands for greater closeness may, paradoxically, be a defense (reaction formation) against his own need for distance, which can now be claimed to be his partner's desire instead of his own, as his parallel partner predictably pushes him away. He protests too much about his desire for a warm, close, and intimate mate. Clinically we must be alert as we view such interactions to see if the romantic does not first cue the paralleler to increase the distance between them. The childlike-parental or any other secondary theme is not as likely to serve as a balancing factor. What does often keep the couple together, however, is the romantic's game involvement with his partner. In this game the romantic—or, if he is defending against closeness, we might call him a pseudo-romantic—does not really want his partner to be a romantic too, as that would expose his own fear of closeness. He is satisfied to criticize his partner for being distant, but does not push too hard, thus allowing the couple to sink back into their usual modus operandi until the next round of the game.

Romantic-Parental Partnership

This combination may work well. Many romantics fall into a childlike stance with a parental partner who is not too demanding a parent. This is one of the few combinations that is effectively complementary for the romantic. For both partners the sense of completion comes through the living out of a romantic child-good parent relationship.

Romantic-Childlike Partnership

This partnership tends to be quite unstable. The childlike partner's stance may have been or appeared to be that of a romantic partner in the couple's early interactions but changed later into the childlike role. However, the romantic tends to become uneasy and anxious when his mate persists in being childlike; he prefers a more equal romantic to quell his own anxiety. He wants and needs someone responsible to complement the childlike qualities he senses in himself. A little childishness in his mate is okay, but a really childlike partner arouses a defensive reaction in him. At the same time, of course, the child is struggling to make his romantic partner into a parental one. This type of complementary partnership is a very uneasy one unless a saving secondary behavioral theme is brought into play.

Parental Partner Combinations

The parental partner finds his or her complementary person in someone who will interact with him as a child. The parent seeks to treat someone as a child; the child maneuvers his mate into being a parent. The interaction elicits the complementary profile from the other. When neither partner is ambivalent about his own or his spouse's role, the two tend to do quite well; many good relationships are based on this combination. If life circumstances, such as illness or unemployment of the parental partner, cause a change in roles, there may then be tremendous stress on the relationship. The parent may feel threatened, degraded, or burdensome, or the child may remain a child and become anxious and unable to assume responsibility. Sometimes such crises bring about dramatic changes in which the child emerges as an adult or parental partner, particularly if love has existed between the pair and if the former childlike partner does not now have a need to even the score for earlier real or imagined injuries.

The parent or master partner—Ibsen's Torvald—who seeks to elicit a childlike response, ostensibly desires someone whom he can patronize and feel superior to, and who will cooperate in keeping the parent's cosmos together by remaining in the child's stance. A common version of the parent partner-childlike partner relationship is one in which men perceive their wives as cute dolls who must be treated as children. The man's need for constant reassurance of his supremacy is evidence of his inability to develop a more mature relationship of equality with a woman. Also common, and for the same reason, is the one in which the woman deals with her husband as if he were a simpleton or a bungling, impractical child.

The parent in the doll's house marriage, as Pittman and Flomenhaft (1970) emphasize, is often a person whose rigid stance masks more severe pathology. A change in the dyadic system to one of greater equality between spouses may severely strain this partner's intrapsychic economy and produce reactions designed to restore the prior equilibrium, or, failing that, he may go on to decompensation. Generally the therapist should not tamper with the paired system of a mistress, master, or parent unless the "child" is motivated to change;

he must consider the mental state of the parental partner while not supporting the exploitation of the childlike partner. Judgments should be made on the basis of the motivation, needs, and abilities of both spouses in the system, *not* on the therapist's value system alone. The fact that the partners remain in treatment and wish to change so that their relationship is more fulfilling (even if at the start each wants only the other to change) is a significant barometer of motivation.

The childlike partner is often the more passive and the follower in this interactional set, regardless of the child-spouse's gender. This is important to note because all too commonly assertive-passive traits are thought of as biologically gender-determined rather than determined interactionally. Often a propensity toward a particular trait, talent, or activity has existed previously for whatever reason and is brought to the forefront by the particular interaction. Pejorative attitudes about role functions or talents that are not traditional make the person who has such proclivities believe that he or she is psychologically or even genetically crippled. It is often necessary to clarify this with patients and to give them approval to fulfill their own desires and inclinations without feeling like freaks or needing to be ashamed.

Children sometimes upset the equilibrium of a parental-childlike partnership. Modern children are likely to attack the stance of each of their parents in this kind of relationship, and the ideas they and their friends bring into the household will often set off the first spark of rebellion in the childlike partner. It is not unusual for the child-spouse who seeks to be a "pal" with his or her children to identify with the more liberated thinking of the latter. Gradually the seeds of current thinking take root in the soil of dissatisfaction, and the child-spouse will then begin in earnest the struggle for liberation and individuation. Regardless of where the spark comes from, no one but the child-spouse can carry out his own evolution or revolution. Others can only assist.

Some parental partners accept the changes in a spouse with reluctance but good grace, realizing they cannot halt the growth process; some are even glad to give up the role, if they have been performing as a parent primarily at the behest of the spouse. Trying to interfere with a child partner's determination to change precipitates a profound shift and even a possible severance of the relationship. Hence the parental partner may agree to make the necessary compromises and changes in the contract while actually fighting a series of last-ditch skirmishes that exacerbate the struggle.

The *rescuer-save-me partnership* may continue as such, with new needs for rescue developing, or may shift into other behavioral profiles. When a rescuer refuses to rescue anymore, or a "save-me" partner stops getting into situations that require rescue, a crisis develops. The rescuer may try to undermine the save-me so he can rescue him again, or the save-me, faced with a mate who will no longer play the rescue game, may precipitate increasingly disruptive situations. He or she may use drugs and alcohol in dangerous ways, get himself fired from work, be hospitalized for psychosomatic or mental illness, or attempt suicide—anything to force the partner back into the rescuer role.

Mutual rescue operations, in which each person rescues the other from what both see as a bad life situation and each saves himself in the process, are not uncommon. Each partner is unable or unwilling to extricate himself without the help of the other. Often each can see what the other has to do to escape but cannot apply the same knowledge and will to his own situation without the other's help, support, approval, and promise of reward. After the mutual rescue operation, such a couple may move on to any other type of relationship. More often than not they do not establish a permanent relationship together because the necessary shift to peacetime interactions which do not require unity against a common enemy cannot be made. The new necessities of their peacetime contracts and interactions may make either or both realize that now, when it is presumably available to them, they cannot have and no longer want the type of relationship they had earlier hoped for.

The parental partner, feeling inadequate about his lovability, believes he can be loved only if he is needed. The parental-childlike partnership, if it does not shift to an individuated level based on the parental partner's own sense of worth and lovability, may begin to elicit the parental partner's dependency needs. Parental partners often refuse to admit dependency needs and hide behind the reaction formation maneuvers of an adult, independent stance. These maneuvers are similar to the masculine-protest maneuvers of the man who is unsure of his masculinity. This defense against normal dependency needs is destructive to efforts to have the relationship progress to another phase. It sets up the basis for eventual revolt by the childlike partner, who no longer wishes to act as the immature one and feels the effects of his partner's unacknowledged dependency needs.

If the parental partner's dependency needs begin to be met by the spouse, the latter may become an equal partner or there may be a gradual reversal of roles, so that over a period of time the parental partner may become a childlike interactor. In such a transition there are usually many stormy periods as the couple's center of power and control shifts back and forth.

When spouses are able to be aware of their own and each other's contracts (through their own experience or with the help of therapy) and to negotiate their differences without being destructive, the relationship may find a new and healthier level of integration. The revised single contract would need to be based on acceptance of each other's interdependence and the ability to shift back and forth from dependent to parental roles.

Parent-Parent Partnership

Sometimes two parents, each of whom has some childlike components, become mates. The sameness and ambivalence in each usually lead to a poor and stormy relationship, unless they shift into parallel living, or unless one truly "conquers" the other and the latter assumes a more constant childlike stance. A more constructive development would be a modus operandi of shifting roles and dividing responsibilities for different areas of marital duties. At best the combination may become or approximate a mature, equal partnership relationship.

Essentially the parent-parent partnership is an unstable one. There is a common misconception that is based on this observation and/or on the concept that marriage inevitably is a *war* of the sexes—that is that one partner must be dominant and the other submissive. This is not true or demonstrated by my observation and description of some of the other partnership combinations.

Other significant profile types that the parental interactor connects with are discussed later in this chapter. The examples above are intended to give an adequate conceptual approach to understanding how other behavioral types may interact with the parental-acting partner.

CHILDLIKE PARTNER COMBINATIONS

Several facets of the *childlike-parental partnership*, which is a naturally complementary one, have been described in the preceding discussion of the parental-childlike partnership. I shall add only a few ramifications.*

The childlike partner, as in some actual parent-child relationships, may sometimes become the true wielder of power in the relationship. The child's power is vested in the parent's overwhelming need to have the child in order to define his or her sense of self as an adult. Without the child the parent's fears of his own anomie and lack of sense of worth roil up, leading to anxiety and an intense need to force the other into a childlike position. Most childlike partners sense their power and may sometimes use it by threatening to leave. This struggle for control is the basis for much negative interaction. Although it is often present in heterosexual dyads, the childlike partner's power of the threat to leave is seen even more clearly in homosexual dyads, where the older homosexual frequently lives in fear of losing his controlling childlike partner.

The childlike partner has many interesting aspects and should not be regarded simplistically. Persons of both genders retain aspects of childhood dependence despite proved competence in a variety of areas, and the ability to evoke the creative child in themselves is the basis of many people's charm and talent.

I referred earlier to the instability of the rescuer-save-me relationship. As one crisis situation clears—unless other crises are precipitated by life exigencies, by the partner, or by the save-me's own

---

* From here on in this discussion an increasing number of partner combinations will have already been discussed. Hence only brief or supplemental remarks need be made about these combinations.

ambivalence—the save-me moves on to seek greater control of his own destiny. This may mean movement toward a more equal relationship. If interaction with the rescuer allows this move toward individuation and growth, the union can become more stable. On the other hand, the couple may find that, with growth, they no longer have a viable basis for a relationship.

Many save-me's do not move on, however. Having found that their stance has rewarding secondary gains, they provoke crises or, as we see so often, continue to play a game with the rescuer of allowing themselves to be rescued "whether they need it or not." When this occurs the partners become locked into their positions.

Childlike-Childlike Partnership

This has been referred to by a popular writer as "the sandbox marriage" (Welch, 1974). These two adults are like playmates or children who conduct their life together within a matrix of a child's world that has no tomorrow and requires no significant responsibility. For a while all may go on as play and fun. But when crises and frustrations develop, each then wants the other to be a parent. Disruption and breakdown of each one's individual marriage contract occurs with the disappointment of each at not being able to make the other into a parent. They compete at being the child, neither wishes to be the parent, and hostilities ensue. Couples who can adopt flexibly alternating parental roles often lead a good life. Others wrap themselves in the cotton wadding of their relationship as protection from the rest of the world. Not infrequently such persons will call each other "Mother" and "Father" when they have worked through a good complementarity for themselves. Others go through life much like brothers and sisters playing house together—incest without guilt.

Two actors who came to see me as a couple had made a good sandbox relationship by developing the ability literally to act the role of parent to the other mate when he or she needed a parent. As long as he could feel that he was playing *as if* he were a parent, the parental-acting mate was able to handle the role and successfully accomplish what the reality of the situation required. But when either thought he really was parental, and forced to be, he would become anxious at the realization and would abdicate. In therapy I encouraged them to play-act as parents and we even rehearsed several situations. One such episode involved the anxiety aroused in the wife, who had an audition coming up with a director and a producer whom she feared. I asked the husband to be the father; he too feared these theatrical notables. His role was to be a "good father"— to evaluate the situation objectively, support his daughter, reassure her, and advise her how to handle the situation, if he saw fit to do so. He first embraced her, held her for a while, and was then truly supporting and constructive. Later, at home, they played out the parenting scene several times, so that the line between acting and reality became nonexistent. The audition went well.

RATIONAL PARTNER COMBINATIONS

The rational partner often forms a complementary relationship with someone who will supply the emotion and spontaneity that he or she is afraid to experience directly. He will often choose a partner who has the potential to act as a romantic or childlike partner. Occasionally a relationship with an equal or companionate partner works out well. In therapy an apparent rational-rational partnership often turns out, on observation, to be a parallel-parallel partnership. Unlike the parallel partner, the rational partner has the capacity for closeness and passionate love—but he has to deny it in himself—and he likes a partner who struggles to move in and to stay close with him. He can then vicariously enjoy his partner's passion, and any "mishaps" will be due to the mate's emotionalism or to the rational partner's kindly indulgence of the mate.

The clinician should not underrate a rational partner's capacity for love, affection, and loyalty. The partner who appreciates and understands him knows his fine qualities and learns not to try to get him to accept responsibility for being more emotional or imaginative. The rational partner does remain earthbound—which can frustrate and enrage some partners—and his characteristics can set the stage for games that will make life miserable for both if he is scapegoated by his partner.*

A *rational-equal partnership* may go well if both wish to establish equality and adhere to their contracts. A rational partner becomes perplexed and upset at what he considers a breach of contract. A *rational-parental combination* can work well, too, if the contracts are clear and not ambivalent. The rational partner can also do well with a companionate or a parallel partner. All depends on clarity and bilateral acceptance of the contractual terms. An important clause must specify that the spouse of a rational partner not demand that he give what he cannot give. Further, the mate should take care not to injure his self-esteem. In other words, the game is to be played by the rules. A change of rules by either party may, of course, either precipitate problems or move the relationship to a different and perhaps more satisfying homeostasis. As in all marital relationships, love, commitment, and the will to make the relationship work make the difference.

A *rational and rescuer partnership* sometimes works when the rescuer offers a rich play of affect and social vitality that the rational partner may lack, thus rescuing the rational one from a relatively isolated and dull life at least for a time. This quid pro quo works satisfactorily for many couples. In exchange the rational partner brings order, certitude, dependability, love, devotion, and often financial stability to the relationship.

Thus the rational partner may mate constructively with almost any of the other partner types, provided that the contracts are reasonably consonant and that his self-esteem is not violated by the partner. He is vulnerable to attack because he loves and cares but finds it difficult to be in touch with his feelings.

The *rational and "save-me" partnership* is obviously a common union. Contracts and changes in contracts after the rescue become the crucial area on which many of these relationships founder.

---

* I appreciate that this paragraph about the rational partner sounds a great deal like Roger Caris, the wild-life conservationist, talking about a particular breed of dog that is excellent when properly understood. However, I think it is an accurate portrayal of the rational partner and how she or he can be misunderstood and even ridiculed by those persons in his life who most need him as a braking force on their anxiety about their ability to control themselves.

The same holds for the childlike partner with a rational partner. The rational partner may shade over into a parent as the child's transferential manipulations elicit a parental response. If the rational partner does not accept a parental role, the couple is in severe trouble. The interplay of the power of transference to elicit desired responses in mates is a very potent force that lies at the bottom of many "violated" contracts.

COMPANIONATE PARTNER COMBINATIONS

The *companionate-companionate partnership* is the most common and most satisfactory for the companionate partner. The two partners have a contract to be good companions, to respect and take care of each other. Love is not expected, but kindness and consideration are. Each partner asks and offers the same.

Problems arise when there are hidden clauses in the companionate partner's contract; for example, a man acting as a companionate partner may at first offer his spouse economic security but after a while he wants a pooling of the woman's and his own financial resources. Sometimes the unbargained-for invalidism of the mate puts an unbearable strain on the companionate partner. More subtle sources of disharmony arise from one partner's need to be loved or to be unique. If a low level of sexual activity was in either or both contracts and this changes to a desire for significant sex, or vice versa, this too can become a focus for disharmony.

Living in the past, rather than for the present and for the future, is often the most destructive element of companionate interactions among couples who marry at middle age or later. Spouses may compete for who had a better life before or who is now more loved and catered to by their children or grandchildren.

The companionate contract is based on genuine deep needs plus consciously made reality compromises that are acceptable on all levels of awareness. It is not to be confused with the unilateral contract of a person who rushes into an ill-considered relationship out of fear of being alone or unloved, or of one who still demands romantic love and is not prepared to accept a considerate, mutually companionable relationship.

This contract is markedly dissimilar from that of parallel part-ners, whose lack of intimate contact reflects a vastly different basis. Companionates desire a warm, close relationship but are willing to settle for the absence of romantic passion. It is a relationship rarely seen between young people, except when both have strong fears about expressing their heterosexuality or are homosexual.

PARALLEL PARTNER COMBINATIONS

The parallel partner does best with another parallel interactor. If both respect each other's defenses and are compatible in other areas, as they often are, they can have a comfortable and satisfactory relationship.

A *parallel-rational partnership* may work well too, provided each is at ease with the accommodations that are being made. But either of them—and especially the rational partner, who needs warmth to warm him up—may use their interaction to demand more (or to demand by withholding) because they need more from their partner. Similarly, a parallel-companionate partnership may work out well if the companionate partner does not demand greater closeness.

With a parental or childlike partner the parallel partner is likely to be involved in a difficult struggle. Either of these two will try to maneuver the parallel interactor into the role that meets the child's or parent's needs, which the parallel partner will vigorously resist. He *must* be accepted as is! A childlike partner who originally had parallel-acting parents (or whose contragender parent was distant to him as a child) might find a parallel partner just right because the paralleler fits into the childlike partner's unconscious needs. If the childlike one must then continually try to win close, intimate love from the "distant parent," this can be a very stormy relationship.

Trespassing beyond the intimacy threshold of the strongly parallel partner is cause for trouble. He or she may deal with the anxiety that develops when his perimeter is penetrated in a variety of ways, consistent with his style. He may distance himself further, develop psychosomatic symptoms, have apparently irrational outbursts of temper, find fault, or become punitive. If the spouse continues to insist on closeness, he may find cause to develop a "safer" relationship

or may even become psychotic if the conflict aroused is too great
and irreconcilable. The parallel partner's defenses must be treated
with the greatest respect and are not to be tampered with lightly
by his mate or the therapist.

It is not uncommon for a paralleler to marry someone who perceives his need for distance but believes that love will bring them
closer in time. The need for distance is not only perceived but is the
essential challenge. Giving love to a parallel partner with the expectation of reciprocity from him produces anguish in the paralleler,
who cannot reciprocate and is put further on guard to remain aloof.
The romantic, who must push for closeness, feels unloved when the
desired response is not forthcoming, and reacts with his defensive
system. In turn, the paralleler reacts with his defense, and a very
unhappy couple, bewildered and perplexed by forces they cannot
understand or control, appear at the therapist's office.

A parallel partner need not always be such. He may merely have
a tendency to be emotionally removed, which may surface in his
interaction with his mate. For example, his mate, having helped him
to be close, may then be intolerant of the closeness and push him
away. After several such conditioning incidents, the parallel partner
in the making may then react in a stylized distancing manner to certain signals (usually unconscious) from his mate. In a sense the intermittent conditioning reinforcement he received in these interactions
has fallen on the fertile soil of a person whose earlier life experiences
prepared him to be wary of emotional closeness. With a more con-
sistently receptive partner, he might, in time, have felt safe to remain
close.

A common basis for a sadomasochistic love relationship is the
interaction of a paralleler, who wants to control the degree of emotional closeness in the relationship, and a pseudo-romantic, who may
really be a paralleler but considers himself a romantic seeking another
romantic. The "romantic" is drawn to the potentiality of the paralleler, apparently seeking an "intimate" relationship with a person
whose unavailability provides the stimulus of challenge and therefore
great desirability.

Consciously the romantic-acting partner believes he wants a romantic relationship, but unconsciously he wants more of a parallel rela-

tionship or a back-and-forth, "push-me, pull-you" way of relating
—the seesaw syndrome. The "romantic" persistently tries to prove
his own self-worth as a sexual and lovable person by winning the
unwinnable person whose lack of ability to give romantic love and
commitment is exactly what makes him so attractive. The pseudo-
romantic goes to any length to seduce the paralleler, attempting to
be indispensable, satisfying every expressed or guessed desire and
whim of the parallel partner. In this process, the pseudo-romantic
takes the masochistic stance in the relationship and suffers terribly.
As Lois Gould described it in her novel, *Final Analysis*, this type of
"romantic" (masochistic stance) may even be grateful to be turned
on sexually by being allowed to masturbate in the withdrawn presence of her beloved, unattainable lover.

I will dwell on this situation because elements of this sadomasochistic mechanism may appear as a minor motif, and in a less virulent
form, in almost any partnership combination. To quote a Caribbean
saying, "No have, want, want; have, no want, no want." The
sadomasochism that sometimes develops between the parallel partner
and the pseudo-romantic counterpart is an almost inevitable part of
the dyadic dynamics of such a couple. The suffering is not enjoyed
for its own sake but it is a concomitant of the pseudo-romantic's
partial and intermittent fulfillment of being accepted and loved, always with just enough "love" offered to keep the pseudo-romantic
locked into a destructive and undesirable relationship, and with the
parallel partner keeping the other suffering by neither firmly ending
the relationship nor allowing himself to love.

Some parallelers do not allow themselves to love because they
fear the tables would be turned on them. Without some rewards and
encouragement the pseudo-romantic would discontinue the relationship, suffer depression for a while, feel rejected and unlovable, and
then perhaps start over again with someone else. However, if the
pseudo-romantic wins the love he seeks, he is likely to destroy or
push away the former parallel partner because he cannot respect the
person who loves him. He now finds unbearable flaws in his partner
and must go on to find another victimizer—to once again prove
what is unprovable to himself, that he is really lovable. Winning the
love of the unattainable parent is often the basic etiological factor

in this syndrome. The sought-for characteristics in a mate are usually those having to do with power and distance in the parent of the opposite sex.

The parallel partner's need for distance is often a reaction to a tremendous dependency need which is inadmissible to his awareness. Such a person appears as ultraindependent, a person who must have charge of all situations; he may be narcissistic and overinvolved with appearances. If these defenses are successfully penetrated—and perhaps this is why he usually maintains his defenses so well—he may melt into a romantic with great dependency needs—thus, as he sees it, becoming extremely vulnerable to his mate.

In most partnerships, the mate who needs the relationship more has the greater potential for being hurt or for being maneuvered into a masochistic position if the other partner plays upon this vulnerability. The struggle of the paralleler is never to allow himself to care enough to be vulnerable to the loss of his mate. If he becomes able to give love and the mate remains a romantic partner they may then "live happily ever after"; if the partner is a pseudo-romantic and now becomes distant or punitive, the former parallel partner may have to pay for his former stance (considered to have been sadistic by the formerly suffering pseudo-romantic). The pseudo-romantic can often be recognized by his selection of "unloving" partners and his loud vocalizations of his desire for a romantic partner.

Another solution that requires understanding and love may be for the paralleler and his partner to perform a reciprocating closeness-distancing dance that does not humiliate or injure either one. This almost ritualistic reciprocity can then be used to enhance their interaction within the security of what may be a mature relationship with some mild and mutually agreed upon sadomasochistic play that provides an extra excitement in their life together.

Nuances and complexities of interrelationships are the spice, passion, anguish, and joy of dyadic love partnerships. With understanding and compassion, abetted by the skilled therapist who comprehends the couple's life style and is not hampered by countertransference, many relationships heading for destruction by either or both partners have a chance to be constructively redirected.

8

Congruence, Complementarity, and Conflict

THE VARIOUS TERMS OF each person's marriage contract may be congruent, complementary, or in conflict with terms in his or her partner's contract. In addition, some clauses of an individual's contract may be internally congruent or conflictual with other terms. This is a common cause of conflict and of ambivalent messages and behavior.

Ideally each person's contract should be consistent within itself and congruent with or complementary to the partner's contract. Contracts that approach this ideal evolve into a single effective contract that both spouses subscribe to consciously and freely. It is not necessary or even desirable for all terms to be identical, so long as the partners know where differences exist and are able to negotiate compromises in a way that either resolves or prevents serious disharmony or dissatisfaction. When dissatisfaction does occur, as it inevitably will, mates must be able to express themselves and their feelings, communicate well, and verbally fight through differences to some equitable solution.

The goal of therapy and the role of the therapist are twofold: 1) to help partners identify and resolve ambivalent or contradictory terms within their own contracts, and 2) to initiate a process whereby the partners begin to work toward a common contract. In other

164

words, a goal of treatment is to turn areas of conflict into areas of congruence, in both the intrapersonal and interpersonal spheres, and to arrive at quid pro quo agreements or other satisfactory resolutions. Not all differences can or should be resolved—some must be accepted and lived with, if they are not pervasively destructive.

The individual contract of each spouse may be regarded structurally from at least two frames of reference. The first, described in Chapter 2, concerns the three categories of contractual clauses: 1) parameters based on expectations of the marriage, or what one wants from the marriage; 2) the intrapsychic and biological determinants of the individuals' needs, conscious or unconscious; and 3) derivative or external foci of marital problems, or the specific issues that couples commonly battle over. These issues are not the causes of the strife, but the arenas in which it is safe and convenient for battles to be waged. The more basic determinants of conflict generally result from differences in expectations of the marriage and differences in biological and intrapsychic needs.

The second frame of reference for the examination of contract terms consists of the three levels of intra- and interpersonal communication and awareness: 1) conscious and verbalized; 2) conscious but not verbalized; and 3) beyond awareness. It is obvious that an unconscious need may be a potential source of intrapsychic and interpersonal conflict, but even conscious and verbalized needs can cause conflict to the degree that partners cannot hear, or will not or cannot fulfill the verbalized need. For example, in the Smith case Mr. Smith was very clear about how he wanted his wife to feed his ego. She refused to, because she felt he was not giving her the support and care she wanted from him.

There may also be contradictory clauses among the three parameters of contractual terms, within one of the parameters itself, or within the three levels of communication and awareness. There may be conflict among any of the parts of the two frames of reference, and there may be internal conflict within an individual's contract along with congruence, complementarity, or conflict between his contract and that of his mate. Since an object of therapy is to improve the relationship, I try to do so by working *toward* a single marriage contract that fulfills in increasing measure the individual's, as well as the marital system's, goals and purposes. The *process* of working together toward this contract serves not only as a means to an end but as an end in itself. The single marriage contract, like infinity, can only be approached, never achieved.

A marriage contract is alive and meaningful only in terms of a specific other person with whom there is an intimate and meaningful relationship. One's desire for particular qualities in a mate or marriage is usually altered significantly from one's fantasy or projection as one becomes involved and begins to interact and form a relationship with that person. As communication becomes established, so do rules, roles, patterns of behavior, and even common myths. The interaction may elicit unsuspected abilities, traits, and needs within each.

Most people function somewhat differently in each relationship. Even those who have been married previously and believe they know what they want in a new mate are often surprised by the extent to which they modify their terms in the crucible of a new relationship. Thus, as two people become "significant others" to each other, they automatically begin to work toward a single contract. As the relationship deepens, each person formulates and elaborates, consciously or unconsciously, the framework of a marriage contract. In good relationships the couple may consciously or unconsciously evolve their single contract themselves.

Therapists help the couples to eliminate hidden terms, "fine print," and implicit clauses from their marriage contracts, but we do not expect two people to adhere invariably to the letter and spirit of their newly emerging single joint contract. We hope instead to teach partners how to negotiate with each other, since the terms of their contract and goals of their marriage will constantly evolve to reflect changes in life situations. Most therapeutic time is spent in changing the need for a counterproductive clause, not in examining and talking directly about contracts.

As in commercial contracts, both parties cannot be expected to be overjoyed by every clause. One may accept a "less advantageous" clause in exchange for a more advantageous one further down the page. The objective is for both partners to agree to the *same* clauses and to find the *overall* contract congenial. As marriage is a dynamic system, a marriage contract is never signed, sealed, and delivered to stand unchanged forever. Many of the ideas set forth here get worked through operationally in therapy; they are not necessarily discussed directly, as the foregoing may suggest.

In Webster's New World Dictionary "congruence" is defined as agreement, correspondence, harmony. Thus congruence of terms or clauses signifies that parameters are internally consistent on all levels within the individual's contract and in relation to the partner's contract. For example, one partner may consciously and unambivalently want responsibility for major financial decisions. If the other partner, without ambivalence, is willing not to vie for financial responsibility, although competent to do so, then the two contracts are congruent in this area. We then would anticipate that this parameter would not be a source of disharmony.

"Complementary" is defined as 1) serving to fill out, complete, or make perfect; 2) mutually supplying each other's lack. Complementarity here refers to the degree to which the needs and abilities of both spouses dovetail effectively. Ackerman (1958) defined complementarity in the sense that it is used here. He saw complementarity as referring

> to specific patterns of family role relations that provide satisfactions, avenues of solution of conflict, support for a needed self-image, and buttressing of crucial forms of defenses against anxiety. Complementarity in family role relations may be further differentiated as being either positive or negative. Positive complementarity exists when the members of family pairs and triads experience mutual fulfillment of need in a way which promotes positive emotional growth of the relationships and of the interacting individuals. Negative complementarity in family relations signifies a buttressing of defenses against pathogenic anxiety but does not significantly foster positive emotional growth. Negative complementarity mainly neutralizes the destructive effects of conflict and anxiety and barricades family relationships and vulnerable family members against trends toward disorganization (pp. 85-86).

An example of positive complementarity would be for a wife and husband who are faced with a long automobile trip that neither wishes to make alone to decide to go together, to make it a pleasure trip instead of an anxiety-producing duty and to cooperatively share the driving. An example of negative complementarity would be one partner believing he must have financial responsibility to avoid becoming anxious, while the other spouse fears financial responsibility and becomes anxious and depressed if forced to assume control of fiscal matters. In this parameter the partners complement each other negatively: One wants control, the other eschews it. If neither is too ambivalent, an effective complementary collaboration results, which wards off the anxiety of each mate, although neither grows very much in the process. It is not necessary for each to strive to be able to assume all possible tasks; however, if we use the financial item example for positive complementarity, the partner who had to have control would teach his now willing-to-learn spouse how to handle the family's basic financial matters and they would pool energies and ideas, thus complementing each other in a positive way.

Dictionary definitions of "conflict" include 1) competitive or opposing action of incompatibles—antagonistic state or action (as of divergent ideas, interests, or persons); 2) mental struggle resulting from incompatible or opposing needs, drives, wishes, or external or internal demands; 3) hostile encounter, fight, battle, war; 4) the opposition of persons or forces. The term "conflict" is used here to connote the existence of 1) opposing or mutually exclusive tendencies within oneself in relation to particular contractual parameters, or 2) implicit or explicit needs of one partner that stand in opposition or contradiction to those of the other. For instance, one partner may consciously want to assume financial responsibility, although unconsciously this power engenders such anxiety that he really wants his partner to take control. His *internal* conflict may manifest itself in terms of ambivalent behavior that in turn provokes external conflict with his mate. Such *external* conflict can also result when there is no ambivalence. For example, both partners may insist on having financial responsibility and ultimate decision-making power, in which case conflict will be avoided only if they can arrive at a compromise solution.

These various ways of handling financial matters illustrate: that in *congruence* there is nonambivalent willingness on the part of one spouse to take over without any threat of problem to the other, who feels competent and is not threatened; that in *negative complemenarity* one is anxious if he does not do it, the other if he does—the two neurotically complement one another's needs, and it works out well—whereas in *positive complementarity* they each grow as they share the function and conquer their anxiety; that in *conflict* they both want to be in charge of fiscal matters and turn this area into an arena for their power struggle.

CONGRUENCE

When true congruence of contractual terms exists, gratifying marital situation generally results. Lederer and Jackson (1968) emphasize that marriages are most likely to succeed (as measured by low divorce rate) when spouses come from similar social backgrounds. Of course it is difficult to determine whether social pressure helps keep together the marriage between the boy and the girl next door, or whether their marriage is actually on a sound basis due to commonality of culture. It seems likely that congruence of values and goals provides a solid foundation for a marriage and augurs well for its stability, but with the increasing number of cross-cultural marriages and the greater mobility of American families, we do not have enough recent studies to indicate the precise weight that should be given to this kind of congruence.

Congruent contracts are more characteristic of equal, companionate, and parallel partner relationships than of rational, romantic, parental, or childlike unions, since members of the former groups depend less on complementarity to make the relationship work. The Waldens, who are equal-equal partners, have congruent contracts.

Mr. and Mrs. Walden are working professionals who make every effort to insure that each has equal opportunity to work and to achieve. When their child was a few months old, each began to work half-days and spend the other half of the day at home caring for the baby and the household. Each has the opportunity to care for the child as well as to help provide for the family and advance professionally. Despite this couple's considerable independence, each spouse has dependency needs that are fulfilled by the other in an interdependent fashion. They can accept each other's independence as well as dependency needs. In addition, the Waldens are part of a quasi-communal group that has similar ideological interests and is devoted to a humanistic cause. This aspect of their life provides the support of an "extended family," in which their positions, both as individuals and as a couple, are respected.

Genuine congruence on all significant contractual parameters is rare, and it is unnecessary when both mates have the maturity to respect each other's differences. The most common areas of congruence are in the sphere of cultural values and mores, where the couple "speak the same language." When congruence also exists in psychological needs, a rich and durable relationship is even more likely to evolve.

An example of congruence from a different socioeconomic group is a couple, both from second-generation Italian working-class families, who were brought up on the same block in New York's Little Italy and now live two blocks away. Their relationship and ambience continue to have an old world flavor. Their neighborhood is their village; they know every shopkeeper and have a nodding acquaintance with everyone within a radius of four blocks. Their conflict was ostensibly over child rearing. The oldest of their three children, a boy of 15, was truant and failing at school; he attached himself as a hanger-on to a club of older "tough guys." This son was the one originally designated as the patient.

The mother had completed high school. The father had two years of high school and then got an equivalency certificate and a job in the sanitation department of the city. His need to be the important and catered-to person at home was respected by his wife. The two were compatible in all respects. She understood her husband's need for respect and was able at the same time to respect herself and her own role as a person. Their major difference was over education for the children and her fear that her son would become truly delinquent. She wanted the children, particularly the older son, to have a college education. Her husband saw no need for this, and, as it turned out in therapy, took his wife's insistence on higher education for the children as a criticism of him.

The son was acting out much of what he sensed as his father's masculine protest against a world that was rapidly changing around the family as the island of Little Italy was invaded by outsiders. Growing up on the streets as a young male supremacist, the boy reflected his father's uneasiness and insecurity. On an unconscious level he was expressing his father's deeper questions about himself in relation to the strength of his wife.

These parents were a loving couple, devoted to each other and their family, but the father was fighting to maintain the status quo ante. He and his world were threatened on a most basic level, and to make matters worse, even his wife seemed to be changing. As a sanitation worker he had security, a relatively good income, and position in the community. This position still held up well, but other neighbors and friends had become middle-class owners of businesses, a few were wealthy, and several had children who had become professionals. His wife was aware of what was happening in their relatively isolated village within the restless, heaving mass of New York, and she knew that the changes could not be stopped. This village was their security, but she saw it would not be so for their children. While she wanted to continue living there, she knew the children would eventually "move out." To "move out" meant to be assimilated, really to leave the old country.

With the help of the two older children and the parish priest we were able to resolve the family problem. The husband was able to accept the reality that the world would be different and that he should encourage his son to go to college, that it was up to him to try to show his son why this was important. In doing so he could finally realize that his wife had not been demeaning him, that she was well satisfied with their social and economic position in the community. Even her desire to find a part-time job was not an aspersion on his earning ability and masculinity; she wanted to work primarily in order to feel better about herself as a person. The wife's role in the change in the family was fully acknowledged by her husband—he was grateful for it. He did not have to find a way to put her or himself down.

As the father resolved his conflict with himself and with his wife, the son changed too. During therapy he was sometimes the interpreter of the new to his father, enabling the father to change as the son changed. The family accomplished this because of the great respect they had for each other's dignity. Husband and wife came to feel more realistically secure about themselves individually and as a unit.

This family—the couple in particular—was very moving to work with. To see the breakdown in the third generation of a stable, extended-family village life occur in the middle of New York, then to be able to pinpoint the problem (the contract concept was used verbally and extensively with the couple), and to enlist the help of other family members and the priest, while maintaining and reinforcing the positive aspects of the couple's essentially fine single marriage contract, was a most rewarding experience.

This case illustrates not only some of the gratifications of being a therapist but the importance of being flexible in theoretical and modality approaches. I worked with this family as a unit, seeing members of the families of origin, as well as working with the husband and wife in conjoint sessions, and with the father and son. Helping this man and his teenage son begin really to talk to each other for the first time in many years was one of the most fruitful experiences I have had as a therapist. When the father was able to put aside his defensiveness and tell his son about his fears, the son was able to put aside his defiance and challenge to his father. The son's explanation of how he felt caught between the "old world" of his father and mother and "what's really out there" reached his father as nothing else could have. The two were then able to work through to a wisdom that may seem very simple to the professional who is not a living member of the situation, and who may never have had to make a similar bridge in his own life, but is in fact very rare and difficult for many people to achieve.

We often observe the phenomenon of superficial congruence or pseudo-mutual congruence (to adapt a phrase from family therapy). In pseudo-mutual congruence, congruence on deeper emotional levels does not exist but there is a mirage of surface agreement. Marriages characterized by pseudo-mutual congruence are frequently the "model marriages" that suddenly explode when one partner blows the whistle on the hypocrisy of the situation.

An example was painstakingly shown in Ingmar Bergman's film, *Scenes from a Marriage*. In the opening scene the couple is being interviewed for a popular magazine. They are depicted as an ideal (if somewhat stuffy) couple by the seemingly glib and anxious husband, while the wife sits by, demurely reticent. The couple have similar backgrounds socially, economically, and culturally. They seem to love their parents and to be involved with their own and the mate's family of origin. As the story unfolds, the falseness of the apparent congruence is exposed. The couple remains unable to deal directly with the partners' differences. The husband verbalizes and acts on his discontent with the ennui and shallowness of their relationship, but the total lack of congruence on deeper, more significant levels of consciousness and needs precludes their taking constructive action together in the interest of the marriage. Only much later in life, when after divorce, remarriages to others, and various affairs they come together for one of their irregular trysts, do they finally really find each other and, at least for the moment, become open, nondefensive, and loving.

COMPLEMENTARITY

More good-to-excellent relationships are based on complementarity than on congruence. True complementarity, including the negative complementary fulfillment of each other's neurotic needs, frequently provides the basis for the best long-term marriages. It is somewhat easier to find someone whose neurotic needs dovetail with one's own than to become free of neurotic behavior and misperceptions. When the couple can complement each other positively in some areas, that is even more gratifying and obviates dependency and anxiety.

In marriages based on complementary contracts, the couple's neurotic and realistic needs fit together to complete a Gestalt that is positive for both. This may lead to a different and perhaps less mature resolution of conflicts than the quid pro quo basis, in which the partners know and accept each other's abilities and limitations and work out conscious agreements whereby "You do for me in this area and I will do for you in that area." This form of negative complementarity creates a relationship in which traits or needs of one partner are used in the service of the other with a deep sense of reciprocity, not exploitation. This is not necessarily "mature," but it is realistic and is the cement of many marriages. In many cases complementarity is not only appropriate; it is necessary to provide the combination of talents needed to make that partnership work well. People are neurotic; we have different needs, abilities, and proclivities. Complementary contracts permit the utilization of certain traits and needs in a relationship. This is apparent in parent-child combinations, romantic partners (who "complete" one another), sadomasochistic marriages, doll's house marriages, and so on. Of course complementary relationships are not always neurotic. They may be unions of relatively healthy persons whose character traits are enhancing and who are able to achieve a positive form of complementarity. Nevertheless, negative complementarity allows some very disturbed people to live together in relationships that are gratifying to both partners.

Mr. and Mrs. York have an excellent marriage in which she is very much in charge of ultimate decision-making and taste-setting and he is at ease with her quiet management of their affairs. In many ways they appear to have reversed the stereotyped male/female roles. Yet each respects the other and is devoted and loyal. They prefer to be together when possible, but they also function well on their own. She accepts her own assertiveness and his relative passivity without ambivalence. He does the same. It is this lack of ambivalence that is essential for this type of complementary relationship. If Mr. York were ambivalent about his passive role there would surely be disharmony. He would be angry or disgusted or feel inadequate as a male; or he might turn his self-denigration against his wife and blame her for making him passive. Similarly, if the wife resented her husband's passivity or was angry because he "made" her be assertive, conflict would be generated.

The completeness of the Yorks' lack of ambivalence about traits that are not consistent with the social norm is extremely rare. It is indicative that each of them has arrived at a modus vivendi that allows a good relationship with the other. Internal conflict or ambivalence over a need or trait can be a terribly destructive force; a self-imposed double bind is as destructive as that imposed by another person. For example, a man who has a deep need to be dependent on his wife is in grave conflict because he also feels driven, because of cultural values, to be independent of her. If he gives in to his dependent needs, he does not respect himself. If he acts independently, he feels he is acting against his wife and becomes anxious, fearing reprisals and loss of love for such independent action. As in any double-bind situation, his conflict may immobilize him or cause him to act impetuously in a defensive, defiant, or inconsistent fashion that is likely to bring censure from himself, his spouse, and others. The double-bind conflict generated within himself could be schizophrenogenic if he is vulnerable to the schizophrenic process. Thus complementarity works well when it is relatively nonambivalent for both mates. To the extent that ambivalence accompanies the complementarity, it can be destructive.

Surface complementarity often leads a couple to marriage. People generally choose mates for the positive qualities (strength, social ease, decisiveness, drive, and so on) that they believe they lack themselves. The desire to please during the courtship period can cause consciously or unconsciously motivated behavior that complements the needs of the courted person and fulfills expressed or subliminally cued needs. In time, though, the truth unfolds and disillusionment follows. We then hear the common complaint: "If I had known what he was really like, I would never have married him."

Often the cause of disharmony is not clear until work with the marriage contracts reveals that each was searching for a partner with the qualities he thought he lacked. Each compensated for his "shortcomings," hiding them by some defensive maneuver, and chanced exposure only as a last resort when the mate repeatedly failed to respond to subtle requests or manipulations demanding that the other supply the deficient quality. This mechanism, which is at the root of much marital discord, causes bitter disappointment and reawakens primitive needs related to the child's fear that he will not survive if he is not taken care of by the adequate parent. The disappointed spouse sees the partner's deficiency as compounding his and thus paving the way to joint destruction. It sometimes takes years and several life crises for people to be ready to perceive the similarity of their partner's "deficiency" to their own. They then have a sense of disappointment, betrayal, or having been duped. The destructive dynamics of this type of system function beyond awareness, with a great deal of pain and disharmony that is usually displaced until there is readiness to confront the true issue in oneself as well as in the mate.

It is quite common to choose a mate whose basic anxieties are similar to one's own. Often it is one's own defense against the anxiety that creates the illusion that the mate has what one lacks oneself. The case of Carol and Walter in Chapter 3 (p. 44) illustrate this complex very clearly. Both these mates had a deep fear of abandonment which they defended against in different ways. The defense of each one then served to escalate the fear of abandonment of the other. Only when they understood the similarity of their underlying fears could they begin to deal with each other more constructively.

CONFLICT

Conflict need not be a frightening or negative term. The existence of conflicting clauses in a couple's marriage contract does not mean that the relationship is doomed. Growth often results from identifying, confronting, and dealing with (not necessarily "resolving") significant conflicts or differences. Greater damage is done to relationships by trying to ignore conflict, or by one partner's passively acquiescing to the other's demands in order to avoid conflict, than by bringing the differences out into the open, acknowledging their existence, and coping with them.

Some conflicts are based on biological or intrapsychic needs that cannot be met by partner A and are so necessary for the security of partner B that either partner B will judge his needs to be ego alien and will request long-term therapy or some other form of treatment to change them, or both partners will realize that they are not basically compatible. B needs someone who will complement his needs in a better fashion, or perhaps no one person can meet B's needs over a protracted period of time in a committed relationship. He may need help to find another life style that will better meet his requirements.

The contemporary therapist should certainly accept and examine alternative life styles with his patients and not feel compelled to fit everyone into a conventional marriage. Communal living, living alone, serial monogamy, multiple simultaneous relationships, and homosexual relationships are among the many alternate possibilities that the therapist and the patient may consider.

When conflicting contractual clauses are brought into the open, they may have a refreshing effect and create a potential for health in the same way that opening an abscess may lead to healing. Sometimes the realization or confrontation is difficult to accept and anxiety-producing. The therapist must use all possible skill to deal with the problem and urge the couple to keep working at it, while evaluating the anxiety that is aroused. It is sometimes too easy to side with the patient's defenses and not deal with anxiety-provoking material. Conversely, sometimes we can be too heavy-handed or our timing may be off because we are insensitive to priorities that should have precedence over the therapist's agenda. When my own approach causes closing up or pushing away, rather than leading to opening, examination, and change, I find the misfiring is usually due to countertransferentially determined activity on my part.

Even when the conflicting clauses concern biological or intrapsychic needs, each mate's needs, expectations, and desires can be discussed in an honest and straightforward fashion. Often the first step is for both partners to understand their own needs and to share this understanding with the spouse. Then quid pro quos can be arranged by the couple themselves or with the help of the therapist (Lederer and Jackson, 1968), or reasonably complementary solutions can be created. Frequently just perceiving and understanding what a partner really desires or expects cause the mate to modify prior positions or attitudes. In task-oriented, goal-directed therapy, clarification of contracts by the therapist, whether or not the information

is shared with the patients, will suggest tasks that will bring movement toward the agreed-upon goals.

If the partners arrive at a realization that they cannot give or
receive what they want, they may decide to separate or divorce.
This is often a positive outcome of treatment. The Joneses were a
couple I saw some years before the development of the marriage
contract concept, but it is easy to reconstruct the significant negative
parts of their contracts.

In the early years of their marriage, as Mr. Jones struggled to become successful in his field, his wife helped him in the family business. They had good sex, enjoyed each other's company, felt engaged
in a common cause, and loved one another. They had three children.
Mr. Jones became quite successful, on the basis of his own ability.
Mrs. Jones felt that he had become more distant and removed as he
ascended the ladder, that he gave her objects and money but not
love. She felt relegated to the home and the PTA, but she made no
effort to return to school or to develop interests of her own, although
it was financially possible for her to do so. Mr. Jones felt that his
wife was envious of his achievements and had taken on as her personal mission the job of cutting him down to size, that she did not
appreciate his accomplishments and wanted to turn the clock back
to when they were poor and had worked closely together. Both had
had extramarital experiences that indicated to each that they could
get more affection from others than from each other, although
neither had developed a deep involvement with anyone else.

Mrs. Jones believed that the man she had loved and married had
become materialistic, unloving, ungiving, and essentially hostile to
her and therefore to all women. The husband felt that he was not
appreciated or loved, that his wife constantly looked for opportunities to put him down publicly and privately, and that she was therefore hostile to all men. Neither could support the other anymore
and neither cared to communicate. Each wanted love but insisted the
other must be the first to change.

They arrived at a mutual decision to divorce. An amicable property, child support, and alimony agreement was quickly reached.

On the plane to where she was to establish residence for a divorce,

Mrs. Jones met a man whom she married within a year. Mr. Jones remarried within eight months. His new wife admires and loves him, protects him from others and supports him where and when he needs it. He reciprocates. The same is true for his former wife and her new spouse. Each quickly found a new partner who could give the necessary love and acceptance and who could fulfill the desire to be loved and needed that they could no longer meet for each other. Positive feelings were and are central in each of the new relationships. After more than 12 years, both new relationships continue to do very well.

Not all divorces have such a happy outcome for both partners. These two were wise to end a relationship in which neither could fulfill the other's needs and in which hatred and paranoia had begun to set the tone of their household. In their new relationships each found a partner with whom he/she could develop a reasonably good complementarity. The original partners still dislike each other.

There is no doubt that certain conflicts cannot be resolved or dealt with creatively to form new and acceptable solutions for both parties. When opposing positions or needs remain as serious sources of anxiety or discontent, either or both partners may conclude that they are in an untenable relationship. In such cases they may decide to separate and eventually divorce.

When the primary conflict is due to neurotic factors in one or both mates that cannot be handled effectively in couple therapy, individual treatment may be indicated, with a return to couple therapy when the threshold of the neurotic reaction has been raised. Conflicts cannot be reconciled easily when they are intransigent manifestations of opposing biological or intrapsychic needs; when either partner is severely mentally ill; or when the conflicts are rooted in a significant difference in intelligence between the partners. Other second-category conflicts that often cannot be dealt with adequately in couple therapy include the question of sexual attraction—why one person, as opposed to another, is found sexually attractive—and the problem created by the cessation of previously intense sexual feelings for a partner.

Another difficult area is the situation in which one partner transmits a high anxiety level to the other and neither one has the qualities (or desire) to relieve the other's anxiety. For example, a person may not know how to react to his partner's dependency needs or other sources of anxiety. He may, in fact, be insensitive to these needs or may feel helpless in the face of them. Worse yet, he may become anxious himself and act in a destructive way. When a partner finally accepts the fact that the anxiety is his mate's problem and that he has done everything possible to fulfill his responsibility, there may be nothing to do except listen and continue to give loving support. Although it is up to the disturbed one to try to work through the problem, it is helpful to know that the partner is there for support and understanding.

When both partners are well motivated, many marital conflicts can be resolved as the couple work toward a single contract. For those who have built a life together it is well worth making the necessary effort to try to achieve a closer and more fulfilling relationship.

9

Therapeutic Principles and Techniques

To UNDERSTAND WHY SPOUSES are unhappy and to provide a rationale for helping them as a couple, as well as each individually, are the central themes of this volume. Conjoint therapy is useful for treating the emotional problems of each mate as well as their relationship difficulties with one another. This chapter indicates how the individual and interactional contracts can be useful with any theoretical approach or modality of treatment, focusing more directly on those aspects of treatment that have not been emphasized or made sufficiently explicit in earlier chapters.

One point bears repetition: The individual marriage contracts and the interactional contract help make sense of the wealth of material we collect from patients. We are free to work therapeutically in keeping with our own bias. Mine is eclectic and (I hope) flexible. The following therapeutic approaches are suggested for the therapist to reflect on, test out, incorporate, modify, or reject as the situation indicates. Each therapist can work most effectively by developing his or her own style. He should, however, give himself and his patients the benefit of becoming familiar with new developments of theory and technique so that he is able to make his own choices and not be bound by the limited number of therapeutic alternatives that were available at the time of his training.

181

Using the marital contract concept makes it relatively easy to pinpoint the factors responsible for marital discord that are significant within the framework of one's own theoretical constructs. The individual contracts facilitate deciding where, how, and when to intervene therapeutically. In addition, the contracts provide the spouses themselves with a frame of reference with which they, as well as the therapist, can periodically examine themselves and their relationship. This is analogous to helping a psychoanalytic patient learn to use his dreams. The analytic patient acquires a valuable added dimension for personal examination, critical ability, growth, and even delightful discovery and self-help. The marital contract can play a similar role for the couple in their future together.

Correct diagnosis is essential for proper therapeutics, so I shall deal first with that perplexing problem.

CONTRACTS AND PROFILES IN DIAGNOSIS AND CLASSIFICATION

No generally accepted or widely applicable system for classifying and diagnosing marital relations exists. The structure I am suggesting must be used with sensitivity and artistry as well as a recognition of limitations.

Berman and Lief (1975) have reviewed four partial diagnostic approaches to marital problems. Each of these approaches is predicated on one factor alone. These include the one by Lederer and Jackson (1968), based on rules for defining power; Pollak's (1965), which is based on parental stage or inclusion-exclusion; Cubor and Harroff's (1966), based on level of intimacy; and a fourth, based on personality style and psychiatric terminology, which has had syndromes of complementary patterns added to it by several authors as they describe a particular dyadic complex. Mittelman set the style for this diagnostic approach in two pioneering articles in which he described four complementary patterns (1944, 1948). These may be summarized as follows:

1. One partner dominant and aggressive, the other submissive and masochistic.
2. One partner emotionally detached, the other craves affection.

3. Continuous rivalry between the partners for aggressive dominance.
4. One partner is helpless and craves care and consideration from an "omnipotent" mate while the mate tries to live up to this expectation but periodically wants to assume the role of dependent partner (Sager, 1966a).

A fifth schema might be added—Ravich and Wyden's (1974), based on the couple's interaction in the railroad game, which tests a couple's ability to interact cooperatively. It offers to predict the prognosis of a marriage based on computerized analysis of the couple's game test findings. All these approaches have merit but each attempts to codify relationships in terms of a single parameter of observation, function, or behavior.

The individual marriage contracts and the interactional behavioral profiles suggest a fresh approach toward an eventual diagnosis and classification system of marriage. The topography I have suggested and the other data described earlier deal with a large number of parameters. I do not offer these as a complete diagnostic system but as a topography, as well as a dynamic interactional approach which moves toward a diagnostic scheme. It is descriptive as well as dynamic and deals with various aspects of etiology that relate to the functioning of the marital system. It avoids the pitfall of trying to explain the remote origins of an individual's behavior, yet it considers the intrapsychic as well as the transactional components. The idea that the source of much anger and disappointment toward one's mate is due to failure to fulfill contractual terms (including those that support one's masochism) is a parsimonious explanation of many of the hurtful phenomena we observe between spouses. It also helps us understand factors that contribute to more fulfilling relationships.

A diagnosis of marital dysfunction cannot be a static label but should be a dynamic evaluation of how the couple function as a unit or system to fulfill the marital system's *and* the two individuals' goals and purposes. As such, it is always in flux. The two behavioral profiles constitute the descriptive topography of the two mates as they presently function together. As the individual and interactional contracts become apparent, and the therapist sees their congruence, complementarity, and conflict, they point the way to a significant operational diagnosis.

On the basis of the congruence, complementarity, and conflict of the marriage contracts we have a complex of intrapsychic and transactional factors that highlights the problems and their immediate causes (even if it does not attempt to deal directly with remote etiological factors), as well as the strengths of the couple and their system. We are then in a position to use these factors knowledgeably in the treatment program, which may or may not deal with remote etiological as well as immediate transactional factors.

It is important early in treatment, even beginning with the first session, to formulate preliminary hypotheses of the positive and negative parameters of the individual and interactional contracts. The therapist's comments in the Smith case (Chapter 5) illustrate the usefulness of these early hypotheses in providing a dynamic organization of data that offers clues for therapeutic intervention. Even initial treatment endeavors may cause the couple's relationship to change somewhat. In turn the intrapsychic dynamics of the spouses are likely to be affected and the contracts may become slightly different almost at once. Thus the dynamic diagnosis (individual contracts, interactional contract, and profiles) may be altered by treatment, which in turn may then require a change in therapeutic tactics. Significant qualitative changes in the marriage depend on the couple's motivation, their biological and psychological limitations, the depth of their love and need for each other, and the therapist's clarity of purpose, skill, and determination. *This dialectic between diagnosis and treatment goes on continually.*

The topography of the marriage is summarized in the partnership appellation that derives from the behavioral profiles the two individuals exhibit in their interaction at any particular time—equal-romantic partners, parental-childlike partners, and so on. The more dynamic aspect can be found in the details of their interactional contracts, which must include the mechanisms of defense they use with one another and that they use together in relation to the world outside their marital system.

The individual contracts supply the rational and genetic material, as it were, for how the two people interact. They show the desires, the ambivalence, the willingness to give in order to get. Individual contracts state what is wanted (including mutually exclusive desires). The interactional or operational contract of the system shows how the two interact to fulfill their contracts as they move toward a single contract. If they are capable of doing this, the interactional contract will become more fulfilling as there is less need to try to fulfill antagonistic, mutually exclusive, or self-defeating needs.

Most spouses do not truly want or desire the strong negative feelings they often elicit in each other. These are an understandable result of the frustrations of those parts of the individual contracts that are not fulfilled in their interaction—just as the interaction can also provide fulfilling and affectionate transactions.

The individual contracts and the interactional one, particularly as we understand the role of the assertive-defensive reactions, are harbingers of a dynamic diagnosis. A fuller comprehension of the assertive-defensive complex and of the persistence of self-defeating and masochistic behavior clarifies why there is often such resistance to change. Planned change is a difficult transformation for most couples for the same reasons that characterological change is so difficult to accomplish in individual treatment. However, with the added dimensions of the systems approach, our therapeutic armamentarium and effectiveness are enhanced.

The topography and the individual contracts are not intellectualized isolates from treatment, useful only for research purposes. They are of prime clinical significance because they directly affect and help to guide the ongoing formulation of the treatment program.

As may be true for any psychiatric label, behavioral profiles are laden with potential dangers. The dangers arise when the description that characterizes a predominant but not singular type of behavior at a given time is regarded as an unchangeable totality, or is seen only as two-dimensional or as black or white without shades of gray or splashes of all the colors of the rainbow. The profile designation should not be allowed to preclude openness to the perception of additional secondary or tertiary behavioral themes. The label describes only one major thrust while most relationships have aspects of various behavioral profiles, not just the two that are designated for the couple. The designation is an attempt to present a picture at a specific point, just as a still photograph of a horse race, taken at 1/1000 of a second, fixes the relationship of the horses at that moment but cannot give a picture of the entire race.

Inherent in the use of the behavioral profile designations as a topography is the danger of oversimplification. The profiles are the therapist's designation. Although often concurred in by either or both mates, the profiles may not be consistent with the image each spouse has of himself or his mate. Spouses frequently resist giving up an image of themselves or their mate that they believe is more ideal or more pejorative. Often two or three profile designations are necessary to capture the essence of a couple's relatedness, particularly when they operate under different external and internal conditions even within the same day, hour, or minute. This caveat in mind, we use the topography with full awareness that it is a description of the way two people have of relating at a specific time. The individual contracts, with all their clauses and parameters, may also change as the interactional contract changes. This provides data for the necessary longitudinal perspective so that we can view the marriage as a *process* rather than an object.

The behavioral profiles are readily understandable to most people. Designating the profile for each partner as it exists in the interactional contract often gives a couple sufficient understanding of aspects of their relationship to encourage them to acknowledge or change parts of their own behavior. It is necessary to be explicit to the couple about the fact that not all their behavior is typical of the dominant partnership profile and that under different conditions each may relate differently. Pejorative attitudes or comments about particular terms or profiles and value judgments about the different profiles are best avoided.

DIAGNOSIS-THERAPY DIALECTIC

When the concepts of the two individual contracts and of the interactional contract are used together, diagnosis and treatment become intertwined as two interpenetrating factors that eventually create a new unity. Diagnosis determines treatment. Treatment, to the extent that it produces change, alters diagnosis. This is exemplified in the two marriage contracts that provide the basis for the interactional or operational contract. Diagnosis of the congruence, positive and negative complementarity, and conflict of the two contracts (as well as internally within each contract) indicates what (but not how) changes occur. The dynamics of the system having changed, therefore the diagnosis will now have changed somewhat too. This, in turn, may necessitate a change in treatment goals, strategy and/or tactics. This back-and-forth process continues until the couple concur in a single joint marriage contract which both are able to subscribe to on conscious and unconscious levels. Such a state of congruence can only be approximated in reality and, except in rare instances, is not maintained as a steady state without being worked on.

When a single contract state is approximated, the diagnosis is then "no dysfunction" and there is no further need for treatment, but preventive attention to the couple's interaction and maintenance of congruent goals and purposes should go on indefinitely. Most couples discontinue treatment when their distress no longer outweighs their gratification and pleasure. As couples come to understand the terms of their own contracts—usually employed quite explicitly in treatment—they tend to use the concept and work on their contract together, even after major obstacles have been overcome in treatment. The major therapeutic role in this period is *not* to compulsively ferret out every conflict but to teach the partners themselves how to deal with conflicts and goal changes, to prepare for the next phase of their life cycle, and to maintain cultural and sexual interests together. Thus, at the end of treatment there is a shift for a short time to emphasis on how to use for preventive purposes what has been learned in therapy.

In summary, diagnosis determines treatment. As the system changes with therapy, the marriage contracts change and hence the diagnosis is constantly amended. The change in diagnosis (contracts and behavioral profiles) then feeds back, producing changes in the treatment plan. Once the couple join the therapist in the common endeavor he or she becomes a member of that couple's marital system. Consequently, the first therapeutic task is to gain inclusion into their system so that he can help to change it. The last is to withdraw from the system, leaving the couple with their own means to prevent trouble in the future and to achieve as much fulfillment as possible.

Some of the modalities that are used in couple therapy, the major theoretical approaches, and some therapeutic techniques are discussed below.

MODALITIES

There are many different methods of working with couples. The following classification of modalities is slightly modified from Greene (1970, pp. 257-259).

> 1. Supportive therapy, which may include crisis counseling, church-sponsored and other weekend couples' encounters that are supportive and focus on improving communication.
> 2. Intensive therapy, which includes all intensive individual forms of treatment; collaborative therapy, in which the marital partners are treated by different therapists, who communicate with the permission of the spouses; concurrent therapy, in which both spouses are treated individually but synchronously by the same therapist; conjoint therapy, in which both partners are seen together in the same session by the same therapist (or a team of two or more therapists); and combined therapy, which may combine several of the above types of sessions as well as individual group therapy, marital group therapy or family therapy.

Berman and Lief (1975) report that at present 80 percent of marital therapy is conducted with both spouses seen conjointly by the same therapist or therapists. I, too, prefer conjoint sessions, and elect not to work with a co-therapist except briefly for training purposes. One reason is that it is not economically feasible for a public or private treatment facility to use co-therapists when this doubles the cost of treatment. Another is that I believe the therapy couple's use of themselves as role models is a dubious procedure based on the treating couple's idealization of their own self-image. I do, however, like to call in a woman co-therapist when my patients or I believe that culturally determined male values or other aspects of my reactions are retarding treatment.

Couples' groups have also been found to be a very helpful modality. I am now developing a flexible approach to structured couples' groups, based on subject parameters of the contracts that are pertinent for particular couples. This application of the contract concept allows me to use the multitheoretical and multitechnique approach with which I am most comfortable. Couples in groups see one another's problems and are helpful to one another in terms of perceptiveness and insight, and of assisting other group members to work toward their single contract. I find that four couples in a group —five at most—are optimal for the way I work.

Berman and Lief believe that treatment in individual sessions is necessary if therapy is not to remain on the behavioral level. My experience differs from theirs. In conjoint sessions I am able to deal with and to affect intrapsychic and remote determinants of current behavior, when it is necessary to deal with these in order to help produce change (Sager 1966b, 1967a, b, c). I often use intrapsychic and historical material concurrently with the here-and-now material and the more directly behavioral and interactional approaches. Psychoanalytic knowledge of dynamics can be drawn upon without necessarily using the techniques of individual psychoanalysis or therapy. Mates are seen individually when one needs to overcome a block so that they may further progress with their work together, but this occurs less frequently as I have come to appreciate the therapeutic power and leverage of the conjoint session. Having the freedom to work with couples conjointly, individually, in groups, and with other family members enables the therapist to use whatever modality will be most effective for a particular couple. However, for me, the major form of treatment delivery is the conjoint session.

In the first session almost every couple demonstrates behavior that is determined by transferential and regressive dynamics toward each other. I will not argue with anyone who calls this behavior a manifestation of parataxic distortions, the introject-projection system of Dicks (1967), or with any other way the therapist wishes to hypothesize the etiology of these observable phenomena; we may see evidence of childhood neurosis and regressive behavior in the first conjoint session that might have required many months or years to elicit in psychoanalysis. It would be a terrible waste of leverage and clinical knowledge if we were not to utilize these phenomena in the conjoint session, along with the theoretical and technical approaches that are based on systems, communication, and learning theories. We do not need to be timid about using our psychoanalytic knowledge in conjoint sessions. Interpretations that are offered as hypotheses or tasks based on our awareness of psychodynamics are important tools in conjoint treatment. Our knowledge need not be ruled out of order nor saved for an individual session.

The systems approach to conjoint therapy can even be adapted to deal with dream and unconscious material. Goldstein (1974) has partners speculate about the meaning of each other's dreams but avoids making interpretations himself. I, too, often have the partners speculate about their own and their partner's dreams, but may also use Gestalt methods of having the individual work with his dream, or suggest connections and offer interpretations myself (1967b). Dreams are also helpful in determining contractual terms on the third level of awareness and in assaying interactional components. They may be used in a wide variety of ways that relate to current and remote factors. One way of using dreams in the conjoint session was illustrated in the Smith case.

Spouses' interactions are very much determined by their acute subliminal awareness of each other's unconscious contractual terms and desires. Transferential phenomena play a significant role because of the many unconsciously determined factors that influence mate selection and ways of perceiving and relating to one's mate. The therapist who has been trained in insight methods of individual therapy, as well as a variety of techniques of marital system therapy, family therapy, and behavior modification, has the advantage of being able to move back and forth between focusing on the interactional system of the couple and on the intrapsychic component of each individual, to see how one affects and helps to determine the content and manifestations of the other.

THEORETICAL APPROACHES

The modalities may be conducted in a way that is consistent with any of the three major psychological theoretical approaches. A mixture of these may also include the organic approach, such as the use of psychotropic drugs. Most therapists employ a mix of two or more theoretical approaches, although they may place major emphasis on one. Our selection is in large part made in terms of what we find comfortable and compatible with our own personalities, what training and experience we have had, which teachers we identify with, and our biases from other influential sources. The only limitation is the number of theories and techniques we permit ourselves to learn. There is usually more than one way to accomplish the same therapeutic objective, and it is rare that any approach can or should be used in a pure form. At the present state of our knowledge it is wisest that we be theoretically eclectic and technically empiric.

The major theoretical approaches are:

1. The *organic*, which uses methods based on treating physically determined etiological factors or their manifestations.
2. The *systems-transactional*, which uses methods based on systems intervention. The aim is to change the transactions between the couple or, in collaboration with them, to change the goals and purposes of the marital system.
3. *Psychodynamic* theory, which employs methods based on any of the forms of psychoanalysis—classical analysis, psychoanaltic psychotherapy, Gestalt therapy, transactional analysis, and so on.
4. *Learning theory*, the theoretical base for the techniques of behavior therapy and behavior modification.

The *organic approach* emphasizes physically determined factors, including somatopsychic effects. It is important for these determinants to be diagnosed and treated with the best of medical knowledge and to use remedial training where this is applicable. When indicated, psychotropic drugs should be judiciously employed. Primary affective disorders, some forms of schizophrenia, and organic brain syndromes strain the marital system to a point that may preclude its survival.

The *systems-transactional approach*, based on general systems theory, views the marital system as composed of two individual subsystems, husband and wife. The transactions between partners, even before the commitment of marriage takes place, have begun to establish a system with its own rules and its own conscious and unconscious contractual terms. It is hypothesized in the systems approach that any intervention that affects a subsystem will affect the entire system. The work of the therapist is to devise interventions that are likely to produce the effect on the system that the therapist and the patients desire. This concept allows for a wide latitude of types of intervention as well as a variety of points at which to intervene. The systems concept is able to incorporate in its general theory most theoretical and technical efforts to understand and change the behavior of the human dyad. This approach is widely used in family therapy, as in Minuchin's method of restructuring the family (1974).

The goals and purposes of individual spouses may be in conflict with those of the marital system. It is common for men, and many women too, to feel they are giving up important rights and freedoms in order to marry. When this is considered a "sacrifice," we can anticipate that there will be trouble. Such a person already feels he has made a poor bargain and is looking for ways to circumvent the marital system and his partner. When one enters a marriage understanding what he is giving up (including the negative aspects of single life for that person), but believing that he will gain something better, he is likely to continue to try to make the marriage work, provided he receives a "reasonable" proportion of what he expected from marriage and his spouse.

Many marital transactions become patterns that often require only a partial stimulus, as the result of experience and conditioning, to set off a predictable reaction. The origins of these set patterns are often lost in the couple's ancient history. To try to pursue who did what to whom first is a fruitless task, although it is carried on with glee by many couples. The transactions that have become set patterns and the feelings that they arouse may be altered by a number of methods. These include restructuring the system or shaping the behavior of spouses so that the motivations, defenses, or impulses of either spouse are altered in a positive way; analyzing the current transaction itself (including video playback confrontation methods); altering the means and effectiveness of communication; prescribing tasks that are designed to change behavior; and a number of other techniques, some of which will be discussed later in this chapter. A recent innovation in the systems-transactional approach is the use of techniques developed by behavior therapists.

Psychodynamics now include much more than our heritage from classical psychoanalysis. The latter encompasses important aspects that should not be discarded when their validity and therapeutic usefulness remain pertinent. There are numerous additional theoretical and technical methods that are also psychodynamic, such as transactional analysis, Gestalt theory, the more interpersonal and cultural theories of psychoanalysis, such as those originated by Horney (1939, 1950) and Sullivan (1945, 1953), and a host of others. Fairbairn's (1952, 1963) object relations concepts, along with Dicks's (1967) adaptation of these to work with couples, and Ackerman's contributions (1958, 1966) to the theory of family therapy, are also included. All these are essentially insight methods, although they usually include some aspects of the other theoretical approaches too.

An individual's psychodynamics are determined by the interplay of his biology and of his environment, which includes more than the influence of parents and siblings or other environmental events in the early years of life. Intrapsychic dynamics can always be altered and influenced by new experiences, including transactions with a spouse. Yet, because of our complexity as people, and because we are open systems that keep changing with our variegated input, the marital system takes on the coloring not only of what each individual brings to it, but of the couple's social environment and the way the rest of the contemporary world impinges on them. It is the latter kind of interaction that made it possible in 1975 for the wife of the President of the United States to say that she would not be surprised if her unmarried 18-year-old daughter were to have an affair before marriage. This comment of Mrs. Ford in turn further influences current mores.

Similarly, as the marital system has its input, so in its turn the marital relationship feeds back to and changes the intrapsychic dynamics of each person. For example, we frequently observe changes in which dominance passes from one partner to the other. It is not uncommon for a man who has been fearful of women to become reassured in a relationship. He then is no longer fearful, nor need he be dominated or dominating after marriage. Presumably his new experience with a particular woman has changed his intrapsychic dynamics as the two arrived at a working marital vivendi.

In *learning theory*, behavior modification and behavior therapy techniques are the particular aspects that concern our clinical work with couples. The interdependence of the two adults in the marital system leaves them ample opportunity to learn to reinforce each other's positive and negative behavior. Therapy based on aspects of learning theory plays an increasingly important role in couple therapy, both marital and sexual. Many therapists now use some techniques borrowed from behavior therapy—for example, tasks to carry out at home, the use of reward systems, and so on. The results of the tasks, the feelings aroused, and the use of those feelings in therapy become part of a multifaceted and integrated technical approach. Increasing numbers of professionals are utilizing tasks along with insight therapy approaches that deal with the resistances and emotional reactions to the task assignments (Kaplan, 1974). The purist approach to behavior therapy, that may have been necessary when these techniques were in their early stages of development, has matured, so that some behavior therapy innovators have begun to soften their positions as more clinicians and theoreticians combine behavioral and insight methods and theory.

My first use of tasks on a wide scale in treatment was in sex therapy. This proved an extremely effective approach when it was combined with insight therapy. The session after the task assignment would deal with the complex emotional reactions the couple had to the tasks carried out at home. I have since incorporated this goal-directed, task-oriented approach into my therapeutic armamentarium for work with couples and their individual contracts (Sager, 1976). Other therapists emphasize different aspects of behavior therapy in their clinical approaches. Stuart (1972) has developed a method of operant interpersonal treatment with couples that modifies the marital relationship by having the spouses reinforce each other's more constructive behavior. Fensterheim (1972) places emphasis on assertive training, while others employ other behavior therapy techniques as their major therapeutic emphasis.

The three basic theoretical and psychotherapeutic approaches—systems-transactional, psychodynamics, and learning theory—are each subdivided into a vast number of discrete approaches to marital therapy. I prefer to remain fluid and try to add to my therapeutic endeavors whatever may be useful. I rarely discard anything totally since I find that sooner or later an opportunity arises to utilize a theoretical approach or technique learned long ago. As healers we must take from wherever we can; no one theory has all the answers for affecting behavior within this most complex of human relationships. The organic approaches are beyond the scope of this book, except to caution the therapist to be alert to the new developments and possibilities that are constantly emerging in this important area.

TECHNIQUES

Specific techniques for couple therapy may be drawn from any or all of the forms of therapy based upon any of the theoretical approaches or on the particular advantages to which some modalities lend themselves. As often happens in psychotherapy, a technique may be developed long before it is fitted into a particular theoretical approach. In a sense, almost every therapist is inventive and adds to the technical repertoire. I wish to indicate ways to approach the application of our basic theoretical knowledge rather than to attempt a complete listing of therapeutic techniques with their indications and contraindications. To attempt to do the latter would be contrary to my understanding of the therapeutic process. There is no one specific treatment for each symptom. As therapists we are dealing with phenomena that are too complex to be approached in a linear cause and effect concept of change. Of necessity we have to use ourselves with our total knowledge and experiences.

For example, I learned the STOP technique (Wolpe 1973) of behavior therapy a few years ago and have used it successfully to inhibit certain types of obsessive thinking and compulsive activity in individuals. Confronted with a couple in which the woman was a compulsive talker, and whose symptom was upsetting to her and her husband, I thought of an adaptation of the STOP technique. With the agreement of both spouses, in order to make it transactional for them and because she was not always aware of when she slipped into her compulsive speech pattern, I taught her husband to use the technique with her to interrupt her when she started on her compulsive track. She was grateful for his help and he was pleased that he could do something constructive. The compulsive talking diminished, and after two weeks she began to use the technique herself and was able to eliminate most of her compulsive talking.

Single Contract

Early in treatment I usually start to orient spouses to work toward a single contract as a means to achieve a better relationship. Often this is at first done implicitly, as the three of us compare the terms of the two separate contracts that have been verbalized or written out by the couple. In its broadest sense the road we travel along toward the goal of a single contract *is* the work of therapy. The terms of the contract must be the choice of the two spouses, not mine. I try to be a guide, a facilitator, a remover of road blocks. I draw their attention to the problem areas as well as those that are congruent and complementary. I devise tasks to change their behavior to each other, and I interpret their intrapsychic and system dynamics to them when I think that will help. I relate the present to the past—to their parents' marriage and their relationships with their parents, to their role assignment in their family of origin, to their relationship with siblings and how this may affect their current marital behavior—and to other life experiences when any of this is indicated. I manipulate their system in their behalf, with their consent and cooperation.

The therapist's role is somewhat similar to that of an experienced fishing guide who has contracted with his clients to help them catch fish but has not guaranteed success. The guide tries to set up the most feasible and expeditious conditions for them to accomplish their goal. He uses all his accumulated knowledge and experience. He knows the haibts of the fish in his locale. He tries to make his clients as comfortable as possible on the journey but they must realize that fish cannot be caught from the terrace of a tenth-floor suite of the local Hilton hotel and that the trip may be arduous and rough, inconvenient and even painful at times but that the rewards are worth it—if they really do want to catch fish. It is the guide's duty not to steer the boat into white water that is too dangerous for his clients to handle. Sometimes the guide is in conflict because he knows the fish may be in a deep pool past the rapids. Then he must make a choice. Usually he does not choose to take his clients through rapids that will endanger their lives. There may be other fish in safer pools, or perhaps this couple will find that their expedition together should end.

Using the individual marriage contracts and the interactional contract, the objective is to work toward achieving a single joint contract instead of the unilateral ones with their hidden and not-agreed-upon clauses. The therapist uses his skill to help reduce the number and the noxious effects of newly discovered, as well as already known, conflict-producing contractual terms. The single contract is not necessarily one wherein each spouse is pleased by every clause or finds all clauses to be optimal. A single contract must involve many quid pro quos, as well as many negative and positive complementary clauses that may or may not be the most pleasing for either spouse but that are at least workable for each and can be accepted without rancor or a sense of capitulation or defeat. Both spouses must have the ability and motivation to fulfill their part of the terms.

To arrive at such a single contract (whether it is spelled out as such or not) it is usually necessary for the couple to become fully aware of at least the most troublesome areas of their individual contracts. Verbal agreements in regard to one parameter may be made but often cannot be carried out for long when there is an underlying conflict in another parameter related to the subject areas of categories 1 and 2. The problem area may then have to be bypassed and the anxiety reduced in some appropriate fashion; alternatively, the remote etiological factors themselves may have to be dealt with.

Once approximated, the single marriage contract has to be reviewed periodically by the couple, since goals, purposes, and needs change in the marriage cycle and for each person.

Communication

There is no need to elaborate on the role of communication. Communication between mates, verbal and nonverbal, is the means, the message, and a goal for couples in or out of therapy. It is the therapist's instrument. The elucidation of the contracts so that they come into full awareness, as well as the working toward a single contract, is intelligence transmitted by communication.

Goals

Goals are essential in treatment and also offer an approach to the rapid initiation of therapy. One way of proceeding in an ordered, step-wise fashion is to set simple goals and then proceed to others when the first are attained. The contract information helps to guide the couple and and the therapist in goal setting and involves the patients as full participants in deciding upon the goals they want. It helps to assure, too, that their priorities, values, standards, and purposes are being met, not just the therapist's.

Goals voiced at the start of treatment do not have to be the ultimate ones. Any goal or purpose husband, wife and therapist agree upon is acceptable if it is plausible and possible to achieve. As therapy continues unexpected goals or problems may come to the fore that must be dealt with. The therapist has to separate the valid goals from those that are distractions or resistance. A step-wise progression is a theoretical ideal that often is interrupted by life's immediate necessities.

Some couples, or at least one spouse, may come to treatment with the goal of separating. If one partner irrevocably wants to leave the other, then the task of the therapist, with the concurrence of the two spouses, is to facilitate a separation with as little destructiveness as possible. However, some couples seem unable to arrive at a workable modus vivendi until their marriage is threatened with termination; one or both partners may use the threat of separation in an attempt to improve the relationship or to force the couple to seek therapy.

My objective is to try to help the couple continue their marriage if they wish to. I make clear to them that the separation or divorce of two persons who loved at one time represents a disappointment, a blow to each partner's self-esteem, and the end of a hope and dream that is painful to accept. It may deeply affect their children and relationships with them; it is likely to cause economic hardships. At the very least, if they decide it is best to separate the couple should understand why they are doing so and learn from the experience they have had together. What can each learn that will enhance the chances for greater self-fulfillment and for the next relationship to work out better, if another relationship is wanted?

The therapist often has to provide firm leadership to establish whether both spouses want to remain together and to improve the quality of their relationship. Couples who at the outset are not sure whether they want to stay together can be helped to use the therapeutic process to clarify their contracts and make a wise decision.

Sometimes one or both mates may have covert goals in seeking out professional help. For example, one partner may want his spouse to be in the "protective hands" of the therapist as a "guarantee" against a depression or a psychotic episode, or a soon-to-depart spouse may fear his spouse's rage when the separation is announced. In such instances therapy may be used by one spouse as an attempt to shift responsibility for the mate to the therapist. Some mates go through the motions of therapy to tell themselves, their mate, children, friends, relatives, and even God that they have tried everything before actually separating. The inevitability of divorce or separation when both mates do not want to stay together is best respected by the therapist.

Just as courtship should take a certain amount of time, a significant amount of time should be spent in working out the emotional and mechanical aspects of separation and preparing for life without a partner—at least temporarily. Whitaker and Miller (1969) make the point that a couple ought to take as much time to decide to divorce as they did to marry.

It is important for most people to learn that they can live without a mate, that they can survive and take care of themselves. Knowing this often removes the need to clutch at a relationship out of fear of loneliness or helplessness. Often this knowledge frees a couple to decide to live together with more ease; neither has to "prove" that he can survive alone or cling to a relationship because he is afraid of being alone.

Any two people who can't maintain a gratifying relationship together need to know that each may be able to do so with another partner. The interaction of two partners is always more important than the psychodynamics of an individual when it comes to prognosis. We cannot predict effectively whether an individual whom we see alone can or cannot have a good relationship with a yet-unfound partner. How the two fit together is the important matter. I have been astounded at times, and gratified, to see how people manage to find a person whose needs beautifully complement their own.

Patients often define their goals at first in terms of their immediate complaints: "We are always fighting. If he would only not jump on me all the time, we would be okay." Or, "I feel she no longer loves me. I can't get overtime work anymore and so money is tight. The minute I come in the door now, she wants me to fix things. She doesn't think about me." Or, a third, "I have trouble with sex, that is, in keeping my erection, and I never used to until these past six months when she found out I had a one-night stand." And, a fourth, "I'm stuck here with this house, the kids, and a station wagon. He's never home. He's married more to that company than to me."

These complaints would be viewed very simplistically if we were to believe that all that is needed to remedy each situation would be: for the first woman, that we instruct her husband to stop jumping on her; for the second, that the man just make more money and his wife give him time to relax; for the third example, that the man be relieved of guilt about his extramarital sexual experience—and that his wife "forgive" him—and then he immediately would be returned to his sexual competence and all would be good between him and his wife; and for the fourth, that the husband be urged to spend more time with his family and give more directly of himself. Of course, no such simple solutions exist.

These category 3 complaints are derivative symptoms, rather than etiological agents. Obviously much more is involved in each instance than can be significantly changed by a common-sense suggestion. If it could be done that easily it would have been, and professional help would not have been sought.

More sophisticated couples may state their immediate goals differently but they may still arise from the third category of the derivative complaints, as the four previous examples do. More subtle versions might be, "My wife and I don't communicate meaningfully anymore—we can talk about things, but not feelings," or "Yes, I can write checks, too, but we really don't have equal responsibility and rights when it comes to making decisions about significant money expenditures. He can decide to buy a new suit for himself, but if I want a coat I have to ask him if it's okay to spend the money now." The presumed goals in response to these two complaints would be to "improve communication" in the first instance and to arrive at a suitable modus operandi for money management in the second. In pursuing these two goals we shortly discover that these complaints are derivative. The first instance, that of poor communication, is a manifestation of the wife's need to maintain distance. In the second example the use of money is but one among many manifestations of these mates' deep struggle for power.

The therapist's task is to help the couple establish goals that will help them get what they really want. This is often best defined in behavioral terms, even when insight is required to help produce the change. It may be important for the partners to learn that the overt expression of their complaint is rooted in fundamental differences that must be solved if the power struggle is to become less crucial in their daily interactions. Or the therapist may elect to bypass the immediate problem and help them work more directly on power, leaving money conflicts to be returned to later if the spouses have not by then resolved the problems themselves. When marriage contracts are used to clarify the underlying sources that produce the marital system's malfunction, the appropriate immediate goals then become clearer.

When therapist and patients are reasonably sure that both spouses, even if ambivalent, really wish to try to improve their relationship, goal setting may then proceed on a step-by-step basis. Some couples are satisfied with traveling a short distance down the road to the infinity of their ideal of the perfect relationship; others want to make leaps—they are too impatient to rest for long at intermediate points. In either case, goals must be attainable if their use is to be effective, as Ferber and Ranz (1972) emphasize in their work on goal reaching and tasks in family therapy. It is the therapist's duty not to accept impossible or destructive goals, such as "I want my wife to obey me," or "Ours must be a perfect relationship without arguments or fights." The therapist must not allow a common goal to be set that one of the partners cannot possibly fulfill or does not wish to accept.

An example of a nonacceptable goal occurred in a marriage in which the husband was subject to depression and fits of uncontrollable rage triggered by incidents that appeared to lack a clear etiological basis. Although already middle-aged and in a profession in which he was successful and well recognized, he had a secret ambition to become President of the United States. His wife supported his ambition semihumorously but underneath she too was serious. They were in a borderline *folie à deux* that embarrassed them and yet was very real to both. At expense to his professional work and family life they became active in local politics. His underlying goal originally was for me to help him change his personality so that he could better achieve his ambition to become president. His wife was more for the goal of eliminating his irrational rages and depressions, which were usually directed against her. After he agreed to work with his wife and me on the more immediate goal of dealing with his depression and rage, we postponed discussing his presidential goal and dealt with the fact he had not been fulfilling his wife's contract regarding his behavior to her.

His symptoms of depression and rage were connected with the fact that he had seen his father at home and in his limited business-world sphere as an absolute monarch, whose slightest desire was carried out by those around him, particularly his wife. He perceived all other people as adoring and admiring his wise and powerful father. His contract was to be adored and for his word to be law, as his father's had been. His wife did not always act in the prescribed fashion. He viewed himself on the one hand as inferior and inadequate as compared to his father, while at the same time he fantasied he was omnipotent. His depression and rage occurred when some event impinged to demonstrate that he was not really as powerful as he was in his fantasy.

The husband's presidential goal came to the forefront again later on, when it could better be dealt with. It was clear that his ambitions had continued to lurk in the background, but to have tried to deal directly with this goal at the beginning of treatment could have created the dilemma Lindner (1955) once found himself in with a youthful patient. As he tells the story in "The Jet-Propelled Couch," Lindner entered his patient's jet-sped delusion and became deeply involved as he made the delusion his own. He therefore failed to perceive when his patient no longer needed the delusion and discarded it, leaving Lindner still riding on the "jet-propelled couch."

It is not uncommon for a therapist to engage in a *folie à deux* with his patient. Lindner bravely offered his classic example to us as an appropriate clinical warning. In couple therapy, countertransference can also lead us into joining a delusional or paranoid system of one mate against the other. Thus I could not accept my patient's goal to help him change his personality so that he could become president on his terms, but after some preliminary exploration that revealed the extent of this need, I asked him to put off our dealing with it, hoping that he would discard the ambition of his own accord. Ordinarily I might have pointed out his illogical position to him, but I sensed that it would be unwise to do so here because of the emphasis he had put on the description of his father as a godlike person whom he could never equal unless he achieved great political power. My pointing out the lack of logic in his ambition at that time could have made him see me as allied with his father to keep him in an inferior position.

To have dwelt on the unreality and inappropriateness of his ambition would have confirmed the "You are like my father who is so superior to me and compared to whom I will always be a boy" transferential feelings that he soon readily developed anyway. In part, his telling me his secret ambition had been a maneuver to get me to respond to him as he felt his father had. It was sometime later that I came to understand why a warning bell had rung in my head when he told me his presidential ambition in the first session; it was too big a secret to tell so soon.

Goal setting is a basic technique applicable to all modalities of therapy and theoretical systems. It implements certain important theoretical assumptions: 1) Goal setting enlists the couple and the therapist in working together collaboratively for a purpose. Karl

Menninger made this clear when he defined the psychoanalytic contract (1958). 2) Goals motivate people and enlist their cognitive and affective systems in the therapeutic process. 3) A step toward maturation is to be responsible for consciously establishing one's own goals in life and to move to achieve them in a conflict-free way. 4) Failure to be able to work toward reasonable goals implies a priori evidence that a negative factor is at work in the marital system or a subsystem. 5) It is the therapist's work to help the couple get by or remove their own road blocks when they do genuinely want to achieve their goals.

Tasks

Tasks that are designed to achieve goals must consider the marital system's dynamics and the needs and psychodynamics of each spouse. Tasks have to be designed that will teach and facilitate change through experience, but that will not arouse so much anxiety or resentment that they are certain to be rejected (unless it is our plan to have the task rejected for predictable therapeutic purposes). By making clear the problem areas and the underlying dynamics, the marriage contracts greatly facilitate our devising suitable tasks. In fact, the contracts serve as a guide for setting tasks that will change behavior or probe areas of resistance, when properly designed to do so, and will help spouses fulfill each other's unconscious needs.

For example, the sensate focus or pleasuring exercises of sex therapy can be used as a therapeutic test in marital therapy to explore with a couple their readiness to accept closeness, their capacity to collaborate, their ability to give and to receive from the mate, their ability to communicate with each other, and their acceptance of directions from each other without feeling put down or ordered about. (See Kaplan, 1975, for specific pleasuring exercise instructions.)

Tasks may include individual ones for one mate, quid pro quo tasks in which each does something for the other, or those that are done together. They are carried out at home or in the course of the day. All are designed to produce behavioral changes; some are expected to produce insight, some are not. An example of an insight-producing task is the paradoxical task, which makes ego-syntonic behavior ego alien. This usually entails having a mate carry out to an absurd extent a behavioral pattern that is disturbing to his spouse (Haley, 1963).

For example, a wife complained that her husband was untidy at home, which he confirmed. His wife unsuccessfully tried to change his ways, alternately yelling at him and picking up after him, much as his mother had done. The man was instructed to be as untidy as he could possibly be—to really mess things up; at the same time the woman was instructed to keep yelling at him and berating him but *not* to clean up after him. Even if she did not feel inclined to do so, she was to yell at him if he left anything untidy or messy about the house. Each spouse heard the instructions to the other in the conjoint session. (The therapist must give such instructions with a straight face and must convincingly convey that he really does want his instructions to be followed.)

When carried to such an extrapolated extent, the behavior of each spouse becomes ridiculously clear to the other; insight into the effects of one's own behavior is almost immediate, and frequently both change their behavior of their own accord. In this case the husband realized sheepishly that he was acting like a spoiled brat and the wife saw herself as the proverbial shrew, which she did not wish to be. Both laughed ruefully at what had happened. Each realized that the exaggeration of their usual behavior was ego alien. By means of this simple task we had changed ego-syntonic to ego-alien behavior. It also was sufficient to make both spouses change their irritating behavior of their own accord.

In the conjoint session following a task assignment, the spouses describe what they did and their reactions to the task. We are concerned with how the assignments were carried out and what the spouses felt. What was good about it, what was not? How did each cope with the other's task as well as his own? Failure—why a task was not carried out—is as important to learn about as is success. Failures, resistances, and emotional reactions form the grist for the therapeutic session. To deal with these requires all our skill, calling on our technical and theoretical knowledge to deal with the immediate (interactive and system) and the remote (intrapsychic, earlier life experiences) etiological aspects.

A fascinating challenge for the therapist is to develop tasks that will tap into the unconscious desires and needs of each spouse. The therapist has to assay rapidly the unconscious terms of the contracts so that they can serve as a guide. This was done, for example, in the Smith case, when each of these childlike partners was trying to make the other a strong but benevolent and giving parent. Each partner's need to be both dependent and in charge was dealt with by putting each spouse in charge of family decisions for alternating periods of three days each, so that the conflict over who was in charge and how to appear to abdicate control while making the other mate do as one wanted was solved.

Problems that originate primarily in the first and second contract categories—expectations of marriage and the biological and intra-psychic determinants—can frequently be dealt with by means of tasks combined with techniques of brief psychotherapy, which are used to bypass or work through the sources of the reactions and feelings that are brought to light in the following session.

OVERCOMING RESISTANCE TO CHANGE

Removing blocks to working toward a single contract is the crucial work of treatment. Some problems are of such a nature that at times individual sessions or more intensive insight therapy may be indicated. Possibly conjoint and concurrent marital sessions, family therapy (with the spouse's children, siblings, and/or parents as indicated), group therapy, or psychopharmacology may be appropriate at a particular time.

Merely making a resolution to change one's behavior is no more likely to be successful than the customary New Year's resolution to stop smoking or start exercising. Readiness and motivation to change must be present on all levels of awareness. This is the quality of readiness that Goulding (1972) refers to as the readiness to make a redecision to change the "life script" that was decided upon long ago. When the individual first adopted his script, it may have been appropriate adaptive or coping behavior. In adult life, however, this same script may be counterproductive and/or masochistic. A couple or one of the partners may not be ready to change at the time help is ostensibly sought. This may indicate that they are not sufficiently unhappy with their situation to try to make the necessary effort, have not confronted themselves with the ultimate consequences of their present behavior, or find considering change too frightening. Once motivated to at least seek out a therapist, the first goal may be to work on becoming ready to change oneself. To accomplish this the contracts may be used in confrontation techniques, which can readily show the couple the effects of some of the remote etiological factors or defensive maneuvers. The next therapeutic step may be to clarify their anachronistic and nonadaptive areas of behavior, feelings, and concepts.

All the therapist's skill, artistry, creativity, and training are required to overcome or circumvent resistance to change. To achieve the necessary interactional behavior changes by whatever means are at his disposal—systems methods, psychodynamic and insight approaches, behavioral modification, or any other theoretical approach —is the central task of the therapist. The therapist usually has to work back and forth, utilizing those methods that he believes will be the most effective. A multifaceted approach allows for greater flexibility.

The authority of the therapist is an important therapeutic instrument. It is a powerful force that should be used consciously, judiciously, and with the full knowledge of its possibilities and limitations. This brings us to the problem of the therapist's countertransferences. These are the same in any form of marital therapy, wherein the therapist is exposed to all the stresses of the triangular relationship with two patients (Sager, 1967b). The therapist may discover that in subtle ways he is sometimes competitive with the husband, or that he is taking sides with the husband against the wife, or that he is prone to male chauvinistic thinking or to feminist or antimale thinking. He has to check his value system constantly, so that it is not imposed on the couple. On the other hand, no therapist should attempt to treat people he actively dislikes or fears. Except for family therapy with children included in the group, there is no form of psychotherapy that is so prone to touch the hidden sources of the therapist's emotions and value systems and to threaten to overwhelm his objectivity.

Systems-transactional, psychodynamic, and learning theories provide a basis for the development of a large number of modalities and techniques with which the individual marriage contracts may be used in treatment. To regard the contracts as diagnostic of the state of the marital system and how the system actually is functioning to achieve its goals and purposes makes clear the role they can perform in marital therapy.

Because the marriage contract is a concept and not a psychological or interpersonal test, its application and the methodology for using the contract concept must remain flexible. It has to be adapted by each clinician for his or her own needs and also for those of each couple. To develop a quantitative "score" for the two individual contracts or the behavioral profiles would be to miss the dynamic essence of the concept. The two contracts that move toward becoming one with the participation of both spouses and therapist cannot be locked into any dogma or schematized analysis. Therapist and patients must remain free to move about within their perception of their necessities and the treatment situation. The desire of two people to remain together out of strength, affection, and love is the best motivational force the therapist can have to work with, and the therapist himself is limited only by his own perceptiveness and ingenuity.

10

Sex in Marriage

To HAVE SEX TOGETHER is universally expected
to be a prime function and even duty within marriage, and many
persons consider sex permissible only in marriage. Yet, the role of
sex in marital therapy has been undefined over the past 50 years.
Until the past decade neither general nor marital therapists made a
practice of inquiring in detail about a couple's sexual relationship.
Confronted by a couple with a sexual problem, the therapist sometimes felt helpless to be of much assistance; often he or she was as ill
at ease or as ignorant about the physiology of sex, as well as the
physical and interactional forces that influence sexual response and
performance, as the patients were.

New developments in our knowledge of the physiology of sex
(Masters and Johnson, 1966) and the treatment of sexual dysfunctions (Masters and Johnson, 1970; Kaplan, 1974, 1975) have led to
an increased awareness of the need for the therapist to inquire into
specifics of the couple's sexual practices. This trend is further
enhanced by increased openness about sex in general and the fact
that now there are more effective treatment methods for the sexual
dysfunctions. The new sex therapy has had a profound effect on
marital therapy (Sager, 1976).

The impact of social and technological changes on marriage and
all dyadic relationships has been translated into a diversity of patterns

for living together, rather than only one universally accepted pattern. Again, marital therapists must be guided by their patients' goals, purposes and values; professionals cannot impose their own values on those who come to them for help.

This chapter will examine the relationship of sex to marital therapy, the question of the couple's sexual relationship as a reflection of their total relationship, and the subjects that are most commonly included in the individual and interactional sexual contracts of couples.

THE RELATIONSHIP BETWEEN SEXUAL AND OTHER MARITAL PROBLEMS

Many clinicians make no clear-cut, sharp distinctions between sexual and marital symptoms. In my practice, among couples whose chief complaint is a specific sexual dysfunction and those with other complaints of marital disharmony, I find, on detailed examination, that three-fourths of the couples from both groups present a mixture of both significant marital discord and significant sexual problems, regardless of whether the chief complaint is marital or sexual.

Sex is only one strand in the cable of bonding, but it is inextricably entwined with the other strands that have kept the couple together. When some of these strands have begun to fray, a number of them must be identified and reinforced if the strained relationship is not to unravel and come apart. Occasionally it is only the sexual strand that needs reinforcing, and in those instances sex therapy is the major focus of therapeutic attention. More frequently sexual dysfunction or dissatisfaction is so intimately connected with other interactional problems that attempting to treat the sexual parameter alone will do little to mend the overall fabric of the relationship. Therefore, it is of primary importance in selecting treatment approaches to be aware of the interrelatedness of the various parameters of the couple's relationship and to define the connection between sexual dysfunction and other aspects of marital disharmony.

The relationship of the discord to the dysfunction seems to be the crucial factor in determining the initial therapeutic focus in the treatment of couples presenting significant marital disharmony along with sexual difficulties. In evaluating the qualitative nature of the discord and the temporal relation of the dysfunction to the discord, I have found (Sager, 1974) three descriptive categories for couples, reflecting the extent to which the discord precedes or results from sexual dysfunction.

In the first group, the sexual dysfunction has produced secondary marital discord. Here it is usually most effective to deal first with the sexual problem, especially when the dysfunction existed prior to the relationship between the spouses. If other parameters of marital dysfunction have dissipated when the sexual problem has been successfully treated, further marital therapy may not be indicated.

In the second group, marital discord in other areas impairs sexual functioning because of the negative interactions that have generated angry, disappointed, or hostile feelings that provide an unsatisfactory matrix in which to find sexual pleasure together. Often something *must* go wrong with sexual fulfillment under these conditions. Many cases seem to fall into this category. Entering the couple's system and attempting to improve their sexual relationship may work in instances when the couple's positive feelings and desire to improve their marriage outweigh the negative feelings and impaired aspects of the relationship. A trial of focusing on the sexual symptoms with such couples may result in rapid relief of these symptoms. The consequent increase in the self-esteem of both partners creates a more beneficial milieu in which to face other pressing marital problems. Indeed, the development or restoration of adequate sexual functioning often enables the couple to confront other problems that their sex problem kept them from perceiving or admitting previously. At worst, an unsuccessful attempt to deal first with the sexual parameter can be turned to good therapeutic effect by using the "failure" to emphasize the need for the couple to deal first with other, more basic conflictual issues between them.

In the third group, severe marital discord, usually with basic hostility, has precluded the possibility of good sexual functioning. In these unfortunate situations attention must first be directed to those contractual and/or interactional factors that create the panoramic negative interaction. Such a couple's hostility would not allow them to attain the level of cooperation necessary for the rapid treatment of sexual dysfunction. Apparent intransigent hostility need not augur poorly for the success of marital therapy, provided there is a genuine desire on the part of both partners to improve their relationship and a willingness to work toward a viable single contract. If the basic hostility is resolved and a sexual dysfunction still exists, this may then be treated more directly.

The necessary conditions for initiating and continuing sexual therapy, using the new sex therapy methods, are that both spouses accept each other as sexual partners; that they have a genuine desire to help each other and themselves; that they can delay personal gratification temporarily, if it is necessary to do so; and that they will participate in maintaining a sexually nondemanding ambience when this is indicated in treatment. The etiology of the sexual dysfunction, its relationship to the concomitant marital discord, and the ability of the couple to fulfill these four criteria for sex therapy must all be taken into account when considering the goals of therapy and the initial point of therapeutic intervention.

When a sexual dysfunction is present and the couple meet the above criteria, unless the couple's goals give first priority to other matters it is often effective to treat the sexual dysfunction first, keeping in mind that the problem is a manifestation of the interactional contract. This was the approach first employed in the Smith case (Chapter 5). Treatment of the sexual dysfunction first is possible because studies of the results of the new sex therapy methods and their theoretical constructs indicate that sexual dysfunctions need not be caused by deep intrapsychic problems that reflect arrest at a particular level of psychosexual development, disturbance in gender identity, or unconscious conflicts. Most symptoms have multiple determinants. Often the sexual malfunction results from the couple's specific interaction; their interaction may then serve as the determining factor in producing symptomatology (immediate cause) in a susceptible individual (made susceptible by remote causes). It is interesting to note that the person with a sexual dysfunction who does not have a partner often cannot be treated effectively for an interpersonal sexual dysfunction because the therapeutic leverage of the interpersonal factors cannot be used as it can be when an involved partner participates in the treatment program (Sager, 1975).

The recognition that the immediate cause of the dysfunction occurs within the matrix of a person with a susceptibility has important theoretical and treatment implications. As in marital therapy, generally, it provides the theoretical rationale for the effectiveness of task-oriented therapy combined with utilization of treatment methods that are founded upon the therapist's knowledge of the remote etiological factors.

I do not think of the sexual area as isolated from other areas of a couple's functioning. All are manifestations of the same two-person system. The specialist in marital therapy must feel as comfortable and competent in dealing with his patients' sexual problems as in dealing with any other area. Thus the marital therapist should have some knowledge of and competency in sex therapy, although he should feel free to refer patients to specialists in sex therapy if he knows he is getting beyond his expertise or into areas that he is not deeply interested in pursuing himself.

SEX AS A REFLECTION OF THE TOTAL RELATIONSHIP

Until very recently many professionals accepted as a truism that the sexual relationship of a couple may be regarded as a microcosm of their marital relationship. Those of us who made this assumption had not, at that time, worked conjointly with couples. We did not observe the couple's interaction but dealt only with the individual spouse. The assumption was based, in turn, on other theoretical assumptions, not on clinical observations. This may have been due to the fact that psychoanalytic writing was founded on a theory of sexual development and arrest that was presumed to have a determining influence on all behavior. Many professionals therefore assumed that the way in which two spouses functioned sexually could be regarded as representative of the developmental level and quality of that pair's total relationship.

Now that we are better attuned to taking a detailed current and past sexual history from a couple, we find that sex, love, and commitment may each be qualitatively and quantitatively different within the same relationship. Some couples who have good sex have a good total relationship all the time; all couples who have good sex have a good total relationship some of the time; but all the couples who have good sex don't always have a good relationship all the time. Conversely, there are those who have a poor sexual relationship but who have a good, loving relationship in other parameters of interaction.

Often the nuances of the parasexual and sexual aspects do mirror the total relationship of the couple. The same power struggles, similar defense mechanisms, the same ability to be close or distant, the same spoiling of one's own or one's partner's pleasure at the moment of fulfillment, the same demands, the same masochistic or sadistic stance, the same dependent, childlike, or parental attitudes may prevail in sex as in other areas of the relationship.

But for many committed couples sex does not reflect a one-to-one similarity to their total relationship. Sex sometimes appears as a unique parameter of their interaction (as other parameters may be unique too), in which either or both spouses may act differently than is customary. Sometimes their sexual activity appears to be dissociated from their other joint activities. There are couples who fight, disagree on most values, have constant power struggles, but continue to have an intense sexual attraction for each other and are able to enjoy and to fulfill each other sexually.

There are also loving couples whose relationships are excellent, whose ways are congruent and whose individual propensities and needs either complement each other's nicely or are at least acceptable and nonabrasive; yet, sexually they do not excite each other. The closeness, openness, and excitement that they can sustain emotionally and verbally are just not there for them sexually. Some of these couples are among those who have a good relationship but have sexual ennui or avoidance.

Another group of couples seen in sex therapy has an excellent overall love relationship but one or both have a sexual dysfunction that clearly is not a symptom of any deep intrapsychic aberration. When such a couple seeks sex therapy and is helped, the sexual relationship may then come to reflect the same qualities as the total interactions. On some occasions we have noted that after successful sex therapy the couple returns later with more generalized marital complaints that have surfaced after sex could no longer be used as the scapegoat or cover-up for other marital problems.

Human sexual functioning can be greatly modified by infant and childhood conditioning and other parental, interpersonal, and societal influences. However, there is a wide variation in the importance of cortical influences and how they affect the older brain center's control of sexual functioning. For reasons not entirely understood, some people's sexual functioning is not inhibited or made dysfunctional in a hostile relationship, nor do they become vulnerable to negative interactional stimuli. These people are able to separate their sexual response and pleasure from minor upsetting aspects of their conjugal and love relationship that might make other individuals dysfunctional. Those who can make this separation without having extensive therapy are a fortunate minority. For others, the discrepancy between poor sexual functioning and a relationship that is good in other ways suggests that their sexual parameter has suffered more than some other parameters that are important in bonded relating.

Thus it appears that sex sometimes does and sometimes does not reflect how a couple behaves in their total interactional systems. Behavioral scientists, poets, and people in general remain perplexed about the importance of the three factors of sex, love, and commitment in bonded relationships. This triadic combination represents the idealized one for most people, but further research is necessary before we are able to evaluate the significance of each and see how they relate to one another. Certainly the three will never be the same for all people. All too often they differ widely even for two partners. If we are to understand better the most fundamental human relationships, research on the triad of sex, love, and commitment must continue on many fronts, and the different disciplines must communicate their findings to one another.

SEXUAL CONTRACTUAL TERMS

Through the ages most states and religions have openly recognized the role of sex in marriage, particularly as it relates to procreation, if not to pleasure or recreation. Thus most have given the relief of divorce or annulment to a marriage that is not consummated sexually.

For some a "barren" marriage or even one that spawned only daughters warranted divorce or at least the addition of another wife.

However, the sexual terms of the marriage contracts we are dealing with go far beyond the basic survival of the race and inheritance of property. A host of subtle influences that affect sexuality is included in individual and interactional contracts.

Some contracts, for example, may include spoken or unspoken terms that one partner will relieve his or her spouse of guilt about sex by that partner taking the intiative while the other is more passive, or a husband may play into his wife's fantasy that the penis is hers, in exchange for which he may fantasy a vaguely sensed but not expressed homosexual need.

In the Smith case the husband wanted to be stroked and have "wanton," uninhibited sex overtures made to him by his wife. She had to feel loved and wanted by him before she could give him what he wanted. She wished him to be strong and active and to take her. Their contracts led to a sexual stalemate except when they were able to work out a satisfactory quid pro quo that gave each more of what was wanted.

In an early case I reported on the three levels of awareness of one couple's contract in the sexual and power areas (Sager *et al.*, 1971). The sexual contracts of this couple were as follows.

On the conscious, verbalized level the contracts were:

Wife	*Husband*
1. I have the ability to help you sexually and will be glad to do so, and will not humiliate you in this respect.	1. You are free and experienced sexually and have the power to help me. I am sexually inadequate and inexperienced and vulnerable. I expect you to help me and to teach me, and I expect to become sexually competent with your help.
In exchange for the above:	*In exchange for the above:*
1. You have the power to help me professionally since you are a professor and a gifted writer. I	1. I have the means and I will be glad to help you develop professionally, and I will not be com-

Wife

am just a beginner and insecure. I expect you to help and guide me to the best of your ability, and then I, too, will develop professionally with your help.

2. I am often depressed and emotionally labile. I expect you not to reject me at these times.

Husband

petitive with you in this area.

2. You are often depressed and emotionally labile. I will not reject you but will try to be helpful and understanding.

On the conscious but not verbalized level their contracts were:

1. You expect me to help you with sex. I want to and I will. I will make you appear to be an adequate sexual male before others.

1. I want many women but they will not want me unless I improve sexually. You are my only chance at sexual freedom. I expect you to give me this for everything I do for you.

In exchange for the above:
1. I am anxious and afraid that I can never make it alone professionally. I can't compete. I am helpless and I am jealous of your professional status. I want your help so I can be as good as you and as good as other people, so I can feel acceptable.
2. I am afraid you will leave me because I am depressed and irritable, and you are really too good for me. I am not very good, so you must not leave me. I want you to remain insecure about sex because this is my hold over you.

In exchange for the above:
1. I am willing to help you professionally, and I will not compete with you. However, I will try to get you to go into an area different from mine, because your competitiveness makes me uneasy.

2. I am willing to reassure you, but it really gets tedious. I hope you mature soon and become strong like my sister, who is really my ideal.

On the level beyond awareness:

1. I am nothing, but I want to be supreme. Only through you

1. I am afraid to be sexually free. I want other men to envy me,

Wife	*Husband*
can I achieve this. You will be strong and powerful for me so that I can use your power to control, dominate, and compete. I will submit to you in exchange for the male power that I lack.	but I am afraid of them. I can be sexually free only if I have your permission and protection. I expect you to make me free—not just with you, but with all women. I will make you powerful in return. I will let you dominate me in return.
2. Females are passive—males are active. I want to destroy you for being a strong, active male. This makes me feel inadequate in comparison. I will not abandon you, if you let me destroy you.	2. Women are inferior. I want to dominate you. If you dominate me, I shall be angry at you and I shall despise myself for being so dependent. I will not hurt or abandon you if you will let me dominate you and put you in an inferior position.
3. I am excited by the thought of your having sex with other women. I will make you free, if you have other women for me.	
4. I am afraid you will abandon me, if you compare me to other women. You must not have other women; in exchange I will make you sexually free.	
5. We must be close and intimate.	
6. We must remain distant and separate.	
7. You must acquiesce to *all* these terms. In exchange, I will not leave you.	

The contradictory elements in both individuals' contracts are clear. Their interactional contract, as might be expected, reflected these strong contradictions and they had a stormy time together. Sex was "good" only when the wife completely controlled their sexual activity. The husband "revolted" from this by becoming impotent with his wife but found he was sexually successful with other women. Their constant arguing and sexual dissatisfaction, the wife's episodes of rage and depression, and the husband's anger toward his wife led them eventually to divorce. When I last talked with the husband he told me they were now somewhat amiable friends and that he was much happier, had a girl friend with whom he had a good relationship and good sex, but did not wish to be deeply involved with anyone at this time. He was not sure about his former wife's status. She came to see me a few months later and told me essentially the same story regarding both of them but added that she had some sexual experiences with another woman and felt better and more at peace with herself. She realized that she was more in tune with a woman than she had been with men. She was not sure she wanted to commit herself to a gay life but felt that it was right for her at the moment.

This case illustrates some of the complexities of the sexual clauses of contracts and how they relate to other contractual terms or may be used as quid pro quo trade-offs. If the ambivalence on the third level of awareness had not been so great or could have been resolved, this couple's relationship might have become stabilized at a rewarding level.

There are three major adaptations for coping with the question of fulfillment of sexual desires. These are reflected in the sexual components of the individual marriage contract.

The first adaptation is exemplified by the person who seeks, accepts, and marries the person he or she believes to be the ideal one to fulfill his sexual needs. He is correct in his choice and his partner proves to have the qualities he perceived. Whatever his requirements, the person who chooses successfully in this way is usually not in conflict over his sexual pleasure and fulfillment. Whether or not the couple continues to fulfill the terms of the individual contracts will depend on how the partners deal with each other in their interactional contract.

The second adaptation is made by the person who deludes himself that he is choosing his ideal sexual partner but has conflict over whether he may have the kind of partner he really wants. Hence he will either deny seeing flaws in his idealized picture of his partner or rationalize that they will dissipate under different conditions, or he will behave in such a way that he forces a potentially ideal partner to react in a sexually distressing or only partly fulfilling way with him. He has his cake but can't eat it; he must flaw it or destroy the good in it for himself.

The third type is the person who cannot allow himself to have a partner with whom he can really enjoy sex. He is driven to frustrate himself and therefore makes a negative choice, sometimes with full knowledge beforehand, but rationalizes his decision or feels comfortable with it because he would not want it otherwise because it satisfies a masochistic or defensive need.

Within the framework of these three major adaptations the qualities of "good" sex or of the sexual partner may vary greatly, in accordance with the parameters described in the following section, as well as others that are less common. While this section is intended to give the reader an approach to the problem, it is not encyclopedic in regard to all possible details of the variables that influence sexual object choice or sexual gratification.

INTERACTIONAL TERMS OF THE SEXUAL CONTRACT

In addition to their individual contracts' sexual clauses, the couple's interactional contract clauses establish the essence of their sexual behavior together and determine whether sex will be fulfilling for each. The sexual aspect of the interactional contract is the area largely dealt with in sex therapy, when the couple's interaction has led them to develop a dysfunction or to perpetuate one that existed previously for either partner.

It is important to take a detailed sex history from any couple seeking marital therapy. When the therapist is at ease in asking particulars about sex the partners are usually quickly put at ease and respond as openly as about any other area. The sex history interview should be conducted with both partners present, leaving time to speak alone for a few minutes with each.

A simple and natural way to start the sexual history when patients have not mentioned sex is to inquire, "When did you have sex together last?" And then, "Please describe exactly what happened."

The interviewer cannot allow himself to be put off with vague references such as "I played with her for a while, went in and it was as usual." It is important to know who initiated sex, how the signals were given and interpreted between them, and exactly what took place in foreplay, as well as how they felt, their mood, the ambience, and all the specifics that seem appropriate. How each felt at each point along the way and afterward is part of the necessary information.

I then go back and ask about their sex history together, and with others. Their responses guide the lines of where my probing will go. Quality and quantity are important. Are they free and open in sexual play, what does each like or dislike, do they use fantasy, do they play out roles together? I then want to know what they would like from each other sexually and what they want and like to give. What excites them? What is their wildest fantasy? If it is pertinent, I want to know the sexual history of each from childhood to the present.

Some of the possible areas of contractual terms include those having to do with what attracts them sexually, how they like to have sex initiated, what they consider appropriate roles for men and women in sex, how frequently they want sex, what they see to be the role of sex in their life, what they think enhances or inhibits sexual pleasure, who and what may be included or excluded in the sexual relationship, how each wants sex to be, and where they are in their marital cycle. Do they want the mate to inhibit or free them sexually, to be a playmate, a parent, or a peer? Is sex to be used to gain some advantage or control elsewhere in the relationship? Is it used for quid pro quo trade-offs in other parameters, as was done in the case cited earlier?

Sexual Attraction

The physical appearance of their mate is important to most people and is a key factor in the initial attraction and its continuance. For them, a suitable mate must meet a standard of beauty or handsomeness of face and figure. For others, physical characteristics may not be of primary importance. Special physical characteristics that fit in with idiosyncratic needs are sometimes transferential in origin. For example, a woman may be excited only by men shorter than she, not necessarily because she wants to be physically stronger or to dominate, but because her very desirable (to her) father was shorter than her mother, whom he completely dominated. Style of dressing or wearing one's hair, and so on, can have a special meaning or suggest a complete Gestalt.

The aging process can have a tender or terrible effect on how one regards the physical changes in one's partner as well as oneself. Aging may cause increased anxiety about abandonment. For a man this is often related to anxiety about sexual performance and good health. A woman may feel keenly the loss of physical attractiveness and youthfulness, and dread poor health.

Smell and personal hygiene can also be very important among the expectations or needs of a partner. Many people have strong olfactory reactions that may be either biologically or environmentally determined. These reactions may be used as rationalizations to avoid sex or intimacy. The antiseptic, hygienic, nonsmelling woman or man of the American advertising industry is not necessarily the most sexually attractive to a mate. Our growing knowledge of pheremones, which have now been isolated from the vaginal secretions of healthy young females, tends to support the conclusions of many observers that, like the other animals, we humans are affected sexually by olfactory as well as oral, visual, aural, and tactile stimuli (Michael et al., 1974).

Relationship characteristics have to do with personality and character factors, especially those delineated in the biological and intrapsychic areas of the individual contracts. Further, the behavioral profile that the mate displays or is maneuvered into through the interactional contract may produce added sexual excitement or turn-off. For example, a woman was generally pleased by her partner, who was very much in charge. She enjoyed his sense of power and competence and made herself interact as a child, pushing her mate into a parental position. As they went through their initial sex dance she would almost invariably provoke a situation that caused him to reject her. She would then become very excited sexually and make amends, putting herself in an anxious and humiliating childish position to do so. "Daddy" then forgave her by accepting her sexual advance. This ritual was very exciting to both partners.

Is the attraction determined by a sense of being loved, of being wanted, or does one desire to conquer or be conquered? Is there a need for acceptance, with a sense of being warmly understood? Subtle interpersonal styles and needs are often the most important factors in creating and maintaining sexual attraction between two people.

The person who has such strong sexual attractions that sex is an overpowering force in determining his activities has been discussed in Chapter 6 (see pp. 129-132). For this person, whether he is the addicted type or not, partner choice is often limited to women or men with rather specific characteristics of personality, character, and appearance.

Initiation of Sexual Activity

Some couples work out elaborate seduction or mating rituals for each coital adventure; others are very direct, simple or straightforward with one another; some are ready to give and receive pleasure; some wait to be approached; others prefer to give the first conscious signal, if not the subliminal ones.

Signals and receptivity to signals for sex are an area of study in their own right. Some couples feel that one or the other partner must give the first sign of sexual interest. Some women and men are afraid to initiate sexual activity because rejection is too painful; they find it difficult to understand that there can be nonacceptance of a sexual initiation without its being indicative of a generalized rejection.

Signals may be clear or extremely subtle. Indeed, some are so subtle that they are self-defeating. In one instance a woman would put in her diaphragm but not tell her husband she had done so. When questioned she said she felt that he should know she wanted sex on the nights she inserted her diaphragm because he should have noticed she had been in the bathroom longer than usual. From her husband we learned that sometimes he noticed when she spent a longer time getting ready for bed but assumed she was delaying because she did not want sex, so as often as not he was asleep by the time she came to bed. His assumption, like hers, had not been based on adequate communication.

Some years ago an enterprising linen entrepreneur made pillows that said "Yes" on one side and "No" on the other. All the man or woman had to do was to flip the pillow. Fortunately most, though it seems not all, couples can work out a better communication system on their own.

Although many couples now believe intellectually that the woman as well as the man may initiate sex, some women are not as hardened (or believe they are not) to rejection, and therefore still prefer to have the man make the overture so that they *know* they are wanted. On the other hand, some men do not believe they too can say "No" when approached and therefore they reluctantly "submit." Other men may feel pleased and responsive, whereas still others may feel that their masculinity is being challenged and they *must* respond regardless of how they feel. This latter reaction is akin to that of the woman who feels she *must* accede to all of her husband's sexual requests.

I have not found an increase in impotence among men due to women's increased readiness to state that they desire sex. A liberated, secure woman does not use her rights in order to be hostile to men or to put them down, any more than a liberated, secure male needs to be hostile to women. Unfortunately there are some people who do abuse whatever power they may have.

It is sometimes difficult for a mate to accept the fact that, although the partner may not want to become excited or have an orgasm himself at a given time, he or she may want to give pleasure and gratification to the partner who does want sex. This spirit of giving and acceptance within sex can be another reflection of a couple's loving relationship, but it is difficult for some people to accept pleasure without feeling guilty and pressured to reciprocate immediately. One man was terribly upset when his wife did not want to become sexually excited by him that evening but told him that it would make her feel good to give him an orgasm. He could not accept her offer, but instead felt rejected. It took a while before this man could properly value himself and accept his wife's loving gesture without guilt.

Gender-Determined Roles and Activities

Stereotypes of male and female behavior preceding, during, and after sex have been changing rapidly. These changes tap into deep feelings of gender role as well as transferential feelings and imagery.

It is often difficult for individuals and couples to escape the bondage of early training regarding gender roles in sexual behavior. The woman who fantasizes that she wants a man who is free, imaginative, and loving to her during sex is sometimes unable to accept the realization when it is offered. She may consider her mate too aggressive when he gives her what she wants. Each couple needs to explore what the two of them want and enjoy and to express their desires openly, especially since these will probably change from minute to minute, encounter to encounter, mood to mood, year to year. It is important that both partners feel secure to experiment and follow their fancy with each other.

Either partner may have very rigid ideas and feelings about kissing, touching, and fondling—whether it be breasts, vagina, clitoris, penis, testicles, anus, fingers, toes, ears, or any other body part. These may include very set ideas about the need for or exclusion of cunnilingus, fellatio, anal intercourse, various coital positions, and so on.

In some instances the man may contract to be a "stud," or the woman to be a "geisha girl." What are their feelings about such roles? Must the roles be constant or may they be flexible and changeable? How are dependency, closeness-distance, power needs, and other parameters of category 2 manifested in the terms of the couple's sexual contract?

Frequency

There can be great variations in the quantity of sex desired by each spouse. How is the frequency of sex and sex play determined? Sometimes one partner may use sexual avoidance and reward as a quid pro quo for something in another parameter of the relationship.

Does one partner avoid sex because of a lack of security or fear of his or her "inadequacy"? There may be a collusive sexual ennui or avoidance that indicates sexual anxiety, gender identity problems, a lack of sexual attraction, an inhibition of pleasure or other factors that may require a questioning of the basis for the couple's relationship.

One partner may want sex more frequently than is consistent with the rhythm or desire of the other. This can often be worked out contractually so that it is no longer a problem area for the couple. But sometimes sexual avoidance is related to a sense of futility because of a sexual dysfunction. In such cases the therapist does his best to determine whether either or both partners want the dysfunction to continue or wish to overcome it. If they are prepared to deal with it, the dysfunction should be evaluated by a therapist with expertise in this area to determine whether sex therapy is indicated.

Role of Sex in the Mates' Lives

Sex may play a central or a minor role in a marriage. Its significance may vary greatly at different times in the life cycle. Is it for procreation, or mainly for pleasure or recreation? Some couples use it to relieve anxiety and tension, as a refuge from the slings and arrows of the outside world. Conversely, the sexual experience may reflect the tensions and struggles of their life together.

For some individuals sex is sought as the ultimate in intimacy and openness. Do both want the same in this respect? Can they fulfill, in sex, their need for infantile care and pleasure as well as their adult love and sexual needs? Does one want only holding and petting (parental love) without sexual passion? Do control and power flow back and forth in a nonabrasive manner, or does one person's contract demand that he have complete control or that he always abdicate control?

In exchange for what each partner gives in sex, what does he want in return? Can or will the couple meet each other's wishes? Are their two contracts congruent, complementary, or in conflict? For example, in the following case sex was used to try to meet different needs for each partner. As a result sex was functionally fine but emotionally nongratifying.

The Salems were a childless couple in their late twenties who came to therapy with the chief complaint that they were growing apart. The husband stated that he was subject to depressions which caused him to withdraw; the wife had reacted to his withdrawal first with anger and later with resignation and hopelessness. Compatible in many areas, they believed they loved one another and wanted to make the marriage work.

When the sex history was taken, they both said very emphatically that mechanically sex was fine; both were invariably orgastic during coitus. Emotionally, however, sex was not satisfying to the wife, and for several months prior to their seeking professional help, she had allowed sex only sporadically. She had had sex with other men prior to marriage and with two men when she and her husband separated for a few months. She therefore knew that sex could be emotionally, as well as physically, satisfying for her. She sensed a distance between herself and her husband when they were having coitus, particularly just after completing orgasm. He would turn away and withdraw, while she wanted to snuggle and talk. "That's the time I can be most open," she stated, "and he just isn't there." The husband confirmed this, describing an intolerable desire to get away after they had completed sex. He sensed her vulnerability but felt controlled and threatened by her desire for closeness at these times.

His Sexual Contract	*Her Sexual Contract*
1. Sex is a dangerous act, but I enjoy it.	1. I enjoy sex and will give freely to you.
2. Women use sex (as my mother did) to make men do what they want.	2. I want you to love me, be open and close with me.
3. I will have sex with you, but I will not be trapped by you.	3. I am vulnerable when I open myself sexually to you and I must know if you feel as I do, I must know your thoughts and ideas, I must know if you love me and understand me.

In exchange for the above:

1. You will take care of me at other times.
2. You will help me make friends and provide a warm home.
3. I am secretive because I am evil. I must hide my true self from you. Therefore, I must fight the temptation to be open with you.

In exchange for the above:

1. Sex will be good.
2. I will love you.
3. I will help you be friendly with other people.
4. I expect you to carry one half of the housework. We both have full-time jobs and I will not be your mother.

The contracts just in the sexual area alone made clear the corrosive forces at work in their relationship. Their ability to function sexually was to a great extent independent of their affects. The husband had to see his wife as he had seen his threatening, sexual mother. He used sex for physical pleasure and limited closeness but feared to be drawn into emotional closeness with his wife. He reacted to the anxiety generated by sexual closeness by manifesting hostile depression and withdrawal. The woman's reaction was consistent with her vulnerability to rejection. She wanted to use sex to reaffirm that she was loved and to be close and intimate. She could not get this with this man. She behaved in a way that reinforced his fears, thus assisting in the negative interactional situation. Without major changes in the couple's basic assumptions about themselves, the prognosis for their marriage was poor. In this case individual therapy for each was recommended as the first step in trying to interrupt their circular negative interactions. Marital therapy had been helpful diagnostically but left us at a therapeutic impasse.

Although sex was mechanically good for this couple, it was affectively inadequate and dissatisfying. Affective dissatisfaction in the sexual relationship, despite good mechanical sex, is a syndrome that we are seeing with increasing frequency. Inappropriate feelings, or lack of feelings, experienced during or after sex may be due to immediate causes within the couple's relationship, as they were for the wife in this case, or to remote and intrapsychic determinants, as they were for the husband.

Thus, any of the biological and intrapsychic determinants can have a widespread effect on the sexual components of individual and interactional contracts.

What and Who Else May Be Allowed to Enter the Couple's Sexual Relationship?

Does the couple, or either partner, wish to use stimuli other than just their own presence to enhance sex? This might include setting a particular mood or ambience, the use of stimulating literature, motion pictures, sexual talk between them, the use of fantasy—either not verbalized or expressed for increased excitement of one or both partners, or the playing out of each other's fantasies. Physical aids such as body oils, vibrator, dildo, the wearing of clothes that either mate experiences as stimulating, and so on, are used by some couples to enhance pleasure.

Once a couple is past the first few years of short-term bonding, they may feel the need for more variety and stimulation. If they use a little imagination and are trusting with each other, they can readily discover activities that are pleasurable for them. Deepening understanding of each other and finding new mystery and facets to one another provide sufficient intrigue and excitement for some couples. Others, equally loving, appear to have the need for other stimuli to sustain sexual passion. For example, playing out romantic or sex-in-danger-of-being-caught situations, mild sadomasochistic play, master-slave fantasies, call girl fantasies, Don Juan, gay, or troilism fantasies are included in the repertoire of many married couples.

Monogamy is a commitment that is implicit if not explicit in most marriages. Even the "liberated" couples who believe they can readily accept their spouse's having a sexual relationship with another person are often surprised by strong negative emotional responses when it does occur. Although the change is not always negative, a known extramarital relationship rarely leaves a marriage unchanged. Monogamy is a matter each couple has to decide upon, but few couples today regard an extramarital relationship by itself as sufficient reason for divorce. The extramarital relationship may conform with their contract or they may recognize an extramarital relationship as a danger signal (it is often a hostile act directed against one's mate) and seek professional help together. Many people can better tolerate their mate's having a sexual encounter with someone than having a significant emotional relationship without sex.

The inclusion of other persons in a couple's sex relationship, as in troilism, is also a highly individual matter. For many couples reality is not as pleasing as the fantasy. For others, troilism with another consenting adult may be necessary for pleasure. The psychology of their needs and their sexual expression may require the presence of the third person. The same pertains to some sets of couples who have an ongoing sexual and/or living together relationship, and to group sex.

Partner swapping on a casual basis and group sex experiences in which both spouses participate have been experimented with by couples for many years. Some stay with it, finding that these experiences gratify their needs and fantasies without endangering their relationship, or one or both spouses may require it as an important clause of their contract. It is a way that some couples find to give themselves the sexual variety that they desire while sharing the experience. For some couples it becomes another knot that keeps them together. Others, after some experimentation, find it is disruptive for them or are satisfied that they are missing nothing and discontinue the practice.

The sexual components of marriage contracts and the couple's sexual relationship are often dealt with in marital therapy in too cursory a fashion. The material in this chapter provides a more comprehensive approach to the inclusion of sexual data and its role within the totality of a couple's interaction.

11

Couples in Transition, in Concrete, and in Flight

SINCE THE CONTRACTS of couples who have not had marital or individual therapy have not yet been studied, the cases presented here are a biased sample, as with any patient population. However, I have selected six cases that are as varied as possible in their histories, their contracts, and the outcome of treatment.

The first case—the Greens—was selected to illustrate the contracts of a couple without a significant marital or individual problem. The second couple, David and Pamela Black, were very open and communicated exquisitely. Their interactional behavior was consistent with their contracts. This couple could neither live together nor divorce. The Browns were inevitably headed for divorce and I helped them to realize their need to separate. The fourth couple, George and Penny Blue, were in serious trouble. With marital treatment and their own will to make their marriage work, they improved enormously; so did the fifth couple, the Whites. The Grays, the last couple, are included both because they had individual therapy after evaluation and because they put a great effort into filling out a lengthy questionnaire form that is a forerunner of the reminder list (see Appendix 1). The most favorable prognostic sign for this couple was the fact that each cared enough to fill out the forms honestly and in great detail.

231

The other couples' contracts are not detailed but their essential elements are given. Most of the contracts were not written in a highly structured format. If they wished to, couples responded in writing; in other instances we worked out the essentials together, usually in conjoint sessions. Sometimes we followed the reminder list and sometimes not. Thus the cases illustrate the flexibility of the contract concept as well as various contract terms that point toward a range of possible outcomes.

Although some minor editing has been done to exclude extraneous material, to improve clarity of the individual's intent, and to preserve anonymity, the material is presented in the general form in which it was gathered.

As these cases illustrate, nothing as complex as a marital relationship can be reduced to a few formal sentences—not if we are to grasp the essence of the interweaving of the positive and negative forces that bind two people together, and if we as therapists are to overcome the clichés of our own biases and find a way to be constructive.

THE GREENS—MARITAL HARMONY
WITH MINOR DISCORDANCE

Laura and Monty Green saw me in consultation because they could not agree on a suitable method of contraception. They had three children and did not want more. Mrs. Green had used the pill for many years but her gynecologist now wanted her to discontinue it. He recommended either the diaphragm or an intrauterine device. Mrs. Green did not like the former—she had used it earlier and felt it always necessitated an undesirable interruption of their sexual activity. Her doctor explained some of the possible complications of using the IUD, and she felt negative about that method, too. She thought that perhaps it was time her husband took responsibility for contraception. As neither of them liked to use condoms on a regular basis, this left the alternatives of coitus interruptus or vasectomy. They had both ruled out coitus interruptus and Mr. Green felt very uneasy about vasectomy. They had discussed it thoroughly, were familiar with the procedure, and knew that the likelihood of the operation's being reversible was fair. Although Mr. Green knew logically that vasectomy would not diminish his "masculinity," sexual desire, ability, or pleasure, he still felt that it would make him "less of a man" because his ejaculate would not be fertile.

They discussed this tender question with great respect and feeling for each other. It wasn't that his wife wanted to even an old score— she was honestly looking for a better way of contraception that would not interrupt their sexual activity. When she was on the pill they had both enjoyed the ability to have sex spontaneously. She asked, "Now that there was another method to accomplish this was it wrong for Monty to feel reluctant to use it?" I replied that there was no right or wrong. If he felt that way—and he did, despite knowing the facts—that was how he felt, and to have vasectomy under that condition was not wise. I said that I as a male could empathize with Monty's feelings. We agreed, finally, that if the diaphragm were inserted routinely at bedtime each night, this would be an effective method of contraception and would allow for maximum sexual spontaneity. They agreed to try it and see whether Laura would be resentful at still having contraceptive responsibility.

The love and consideration this couple had shown to each other in our discussion were impressive, and they told me that they had no other marital problem of any consequence. Since I had been looking for a couple without serious marital problems to see what such a couple's marriage contracts would be, I asked if they would allow me to explore their contracts with them. Both, particularly Monty, resisted the idea at first, but when I explained the purpose further they agreed to cooperate. What follows is a summary of our two sessions together. My hunch was correct. They were relatively free of disharmony and had as good a marital relationship as anyone could reasonably expect. They had channels of open communication, respect, and love that they used to resolve differences. For each of them the first assumption was that the other intended no harm or slight and most negotiations were opened on that premise, not that of redressing a presumed wrong.

In terms of gender roles and responsibilities the Greens for 18 years have had a rather traditional marriage. Monty, at 47, is eight years older than Laura. He did not consider marrying until he was making enough money to support a wife and children as a skilled worker in the printing industry. Laura comes from a working-class background too, and did light skilled work in an electronics factory until she became pregnant. Since then she has stayed home to be mother and housewife. Their religious and cultural backgrounds are similar.

They have a daughter of 15 and two sons, 12 and six. They live in a pleasant semidetached two-family house in Queens, an essentially residential borough of New York City.

They do argue at times, mostly over money. Laura feels that Monty gives her a reasonable "table allowance" every week but she resents having to ask and sometimes being refused, although there is always a reasonable explanation, when she needs "extras" for clothes for the children or herself or for house furnishings. They also argue at times because Laura believes that Monty could do better financially than he does. Yet, when he had a chance to go into a printing business with a friend, he discussed it with Laura and they agreed it was too risky a venture in which to place their life savings and borrowed money as well. Monty was relieved that Laura was against it. Monty, who is a union activist and has been a minor official in the union for several years, feels that he has good job security.

Laura feels restless at times; she is bored with housework and plans to find at least a part-time job next year, when the youngest child will be seven and she will feel more comfortable about his staying at school for lunch.

The Greens have a clear sense of being a family. They do many things together, including driving-camping vacations and spending a month during the past few summers in a rented cottage at a lakeside bungalow colony. They visit with friends and with other family members, watch television, go to the movies and occasionally to a Broadway show or sports event. Monty and the older son sometimes go to baseball and basketball games by themselves.

Monty and Laura go out without the children in the evening and on a few occasions (four times in the past six years) have arranged to go to a resort by themselves for a few days. Both were brought up as Methodists but are not religious. They insisted that each child go to Sunday school for a year and then make up his or her mind whether or not to continue. They seem to be truly *laissez-faire* about religion and have refused to change their position despite criticism from relatives and some friends.

Monty feels that Laura is not strict enough with the children, particularly their 15-year-old daughter, who is very attractive and is actively dating. Laura says he wants her to be the disciplinarian, but when it is appropriate for him to set or enforce the rules he backs down and is easier than she. Their family life did not seem to me to be chaotic as a result of this, but to be relaxed and to have adequate structure.

Laura and Monty claim they try to talk through their differences. They do try to avoid arguing in front of the children and often wait until they are alone to air problems that are important and emotionally loaded. They are openly affectionate to each other and to the children.

Overall they are family- and couple-oriented, although each spouse is a person and a force. Although they are in quite traditional gender-determined roles (and the daughter is junior mother to the sons),

Laura appears to be the more decisive tastemaker and pacesetter at home.

THE CONTRACT

Category 1. Expectations of the Marriage

They see themselves as members of a family unit who are loving, loyal and devoted to each other and a support against a world which they do not regard as too hostile. Well aware of current divorce rates, they feel secure that they will stay together. Monty: "I think we keep finding new things in one another. Like in sex, since we started reading and seeing more X-rated films we've learned to have a lot more fun. Even keeps me from wanting to wander." Laura: "I'm still in my prime—that could go for two." (We all laugh.)

They take their responsibilities as parents seriously. Laura feels that at times Monty is not sufficiently responsive to the children or to what she sees as emerging problems—especially with the boys—whereas he is too prone to worry about their daughter's potential for enjoying her attractiveness and sexuality. They look to each other for companionship, comfort, and support.

Although money is tight, they are not insecure about it as many of their friends are, because Monty believes he has excellent job security. It is more a matter of holding off on some of the extras so that they can afford the essentials: Monty just spent a few hundred dollars on repairs for their four-year-old car rather than buying a new one. They both feel they are getting what they want and expect from their marriage. Neither one appears to have unrealistic expectations of the marriage, or any hidden agenda.

Category 2. Intrapsychic and Biological Determinants

1. Independence-dependence. Although both felt they were quite independent, Monty said he would be lost without Laura. "I've often thought, I know it's selfish" (he looks at her) "that I hope to die first. There's enough life insurance. I couldn't make it without her." They more often attend the social events and the movies she prefers, but that's okay with him. He is not resentful later because she made the choice. When he is without her, as when Laura recently visited her sick father in Florida, he fared well and managed the household and children effectively for a week with the help of their daughter. Each is self-actuating; there seem to be reasonable independence and interdependence.

2. Activity-passivity. On basic levels Monty seems to be somewhat more passive than Laura, although he is not a passive man and is respected among his fellow workers. Laura initiates and sees that more of the necessary family activities are followed through on—but they both regard this as her prescribed role. Differences seem to be talked through without continuing resentment.

3. Closeness-distance. Monty appears to seek and need more bodily closeness—he is a toucher. Laura wants more emotional and verbal closeness, which is difficult for Monty to stay with. He frequently jokes when emotions become too warm for him. Laura misses the type of intimacy she wants with him, but she has a circle of close friends from whom she gets emotional support and understanding. She and her friends sound like an informal consciousness-raising group. Laura's desire for greater closeness is troublesome to Monty at times, but she appears to accept Monty's difference in this area and does not retaliate.

4. Power. Monty uses the power of money almost as a manifestation of his masculine protest. He makes it and therefore he is in charge of its distribution. In effect, however, it does not work this way because Monty is definitely a family man and the use of the money is allocated and budgeted away before the check comes home. Yet his having the power to be arbitrary, which he rarely exercises, bothers Laura. She is planning to return to work next year. She considered going to college (she and Monty are definitely of college intelligence level) but decided to "leave college up to the children." When alone with her for a few minutes I asked her about this decision and she said she decided against college partly because it might make Monty feel she was getting ahead of him. She reads a great deal and doesn't feel a great need for advanced study.

5. Submission-domination. There is good give and take and each can accept the leadership of the other. Laura possibly has a slight edge, except for Monty's use of money, but there seems to be an acceptable complementarity.

6. Abandonment. Each seems secure about the other, but I was not able to explore individual feelings sufficiently. Perhaps Monty's statement about wanting to die first is a clue, but this is also a cliché and I am not sure of its significance.

7. Possession and control. These concepts do not quite apply, despite the fact that the Greens are a traditional couple. They expect certain behavior from one another and both give and receive it as a matter of course. Neither appears to be defensively possessive or controlling of the

other. There is a sense of security. They know they are "right" for each other.

8. Level of anxiety is not unusually high for either. Laura is not as well defended and shows her anxiety more directly. She is not as sanguine about their financial security as Monty. An attractive woman, she is also concerned about her appearance and the beginning signs of aging. Her anxiety evokes joking comments or platitudinous reassurances from Monty which annoy her; he then feels manipulated and believes he is expected to give her more money for clothes, which in turn bothers him. This leitmotif may be accentuated for Laura by the emergence of their daughter as an unusually attractive adolescent. To a great extent Monty uses denial to deal with his anxiety. He plays things safe. In general he is the opposite of paranoid, denying the recognition of potential danger or threats to himself from others.

9. Both claim to feel good about themselves in their sex roles. Monty feels he has done well as a skilled worker and is glad that he did not become an entrepreneur: "I get out of work at four and I don't have to think about work again until eight o'clock the next morning—I'm free." (I question his complacency: Contrary to the Peter Principle he has not elected to climb until he reached his level of incompetence.) The changing world has not threatened or touched him very deeply. He is satisfied to move through life leaving the bigger questions to others—but he is protective of his own turf when he recognizes a threat. Laura is more discontent, restless, anxious about approaching middle age and competitive with her daughter. She does feel security in her desirability as a person and a woman, and Monty appears to reinforce her well—as she does him. But she has a growing concern about others' seeing her as attractive. She does not want another man—she wants reaffirmation of herself from Monty.

10. Sexual attraction to one another. Each, objectively, is an attractive person; more important, they apparently remain attractive to one another. They have had a resurgence of sexual activity over the past several years (see Monty's comment earlier). There are no sexual dysfunctions—they are open and free in sex, have tried various positions, fellatio, cunnilingus, and use fantasy and playing out of their fantasies with one another. Laura says that originally she was very uptight about sex but Monty helped her get over this before they married. He was experienced sexually; she was a virgin. Sex improved after the first year of marriage, when Laura became orgastic during coitus as well as during sex play. "Sometimes just looking at him I get turned on

again—that's how I got pregnant the last time. After Claude" (the younger son) "was born it took me about a year to really enjoy sex again—that's when the porno books and movies were good for us. . . . Maybe I'm a masochist or I like Monty being a little bit a male chauvinist pig, but I get turned on most when he really takes charge and sometimes we play rape and I finally must submit to him." Monty smiled appreciatively and added, "I like that and I also like being really passive—like she is my slave-girl and knows just what to do to play with me and excite me—and she does!"

Laura in private said she has been tempted a few times but has never been attracted to any man enough to take the risk of upsetting her marriage. She feels it just isn't worth it. Monty said privately that he has had sex four times with other women since his marriage—always with women with whom he had no relationship and always when he was away from Laura, and never in his own home.

11. Love of self and mate. This couple love themselves sufficiently to have good self-respect and appear to be truly in love with each other. Passion between them has been rekindled.

12. Approach to problems. Cognitive styles, including intelligence, do not appear to be disparate. Laura seems to be overly concerned with not challenging Monty so as not to make him doubt himself. I am not sure if her slight edge of deference to him is due to life experiences with him that cause her to act that way, or is culturally determined (which I doubt), or is "good behavior" for my benefit.

13. Laura feels let down in terms of Monty's not being sufficiently in tune with her feelings and not being willing or able to talk openly with her about his. When first married she "had foolish, kid dreams about our becoming rich, but that was silly—I have no complaints"—yet I felt there was a sense of letdown, that somehow she wanted Monty to be a more effective alpha male, to climb to wealth and glory instead of being content to be a member of the "aristocracy of labor."

The major "in exchange for" contractual expectations are that each will stay in the traditional role. Also, I will support you with love, sex, and reassure you about your masculinity and vice versa. Monty supports Laura's femininity in a teasing way, but for the most part she does not see this as hostile—possibly because she well knows her ability to excite him sexually. This may sound like a pseudomutual type of agreement but I do not believe it is. The Greens are basically satisfied with their life together. Laura cannot get Monty to be as open with her about his feelings as she would like and she accepts this without feeling strongly enough about it to make waves. They both feel that they have a good marriage compared to those of other couples they know. In a sense, their quid pro quos are designed to give them a security with each other and within their slice of the world. They have fun, they argue, they disagree, they make good love, they play out their parental and oedipal roles with their children, and life goes on with ups and downs. The rises are not to great heights but neither are the troughs very deep.

Category 3. Derivative Problem Areas

1. Communication. Generally they send and receive messages clearly—except that Monty turns off when Laura tries to discuss feelings and motivations that may underlie his behavior.

2. Interests. Each has some of his/her own and several that are shared. Each has friends of the same gender. Life centers on family and friends.

3. Each wants the other to be more strict with the children; actually the whole family seems to have a pleasant, relaxed interaction most of the time.

4. Children are not used adversely in any significant alliances. Monty may use daughter and his defense against his sexual responsiveness to her in subtle ways with Laura.

5. The family myth is that Monty is where he wants to be in life—not that he *has* to be there. The myth is that he could have become an entrepreneur but preferred to stay where he is and maintain his "proletarian" value system.

6. Their values are similar. Monty takes pride in Laura's appearance and appreciates that he walks down the street with a sex symbol. In return she wants love and closeness—and gets most of what she wants. She is proud to be with Monty.

I consider this couple an effective marital pair who are fulfilling their marital system's purposes as well as most of their individual contractual needs. In essence they have a single contract. Their individual contracts are congruent and complementary, with minimal conflict. Communication is reasonably good. Above all, they recognize their importance to each other and both are willing to put themselves out to make the relationship work. They genuinely love one another. Recognizing that their sexual and gender reinforcement needs were a source of potential trouble if they did not find sufficient gratification with each other, they turned to a new sexual freedom within their marriage—and thereby enhanced their lives.

The Greens seem to me to be two adult partners, each of whom has a childlike secondary theme. They are able to switch roles and to be unconsciously sensitive when the other is childlike and needs support, although Monty is not quite as adept or giving at this as Laura. At the time of marriage Monty probably was more of a parental partner for Laura than he is today.

Their defenses are generally used in a positive way, eliciting only minimal negative reactions in the partner. Laura has learned to respect Monty's need for emotional distance and not to be bothered by his modest masculine protest (reaction formation). He is often bemused and makes light of her anxiety about her attractiveness, while giving her the basic reassurance she asks for. They respect each other, including each other's defenses and foibles.

THE BLACKS—THE ELASTIC STEEL BOND

When they came for treatment David and Pamela Black, aged 54 and 41 respectively, had been married 18 years; for nine of those years they have maintained separate residences, although they have continued to see each other socially very often. They have two children, a girl of 16 and a boy of 14. Sex is poor. David is impotent with Pamela and avoids sex with her.

They lived together for the first six years of marriage; then David left. He had been impotent with Pam most of the time for three years before they separated, and had a "crush" on a younger woman, with whom sex was fine. They took no legal action to formalize their separation, continuing to see each other from time to time, maintaining constant touch in regard to their children, social activities and so on. They filed joint income tax returns. David fulfilled financial responsibilities to his wife and children, visited, enjoyed the children, and, as they got older, participated with them in more activities.

The first "separation" lasted three years; David returned home "to tell her off and divorce her" after Pam told him she was considering remarriage and asked for a divorce. He moved in and stayed; Pam was glad to have him back. Sex was good for a short time, but then David became impotent again and constantly found fault with Pam. During the three-year separation she had begun to learn that she need not be dependent on David. After another three years he left her again, again ostensibly for another woman with whom he had good sex. That was six years ago. The pattern of his visiting his family and staying with them for a while on and off each year continued, and he and Pam appeared together at various social functions, although each dated others as well. Pam had no sexual problem with other men. She now insisted on professional help, saying, "Let's work out David's impotence with me. Either this time we stay together and make it" (sexually and in general compatibility) "or let's get a divorce once and for all." Her decision was ostensibly precipitated by David's visit to close friends of theirs with another woman. She chose to be insulted by this act, claiming that when she went out with other men she did not flaunt the fact that she had a sexual relationship.

David is handsome, verbal, polished—a worldly gentleman. Pam is beautiful, intelligent, and verbal. She shows anxiety more easily than he but, like him, has great poise and charm.

David is 13 years Pam's senior, and when they married she felt unsophisticated, childlike, and ill fitted to move into the circle of his friends. Sex had been fine premaritally, and after they married, Pam had been readily orgastic with him when he was able to be affectionate and warm with her. But when he was hostile and impotent she had felt rejected and wept, which infuriated him.

Originally he had felt protective of her; now he did not. She was a bright and attractive companion and he still felt that her presence enhanced his prestige. He questioned his ability to love anyone. He was preoccupied, as was Pam, with appearance, form, and doing things with style and élan.

She said she still loved him but would no longer tolerate her unsettled status. He did not feel pressured to change their marital arrangement, and as time went on it became clear he really did not wish to change the status quo, except to have Pam finish her degree at architectural school so she could go to work and partly relieve him of the financial burden.

My treatment plan was first to explore their marriage contracts with them as quickly as possible and see if there was a basis for breaking the elastic bond that kept them "half together." Some systems should not be tampered with unless at least one partner really wants to change. It is important to respect the needs that have kept two individuals locked into what appears to be an impossible situation for both. The question was whether either Pam or David wanted to make the break complete or whether both of them could accept living together again. Both were open and in touch with their feelings, and talked about their situation with ease. Each had had several years of psychoanalysis, but it had not improved their interactional system.

When the couple wrote their individual contracts, they used the three levels of consciousness form (see Appendix 1) rather than the three categories. David prefaced his with the statement, "I have the impression solutions must be found in the third level—Beyond Aware-ness—before the other two."

Husband's Contract

Verbalized Level (Includes 1 and 2)

1. Keep me sexually interested and active. I need that form of ego reassurance—perhaps to ward off some faint lingering misgivings about my masculinity. The arousal of a woman by me seems most often to be the key to my sexual and psychic reward.

2. Don't be overdependent. Make your own way. Make money. I won't last forever and my high earning years won't either.

3. Don't betray me. But do. Although I become more intensely and even irrationally involved with you when threatened by infidelity, I also have a not unpleasantly neurotic need to feel slightly endangered by your actions with other men.

4. Be my child. Pay attention. Learn. Respect my gray hairs. But I'm really youthful, attractive to women of all ages—but I much prefer the younger ones.

5. You've done a good job with the kids, but you've been overpro-tective. It's good to see you loosen up a bit, even if it has only been for your convenience. But you *have* borne the brunt of the time needed to serve them—less than you have claimed, but lots, nonetheless. (Note how he gives and then immediately takes away.)

All I can offer is a show of marital attention. You don't turn me on. But I'm pleasant to guests unless we squabble, personable, bright.

I can't give you love in any dramatic—or perhaps even real—sense. I get crushes, usually related to sex—and can be fond of people. But I don't *love* anyone. Maybe myself?

I'll philander—unless some miracle occurs between us. And maybe even then.

Level 3. Beyond Awareness

All this I know. The unconscious is whatever it is that makes me fear you and other women. With a new young lover I am in charge, wor-shipped. Invariably, as with you, they all learn my weaknesses; then I fear I will be controlled and I become impotent and must become distant. I actually become afraid of your control. I know it relates to my mother

—but five years of analysis have not changed it. And I don't want more prolonged treatment. I won't change if I haven't by now.

WIFE'S CONTRACT

1. Conscious—Verbalized

1. Sense of equality, now—on my part. Not at the time of my original contract. At that time I wanted him to teach me. I think he did.

2. You* give me prestige which I enjoy and profit by.

3. We share friends, interests, children, achievements, pleasures and many common goals. We work well together in many areas—"attractive couple," etc. We enhance each other publicly; there is a sense of helping one another in this fashion.

In exchange for

1. My enthusiastic and rather joyful temperament, which is beneficial to Dave: I first realized this role on our honeymoon. I enjoy this part of me—so it is not difficult for me.

2. Conscious—Not Verbalized

1. I'm insecure and anxious socially and I depend on Dave for initial entrées to people who intimidate me (people more powerful than I am, the "grownups"). I need Dave's nerve—self-starting ability. I feel I'll be rejected—only at the beginning—a hangover from my childhood of feeling insecure.

2. I feel Dave will compare me with others in this respect and I'll suffer by the comparison. (She mentions the names of two women friends.) I'm very insecure because of this—he'll reject me because I'm not good enough. This has changed recently. Yet on the other hand, I know Dave is insecure about his place with these people, too, and he needs me.

In exchange for

1. His protection and social support, I give him support by my general attractiveness, etc. He will also appear sexually adequate.

---

* Pam changes back and forth from second to third person in referring to David. David.

3. Beyond Awareness

1. I am nothing without you. I need you and I love you for that because it means you're so much better than I. I need you like a father protector.

2. Because I need you like a father I'm depressed sexually—hate and love you for this. You won't give to me sexually. You are close in one way to the childish part of me, and apart in the adult fashion. David needs me so much—he'll never love anyone else. I want you as father—my "teach-me syndrome."

3. I want you as lover—I have a sense of extreme deprivation here—but I'm afraid of it, too.

4. Want closeness.

5. Don't want closeness because of father hangups.

6. I won't measure up to your other women sexually.

7. I know I can make relationships with other men—stronger, more powerful, richer and sexually able. I will if I have to but I want *you*. Because you are not available?

8. Sadomasochistic. The games we play out, money, decisions, competition between us, your constantly putting me down. You want me to be humbled, a child. Does it still excite me?

9. My ability to frighten you, consciously on my part. I now know my strengths and your weaknesses. I know you are afraid to have sex with me. I want it; I'll help you.

The basis of their elastic steel bond is clear from the Black's contracts. Ultimately both are aware of what they do but not necessarily as the interaction takes place. They have been powerless to alter their interactions. Theirs is a very deep sadomasochistic relationship. They started out 18 or so years ago with David as a powerful parental partner and Pamela as a childlike one. They now take turns reversing these behavioral roles in their interactional contract cycle. One of them says or does something in their interaction and then the roles switch—he becomes the child and perceives her as the controlling mother. She then behaves in a way that is threatening to him. As soon as he is ahead with her he feels frightened and gives up control, thrusting it upon Pam. When she has it (and uses it) he then becomes angry and frightened and sees her as his castrator. He does a very neat job on himself as she falls into her role assignment. Aspects of this game continue, although he now is less of a father image for her.

Now an accomplished woman, she wants to be a romantic child partner but with a man who is powerful and will also be the good father, not the punitive one as David is. (Or does she? Up to now she has not developed a significant relationship with another man.) David's threat and the reality of his having left home play into the fact that her father did disappear when she was three. David's reappearance reinforces the fantasy that Daddy will come back. But soon after he returns she is glad to have him leave again because he is so hostile. The emotional impact of David's ways is lessened somewhat for her by now, because the constant awakening of her warm and hopeful feelings, followed inevitably by disappointment, has begun to desensitize her to her expectations. Rather than serving to give her intermittent positive reinforcement of her warm feelings whenever he comes home again, her reaction now is more like the consequence of a repetition-compulsion that gradually drains off the cathexis of the act. If this is true it may mean that Pam *is* ready for change. This will have to be tested with tasks, not just words, so that both of them can confront their actions with me.

David depends on Pam to give credence to his masculinity, just as his handsome and urbane presence reinforces her public image of femininity—as each sees it for him/herself. Meanwhile, he is free to try to reinforce his self-image and defiantly show his independence of Pam by having crushes on young, beautiful women with whom he is sexually competent until he feels he has conquered each. At that point he makes the woman into a mother and becomes impotent. He feels the woman "will stomp on me with iron boots" (a fascinating and at the same time frightening prospect to him—his masochism loves it; his defensive sadism makes him act first by attacking). Flight, distance—both physically and emotionally—are his defenses. Pam now recognizes that she is "too strong" for him. She knows now that she is in control, except that she cannot control his flight and impotence, both of which infuriate her. She stated that she lost her love for him when she realized he could no longer play the role of strong protector and teacher for her. David's contract in some respects was more to the point about where they are now. Pam's was addressed to the past and did not accurately convey her current feelings.

I asked them to arrange to get together for an evening without the children. This suddenly became a great logistical problem despite the fact that they had two apartments. I asked them, as a task assignment, to pleasure one another's bodies without touching the genitals. As I gave them the instructions David repeatedly said that Pam did not turn him on, that he was a philanderer and couldn't love. I heard his message and explained the sensual and communicative aspects of the exercise; it was not to be sexual and there was to be no coitus or attempt to give each other an orgasm.

Their sadomasochistic picture was clear from the contracts. Whoever is in control must hurt the other—the pleasuring exercise made this clearly apparent as we progressed.

First home session of pleasuring without genital touch. She was anxious. The day they were to see each other she "had an impulse to go to a lawyer and get it over with." She went home, rearranged books, and did needless tasks to master her anxiety. When David came in, he too was anxious. He was not looking forward to the experience even though I had told them to be sure not to have coitus. He questioned Pam's desire to go through with it. Assured that she wanted to, he then assumed the parental role, tried to put her at ease, and quickly moved them to the bedroom.

When they got into bed Dave immediately made it clear he did not plan to stay all night. (This cue put their negative interactional contract into operation at once.) Pam let him know that she felt rejected. He then tried to woo her but he felt annoyed at her feeling rejected. They relaxed, hugged, talked, stroked one another's bodies to some extent—they enjoyed the talk most. After an hour Dave left. Pam cried for a short time and then stopped, feeling she was silly to have expected more from him.

Second pleasuring session one week later (with genital touch, but no coitus, no orgasm). These instructions were designed to remove the pressure of having to produce or perform.

They spent a weekend in her apartment but avoided the pleasuring of each other because the children were there, although her bedroom offered adequate privacy. Pam pointed out in the following conjoint session that she pulls back when he distances himself this way because she so fears his rejection. He says he feels that he had better not come close to her or he will be stomped on "with those iron boots." They therefore slept in separate rooms and did nothing sensual that weekend. He used the children to promote avoidance of any intimate body contact with Pam.

Next weekend. Pam arranged for the children to be away. David felt ill at ease with his protectors gone. When they went to bed he pleasured Pam, but because she felt he was hurried she did not enjoy it. She said it took the heart out of her, so that she was not with it when it came to pleasuring him. (This encapsulates their relationship.)

Their script. Pam: I anticipate that he will reject me and of course he does. I feel angry at him for this. Dave: Pam is angry at me. She (as his mother) will stomp on me. I am frightened. I do not care to give her anything.

In the session in which they described their weekend they each communicated their feelings and reactions openly. Communication was good but it did not have the effect of lessening the anger or anxiety of either. Instead they both used it to confirm that they had reason to be upset.

Third pleasuring one week later (same instructions). They were at my office the next morning, so the events were clear in their minds.

Dave: I am tense in these things (the pleasuring).

Pam: Just your body is there—not this part (she holds his hand tenderly).

Dave (to me): We started to touch—but I got more controlled. Pam touched me—including my penis—and *nothing came of it* (said emphatically and with pathos—as the final proof of their—his—hopelessness). Pam then got sleepy when she did it to me.

Pam: When he did it to me I got excited this time—but when I did it to him he was so distant *I went away further by falling asleep.*

Dave then went on to say that the pleasuring and touching make him tense and that he knows he can't respond—and isn't this sufficient proof that their relationship is no good? Pam said she was willing to go away if he no longer wanted her. I stated that David's feelings had to be respected and that it did seem to confirm that they might as well divorce. As soon as I mentioned divorce they both said that they wanted to continue treatment.

Fourth evening together (pleasuring again). Both felt better because somehow they felt "no need to perform, no gymnastics." It was pleasant for both. (My confrontation of them the previous session had caused them to draw a little closer together as they consolidated against the enemy who was challenging the status quo they had demanded that I challenge.) They were friendlier to each other. He was straightforward and said that an evening like that just helped him to stall. He had finally realized he did not have to perform and therefore felt fine. He had not had an erection, he said pointedly, in case Pam and I misunderstood his message. I then asked them, "What would you like to do the next evening together?"

David: I get an immediate association to a Sartre character. I could cut off my own penis as an existential act. (That said it all! I felt great empathy but I also realized that they had to play out the rest of their script their own way.) He then smiled and said he and Pam had planned that they would play that she would be his date and come to his apartment next week.

Fifth evening, one week later. They went to the theater and then to his apartment—both electing that they would act as new dates and not refer to their long history together. They spent the night together.

David said he had had no sexual response to Pam. Pam said she felt rejected and depressed. As he pleasured her she had fantasized herself at an attorney's office making divorce arrangements. She had realized, as David changed to masturbating her, that he had not kissed her during these past several weeks. She wondered why he avoided this intimacy. She became aware *at that point* that she had become aroused quickly, and as David continued to masturbate her she had an orgasm.

David then stated matter-of-factly that he usually got excited when he turned a woman on—but not with Pam (a devastating put-down that was meant to hurt, yet conversely it was her fantasy of hurting him by seeing the lawyer, plus her injured feeling at the realization he had not kissed her, that made her excited and led to her climax). I pointed out how important it was for each to hurt the other—neither dared to risk a sustained campaign of staying in close. I asked what I thought was a rhetorical question, "Why take turns chasing after each other when you both know you are unattainable to the other?" David responded (although no response was expected) that both of them like to be kicked; Pam answered, "I am bored by simple men and bored by men who adore me."

I told them I did not know how to help them to change. They did not seem to want either to come closer or to divorce, and both of them seemed to want the situation as it was. David immediately said we should stop treatment. Pam acquiesced. So did I.

They left treatment. I doubted that any change had taken place.

On mail follow-up a year later David did not respond. Pamela replied that after their last session with me she had realized that she had no hope or desire for a reconciliation. She viewed David's readiness to leave therapy as justification for her decision. For her all conflicts and anxieties stemming from their marital difficulties had disappeared; she felt released and free. She told me they had now taken legal steps to dissolve their marriage but I wondered if they would ever complete the legal divorce.

The Browns—Splitting

The Browns had been married for two miserable years when I saw them. Thad was 26, Inge, 24. They had no children.

They came in saying they wanted a divorce unless I could change their minds. When I asked why I should, Thad said that he loved Inge but could not stand her infantile behavior, her temper tantrums, lack of control, need for having everything her way immediately, putting him down in front of other people, not respecting him, placing her parents ahead of him. Inge said that Thad did not excite her sexually, that she refused to have sex with him, that he was too tied to his parents. She was not sure she loved him anymore, felt he was "too square," was too worried and concerned about everything, was too much of a planner, could not even go out for a drive without having a predetermined destination. He lacked spontaneity, didn't like fellatio and cunnilingus, and in fact was no fun at all.

Husband's Contract

1. I expect you to be respectful of my feelings and not humiliate me in front of other people. I will treat you with respect and not ridicule you in front of others.

2. I expect you to try to be more patient when frustrated and exercise self-control rather than giving way to temper tantrums. I expect you to try to discuss what bothers you in a rational way rather than resorting immediately to angry insults. On my part I will try to be more alert and cognizant of your desires. I will also try to be less sensitive about occasional insults.

3. I expect you to accompany me occasionally when I visit my parents' home. I expect you to be courteous to my parents and not deliberately try to hurt them. I will also see that they treat you with courtesy. If they cannot do this I will no longer insist that you visit them.

4. I expect you to be more self-reliant and not attempt to enlist your mother's support in every disagreement with me. I expect you to allow me some privacy in my interactions with you and not report every dispute we have and every action we take to your mother. I, in turn, will try to avoid any interference by my parents in our personal lives. I will also try to be more supportive when you need me.

5. I prefer certain traditionally male roles, such as taking care of the car and handling our finances, over traditionally female ones like cooking meals. I do not believe in inflexible roles, however. In short, where work roles are concerned I have preferences but make no demands. My only expectation is that neither one of us will take advantage of the other.

6. I expect you to have sexual relations with me more frequently than you have in the past. I am open to any ideas on how to make it better.

WIFE'S CONTRACT

1. I will give you companionship if you will give me companionship, i.e., I must talk to others because I don't really obtain the truth from what you say (i.e., your mother's conversation, always telling a story about someone sicker than my father. And, like Tony asking me to sleep with him—your telling me, a 24-year-old, that I misinterpreted what he said).

2. I will give you respect if you fulfill the small obligations of normal living. If you act like a responsible human being, i.e., lock the house door, put radiator cap back on the radiator before we go on the highway, have car inspected so police don't have to have tête-à-têtes with you, remember car keys, buy yourself a key chain.

3. I will give you love if you stop telling me that you're paying me to make your dinner, fold your socks, cook breakfast—i.e., I told you that if you didn't cooperate and clean the table off properly after dinner, I wouldn't cook dinner anymore—your retort, "Well, then, I'll stop giving you money." Don't you understand that I have a full-time job too?

4. I will give you love if you quit being such a killjoy: "There's too much traffic on the road"; "the egg is too salty"; "the French bread is just not as good this time." If you stop saying to me, "I'm disappointed in you." People who love each other don't call each other names ("moron," "idiot," "shithead").

5. I will give you sex if you don't turn me off by doing all of the above. I would like sex too; it doesn't make me happy not to do it. You just turn me off and I don't want it.

Discussion

Sessions were tempestuous with Inge very hostile and provocative to Thad. She was an attractive, sexually seductive woman who was seductive to me in front of Thad. She tried to enlist me to agree with her about his being square, too serious, no fun, and so on. Thad was a good-looking, earnest young man who obviously could not contend with his hypomanic wife, who appeared to be bent on destroying their relationship.

He was a rational partner, she a childlike partner, with the child very much in control of the downward spiral of their relationship. Inge needed limits to be set for her, which Thad was unable to do. His rationality was not backed up with sufficient strength to control her chaotic behavior. His inability to control her made her act out more, and she heaped more ridicule on him.

Most of their time in sessions was spent on who did what to whom. It was obvious that each was overinvolved with his/her family of origin. She had made herself so objectionable to his family that she was not really welcome in their home. She may have done this, in part, to keep him away from her family of origin. She certainly fought hard to exclude him from them. The areas covered in their contracts were few and these were dealt with in the most superficial way. Each had little understanding of his/her own behavior but focused on the other.

A month after they wrote their contracts I asked them to write additional contracts about their parents. In his, Thad also repeated his plea for consideration.

CONTRACT 2—HUSBAND

1. Respect. I expect you to treat me with respect and not humiliate me in front of others. I will do the same for you.

2. Understanding. I will not serve as whipping boy when things go badly for you. I will accept a certain amount of criticism but expect you to differentiate between major and minor offenses and take the minor ones more in stride. When I do fail you, and inevitably I will, I will not allow you to torture me over it indefinitely. I will try to comfort you and please you as much as possible, but you must realize that I am only human.

3. Your parents. Our own relationship is of primary importance. It takes precedence over the relationship between your mother and yourself. Your mother cannot be the prime consideration in such matters as

where we ultimately settle or whether you move with me when I get transferred. (A company transfer was imminent for him in the next year.) It is not necessary that she know our situation and state of health every three hours and be aware of our every feud. You cannot side with her 100 percent of the time when her opinions differ from mine. I do not stop being your husband when you are with your parents; therefore you cannot exclude me from your relationship with them. I will try to be respectful and considerate of your parents, but they must not interfere with our relationship.

4. My parents. Our relationship takes precedence over the one between my parents and myself. I cannot allow their concepts to interfere with our relationship. I agree to restrict the amount of advice and guidance that they give to me in order to insure the independence of our relationship as well as the separation of my life from theirs. If they wrong you I must defend you. On the other hand, I expect you to be courteous to them. I expect you to visit with them occasionally and be friendly rather than belligerent on such visits. I expect you to relate to my parents with an open mind, rather than looking to find fault with them.

5. Sex. I expect you to have sex with me—any way you want it as long as we have it. I do not want a wife who merely wants to be cuddled. I want one who wants to be screwed.

CONTRACT 2—WIFE

I will visit your parents if you stick up for me, not allow your parents to talk to me as if I were a child, not allow your parents to speak to you as if you were three years old, not allow your parents to treat you as an embryonic form of life, not permit your parents to bully, lecture, instruct, or soliloquize before us.

I will allow you to visit my parents if you are fully interested in their well-being—not out of a mere form of duty or politeness. It is not important to me whether you see them or not.

I don't believe your interaction with my parents is important to our marriage.

Inge showed no will to change, and she regarded Thad's more conciliatory attitude as evidence of his weakness. Clearly there was no congruence or complementarity between their contracts. Inge, when alone with me, told me she was wildly turned on by an older man with whom she had sex regularly and that Thad just left her cold. I asked her if she definitely wanted to break up her marriage. She answered, "Yes." Thad, when seen alone, seemed to want permission to dissolve the marriage, and to make sure that all possibilities for a reconciliation had been explored.

I then talked with both of them together and told them I saw no reasonable hope of their being able to arrive at a good marriage and that they should, perhaps, follow their original idea and get a divorce. I told Inge that Thad did not meet her idea of what she wanted, and to Thad I indicated that Inge was exciting but that she brought upsetting disorder and unpredictability into his life. She also acted as if she did not like him and would continue giving him a hard time. In view of her adamant position on almost every point of difference between them she was not likely to change, and she did not show him any respect, as I had pointed out several times before. Alone, I suggested to Inge that individual treatment was indicated for her, but she felt that to escape Thad was all she wanted or needed.

They both called me in two weeks to say they had become more friendly after starting the wheels in motion to get an annulment. They both thanked me and both agreed it was for the best.

It was clear to me that this couple had come to see me in order to be convinced that it was all right to separate. We all had to go through the "sincere" motions of exhausting all possibilities. Bound as they were to their parents, they needed an authority to tell them they could split. I was glad to play this role for them and to put my stamp on their conclusion that they could not live well together.

Two months later I received the following note from Thad.

> Once again I'd like to thank you for your help with my marriage. I think I developed a clearer understanding of what was really going on in our marriage after talking with you, and I know I felt better after airing some of the problems that were weighing on my mind. Given Inge's and my own personalities and attitudes I believe the outcome was inevitable, and I appreciate your having been frank with us.
>
> Though the transition to a single life has been difficult, I have no regrets that we took the action we did. Quite frankly I'm happier than I've been in a long time.

THE BLUES—MAKING IT

When I first talked with George and Penny Blue they had been married four years and had a daughter of two. George was 29, Penny, 27. Their complaint was that George had just confessed to having an affair. They were both unhappy about it because it confronted them with the fact that although many things were good, each had some dissatisfactions in the relationship. As it turned out, George's dramatic action was timely in halting the deterioration of their marriage.

They had consulted a colleague of mine two and a half years earlier, when George was depressed for no apparent reason. Their communication was poor even then. It became clear later that George was depressed because he was doing poorly in the company he worked for and was beginning to realize that he did not have the will to make it to the top of the ladder in the competitive structure of a large corporation. At that time he had been avoiding decisions that soon would be thrust upon him. He had always believed he would be a big success and eventually would become part of the power structure of the country. To readjust his ambition was too threatening then.

Penny had been an independent woman when they met; she had her own home, traveled, had friends, enjoyed sex, and felt liberated. When she married she had felt she was giving up her freedom. A few months later the couple moved to New York, and she felt she was giving up her home and friendships, and was moving to a lonely apartment. She could not find work in her own profession when she came to New York. George came out of his depression when he decided to resign and found a position with a much smaller company in New Jersey. The Blues had to move to New Jersey because George's new office was too far from the city for commuting, and eventually they bought an old rundown house in a pleasant, rather fashionable rural area near George's job. Penny now felt more and more fenced in by her life and obligations. She had a house and a baby to care for and another on the way. She felt boxed in by marriage, by decisions that apparently had to be made to accommodate to George's needs. Although she felt like these were necessary and correct decisions, they left her in a position very different from what she had anticipated when she married.

Contracts were developed in the course of our sessions, rather than written out by the Blues themselves.

WIFE'S CONTRACT

Category 1

Marriage is sharing all those things and I agreed to get pregnant— but I am so tied down. I don't like to take care of house and child—I now know I do prefer to work, and to have the freedom I had before I married. I know I had to "settle down"—but it's wrong this way. George works like a dog to make enough for us. And I know he will do okay here; he likes it. I'm a household drudge on a suburban hilltop that we can't afford. I can't even look for a job now. Marriage just is not supposed to be like this.

George was supposed to stay in New York and I thought he could shoot to the top. At times I feel I shouldn't have hitched myself to his star but stayed on my own—I was my own boss, came and went when I wanted to. I do feel he let me down. I know I sound awful and that makes me feel terrible.

Category 2

1. I'm independent but I'm forced to be dependent on George now— and I do not like it. He is good—but he is moody and so am I. In some ways he is dependent on me and I know I let him down—I don't keep the house well organized and dinner isn't always ready—but I *do not like this life*. I guess maybe that's why he had this affair. I haven't been too turned on by him.

2. Active-passive. I feel negativistic and that's wrong. I don't want to be that way but I do feel cheated—like I got a dirty deal. Not that he doesn't work hard and try, but he will always be a plodder and I see a life of dullness and drudgery ahead—and soon I'll have another baby. I'm basically more active—he is passive when it comes to taking over at the important times. That's why I have lost respect for him but I can't tell him that.

3. Closeness-distance. We both tend to be removed and not in touch with our feelings as you talk about it. If I let mine out I know I'll

slaughter him and he likes to keep everything so intellectual or he feels depressed and moody and just withdraws. If you can help me talk it would help. (In sessions he is intellectual, she silent—answers briefly, does not open up—sits on the feelings she expresses to me when alone.)

4. Power. I feel powerless. I used to be so in charge of myself—it's like I've been gradually engulfed and overpowered by a sea of molasses called George. He's "sweet"—how can I be a nasty bitch? I feel trapped —a sea of molasses is right—you just can't fight it. Even his playing around with this girl—I understand it and am not really angry about it. I do love him—I just don't like what my love has led me to.

5. Abandonment. That's not it. I'm not afraid to be alone although I think he is. That's not the answer—*how to make it work is.*

6. I don't want to control or be controlled—unless my wanting him to have more drive for success is control; if so I want to control his goals in that sense. But it's not real control, nor do I want to be controlled. I resent the control imposed on me by these circumstances and indirectly I do blame George for that. It was not our plan to have it work this way!

7. (Both are defended. She quietly simmers with her anger and is in a moderate depression. Overt anxiety is not expressed much, but her withholding all affect from George, including sexual desire, is an expression of her anxiety and anger. She displaces to child and internalizes to George, her position, etc. She projects her sense of inadequacy and anxiety to George and is terribly anxious as she recognizes his limitations.)

8. I had felt great as a woman; I don't know how I feel now—like a trapped woman. George is physically attractive, but I'm not feeling sexual to him now. Maybe after the baby—but that's not it, that will only close the trap more.

9. Love and accept myself and George. I don't know at this point—I could say yes but I don't like me now and I'm angry with him. Perhaps I should be angry at myself for letting myself get into this. But I felt we both had so much to give and that he could make it and I would have children and my own work.

In exchange for your providing the life I want and the power I can't get myself I will be more responsive and not so bitchy—but he does have to understand where I am at: We did not plan that he would be a simple country gentleman. If he will help me more I'll try to drop this damn bitterness. (She sounds again as if her feeling bitter depends entirely on George—this is an area that requires immediate therapeutic attention.)

Category 3

1. We can't and do not communicate—it comes out all wrong for both of us. I start to and then he doesn't seem to be there with me—like he has his own world he is living in where they speak only Chinese and I speak and understand only Swahili. That's what it's like most of the time except for "pass the salt."

2. We are both intelligent and have enough similar interests, but we are both too busy—he at work and me with fixing up this old house. It's some fun but mostly it's work—it could be fun if it were what I had chosen to do. I feel I was shanghaied into it.

3. Family. His and mine are no problems, nor our baby—it's just this feeling of my being stuck in a world I did not choose.

4. Money, etc., is not used directly for control—everything must go into the house so that is that!

5. Sex. He likes to plan it like a scenario—which turns me off. Sex had been great—he is good and I never had trouble enjoying it with him—had orgasm in foreplay and with him inside. But now he leaves me cold—I know it burns him up but I can't help it. Sometimes I just go off to sleep when he's making love—I can't help it. Basically I know it's because I'm so disappointed with him. I guess disappointment is worse than anger. If you are angry over an act things can be straightened out and amends made, or you go on to the next thing and forget about it. But disappointment is different—it means if I don't reset my expectations it will only get worse and the poor guy has no way, no chance to make it okay because I want him to have qualities he just doesn't have and can't make up. (This clarity raised my prognostic expectations.)

The above evolved over four sessions—mostly when seeing Penny alone at her request. She did not want to express her anger and disappointment to her husband for fear of hurting him. George's failure to meet his wife's expectations and her feeling trapped in a suburban life that has clipped her wings and changed her life in ways she did not anticipate are a common story that is rarely expressed so eloquently. Penny's understanding and insight—as well as her basic insecurity about herself and therefore her expectations that her husband would fulfill what she believed she could not accomplish herself—became clearer to her as our sessions went on.

HUSBAND'S CONTRACT

Category 1

I don't understand Penny. I understand her need to work, not to be in bondage to the house, and she knows that as soon as she can after the baby she can look for a job. I don't want her to be just a hausfrau. She is brilliant and a different person when she works. But she wanted children too, and she knew we were tight about money.

I do help out at home. She is well organized, fantastic in her professional work—why can't she apply some of that ability at home? I know she needs to get out and I want to help and I want her to work because she isn't happy this way. But I'm trapped too, working 12 hours a day six days a week right now—but that won't last forever.

I feel better out of New York and the major leagues. I fit in better here and I'll be a big fish in this smaller pond in a few years.

Marriage does mean sharing most of life together. There is plenty Penny will be able to do on her own, too. That affair is over—I guess it was my way of telling Penny off instead of working it out with her. That's why we're here now with you. I like married life—children—and a wife who I hope will be with me but not under me.

In exchange for her loyalty and trying, I'll do my best to be someone of consequence. I want that for me, too. New York and that company were just too cutthroat for me; I'm not built for that. (His father is an extremely successful businessman, the promoter type, who puts big deals together and apparently does it well.)

I don't want to split with her. We've had a rough time with the change of jobs and less money, two changes of living areas in four years, one baby and another coming. I feel I'm on the right track now and if it's right for me I think I can make it right for us—unless she just wants her bachelor life again. I don't think that's it. I think it's her having realized that the lack of work, the house and the baby aren't what she wants. I do not want us to fail at this marriage. I love her.

In exchange for her understanding I'll give mine and my help—but life together can be tough, and is right now for both of us.

Category 2

1. I'm independent—so is Penny, basically. I feel circumstances, and perhaps I determined those, have fashioned our present life, and Penny resents that.

2. Active/passive. Right now I'm more active and she is depressed. At times it's been the other way around. Like when we saw Dr. H. a couple of years ago and I was down because of my sense of not making it at work. I was wrestling with changing my dream—maybe that's what Penny is doing now.

3. I'm a closed person—I think I'm too insecure to let people in. I've been through this before in treatment, and it's true. Penny wants to be more open, she says, but she can't make it or I don't make it easy.

4. & 5. I don't think either of us abuses power or wants to dominate the other. I do have ideas of what I want things to be like. You know, the perfectly ordered house; Penny meets me at the door beautifully dressed and groomed with a cold martini for me. The way things are now she would pour it over my head!

6. Abandonment. I don't think of it—the idea of Penny leaving me is frightening. I don't want to hang that one on her. I feel (hope?) somehow we will work it out.

7. & 8. Anxiety. Sure, I know it well with my old stomach trouble— that's so much better now. (He had had a gastric ulcer.) I do get tense if I feel something may not go well at work. That damn inferiority hangs on but I'm fighting it. (His major defenses are intellectualization, denial, somatization, and reversal.)

9. Feel about myself? Not too good. I know I did not make the grade in New York no matter what Penny, friends, or I tell myself. Now Penny isn't happy with me, and I must admit her attitude about marriage and her not responding sexually now do make me feel lousy. I don't know what to do—I can't change the way family life is structured. If she worked, good as she is, she can't make what I can—and I know that's not the answer. (Note that he expresses no direct anger at Penny.)

10. Sex. I love her appearance, her body, her ways when she is feeling good—she turns me on then and sex is great. Right now it's a drag—I resent it.

11. Love. I love her; I'm not so sure about myself. I do need her love and support, especially now because this is a tough time; I feel I have to prove myself. In exchange I'll help her to be as free as possible. I'll help at home; as soon as I make a little more money we will get help. I'll cooperate in her getting work. I think she needs me. She has to learn that she is a wonderful person and to feel better about herself. I don't mean the drudgery crap—but she was living the life of a bachelor when we met—which was a life I was fed up with—yet she looks back on that as heaven. Something is wrong with her picture even if I let her down

somewhat financially and on the jet-set picture we both used to joke about. I need her strength to supplement mine. I want and expect a partnership. We are a family now—not just two lovers.

Category 3

Communication is our biggest problem—we both withdraw or do not express what we want.

Discussion

This couple had disappointments with their individual contracts early on. She wanted a man who would give her a style of life and power she felt she could not get herself. She therefore put herself in a typical conventional middle-class configuration of the woman who settles for the reflected power and glory of her husband. Her own work, which she needs because housekeeping and constant child-care are not to her liking, gave her satisfaction but she was content to remain on a noncompetitive level in her industry. Thus she is rather confused about her own identity as a person and the role she wants for her husband.

George, on the other hand, is somewhat compulsive and removed. He is plagued by a vague sense of inferiority which he defends against by his intellectualization. They do need each other, if they can reach each other.

George's behavioral profile is that of a rational partner at times but basically he is more romantic and wants a wife who will "complete" and complement his weaknesses. Penny, who appears at first as a parallel partner, actually has a strong component of the child-like. Therefore her parallel characteristics in the interaction (she really does push him away) are ascendant when her childlike needs are not met. When she drops her parallel partner reaction defense to his rational one, and when he is more romantic, they work well together.

As therapy went on, Penny moved toward a more childlike-equal partner stance and he a romantic-equal partner position. Communication improved. Penny took greater responsibility for herself, and therefore for her home. After the birth of the second child she got a part-time job. Sex improved with these general changes but also when George learned he could express his anger directly to her when she fell asleep during sex play. She awoke, impressed by his commanding way, and found she was sexually excited. He learned from this experience.

Their situation improved. After 15 sessions we discontinued treatment with the understanding that it might be resumed in the future. A follow-up letter was sent three months later and I received the following response from Penny:

> George and I have had a pretty good couple of months and feel encouraged on the whole. Our ups are better and last longer. We both feel we can communicate with each other more easily and about a lot more than we could in the past. Our low points are as bad as they ever were but they do seem to come more infrequently and not to last as long. So, although we have not arrived, we think we are closer than we were and are getting there. So, unless things take a turn for the worse, we would like to see how it all goes for the next few months.

I am sure that not all the Blues' problems are solved, but they have come a long way and are now on a more solid foundation.

THE WHITES—FINDING IT AT HOME

Mary and Norman White were in their late thirties and had been married 13 years when they came for consultation with the presenting complaint of poor communication. By this Mary meant that Norman treated her "like I worked for him—he likes to tell me what he wants me to do and it has to be done his way." She felt that she could not discuss anything with him; he closed her off. He felt that she always wanted to talk "psychological stuff" and that she had no real feelings for him. They had two sons, 11 and eight. Mary had tried to be an actress, had not been successful, and had then married Norman, who was an engineer and now had become a successful building contractor. Mary had recently returned to college. Both were attractive; Norman was very carefully and stylishly dressed in an expensive and somewhat flashy style. She seemed relaxed, he stiff and ill at ease. She talked readily, openly; his speech was constricted.

My first tentative topographic assessment was that Norman was a parallel partner and Mary, a romantic partner.

Norman was having an affair with another woman at the time of the first interview. He had recently told Mary about it and had gone away for a week with this person. Mary said she had not been very upset about it. On his return Norman had told Mary he wanted to consider staying in the marriage but that she and perhaps he would have to change. This was the immediate precipitant for their visit, during which I saw them conjointly, as well as individually for a few minutes.

Four years earlier Mary had had a brief affair because she felt unloved by and sexually unresponsive to her husband. In her individual part of the session she told me she had been open and orgastic with the other man, whereas with Norman she was always tense and rarely felt sexually excited.

In his part of the session Norman said he was not yet sure about staying with Mary, she was so puritanical, would not do fellatio with him, disparaged him before others, called him compulsive and autocratic. He enjoyed sex and if he could not have it with Mary he would just have to find it elsewhere.

When we resumed the conjoint session Norman said again that he was not sure he wanted to make it with Mary. She said she wanted to really try with him, but she felt no vibes from him, just a dead feeling when she tries to get any response from him except a sexual one—for which he is always ready. Norman said he wanted her to want him—he never feels she does. She admitted he was correct, but said that because he treated her as an object or an employee, she could not respond to him sexually or lovingly.

The next session, they both came in smiling. Norman announced, "I fired my assistant and my girl friend yesterday. I want to try to make it work with Mary." Privately he told me that the other woman loved him but he could not reciprocate; she was too depressed for him and six months were enough. "I could see it would be even worse than with Mary. I do want to give it a try."

Mary said she loved Norman but was not "in love" with him, that she was not a masochist. She felt that he did not make her feel attractive—his attitude was, "I know you are pretty and you know you are so why do I always have to reassure you?"

It was apparent that Mary could not be free sexually with Norman in their current way of interrelating, nor could he readily respond to her demand that he communicate more, which apparently meant to be open about his feelings and his uncertainties, as well as to be more patient with her less precise ways of doing things and to reassure her of her desirability.

Their contracts as elicited in the sessions were as follows.

WIFE'S CONTRACT

Category 1

1. Marriage is a partnership with major emphasis on one another and the children but there has to be room for other friends and close relationships too. I don't mean sexual necessarily.

2. If we can make it it will be great—if not, the sooner we know and separate the better it will be for all of us, children included. (Does not sound like a determined commitment—is it realistic?)

3. (Not expressed directly.) We have a good life superficially. Divorce would be tough and no man out there looks any better to me. I must try to make this work but I don't want to give him the satisfaction of thinking I want or need him that much. I want him but I want him to really want me!

In exchange

1. I will run a tighter ship.

2. I will try to let my love come through. But I'm afraid to get dependent on him again. I expect him to really try and not just go through the motions. (But this is what she sounds like she may be doing at this point.)

3. He must stop putting me down or making snide remarks about me in front of the children and our friends and I will stop doing it to him.

Category 2

1. I have been defensively rebellious—not independent—with him. I'm glad I decided to go back to school. He is such a big success and I feel like I'm nothing—or I did.

2. He is such a whirlwind—the most active and determined person I know—but I'm no slouch either, if he just wouldn't roll over me as if I'm not there. I want him to respect my ideas too. I've been trying to make my presence felt in a negative way mostly (sex), which maybe is what pushed him away—*but I had to get back at him or drown.*

3. Closeness-distance. I want more closeness, more feelings from him. He gets me so angry it makes me close off and I don't talk to him—I put him down now and that infuriates him.

4. Power. We both have it. I'm just sore because he is so stubborn about things. I can do most of what I want. He wants me to spend more money even, but that's not the point—he won't respect me as a person. I expected him to be powerful and to take care of me. Basically he is no stronger or less so than I am.

5. He used to be very possessive of me, not only if I talked to men but even with women. I was a social buffer for him, more superficially at ease socially, etc. Now he doesn't seem to care. I don't want him the other way *but I do want him to care.*

6. I have a high level of anxiety; anything that reminds me how insecure I really am sets me off. He does not want to or doesn't know how to set me at ease—when he does I love him for it.

7. No matter what people tell me, I feel inadequate—*I know there are secret parts of me I don't like. I want plastic surgery*—Norman says I'm crazy. I am unsure of myself as a woman.

8. Norman is very attractive and sexual. At first he had premature ejaculations but that cleared up after the birth of our first child. When he was okay sexually he became less loving to me and I turned him away and didn't want him. (Note the switch off of her sexual attraction to him after he becomes sexually competent. Mary blames this on his being less loving. What effect did the child's presence have? What effect did his sexual competence have on the situation? Did she now feel a loss of control?)

9. We approach problems so differently—I tend to use my feelings and he is so well organized—which is fine if he doesn't expect me to be the same. Somehow I do get done what I have to and I do it well.

In exchange for his consideration of me and my needs I promise that I will:

1. Try to be more warm, loving, and sexually receptive.

2. Not put him down.

3. He gives me financial security—I do my part to run the house and our social life. I hate to feel I owe him anything, but I guess I shouldn't criticize him so much.

4. I realize I am a person and should not expect to get my strength and sense of self so much from him. School is helping me with that.

Category 3

Nothing of note here that has not been covered already.

HUSBAND'S CONTRACT

Category 1

1. If our marriage can work, it's best for her, me, and the boys. I want a home where things run well and that I can be proud of. Mary has made a beautiful home even if everything doesn't always get done on time. On the whole she is okay and now that she is at school she delegates things well—she's a better boss than a worker, I'm learning.

2. I know I'm supposed to give my wife encouragement—but she is insatiable. If I tell her her dress looks beautiful on her she thinks I don't think she is pretty because I haven't mentioned that. It's like the guy

who got two ties from his mother for Christmas. When he visits her he makes sure to wear one of them. His mother looks at him and says, "What's the matter, you didn't like the other tie?" In exchange for all I do I just want her to accept me and not make me feel like I'm some freak. I really need her. She should realize that without my having to beg. I want a good home life as well as our having fun together. I think we want the same things in marriage.

Category 2

1. I'm independent but of course I'm dependent on Mary—but not to the point where I'll continue to live with someone who treats me as she does. I am dependent on her emotionally. I want to feel loved and to be considered important.

2. She always talks about wanting me to be closer—but I think she moves away as much as I do or she does things that make me want to move away. I can't spill my guts out all the time. I'm not sure of what she wants but I do know she hasn't been there for me when I have needed her and I'm tired of always reassuring her about how great she is.

3. I don't think I want her to submit to me, but I don't want to be her slave either.

4. I was possessive—it's true. It's also true that I haven't cared since her affair four years ago. I was ready to leave her any time after that until I was really faced with it and we came here. I know I was about to do the same thing with someone else as I had with Mary. Some superficialities would be different but essentially it would be the same type of relationship. I saw that the week I was away with this other woman. It was good for that reason.

5. My anxiety is hidden. I get cold, have sharper control—I've always reacted that way in emergencies since I was a kid. With her it's all up front. At first I thought it was cute and it made me feel protective and like the big man, but after a while it became a real pain. I could spend half my time reassuring her and it still wouldn't be enough. And she didn't seem to understand when I needed her support. I don't like to have to ask for it.

6. I feel good about myself as a man now. I didn't for a long time, but once I began to make it okay in business everything came together—I even got to be good sexually. I feel Mary resents my success. That's why I've encouraged her to go back to school and told her to get full-

time help. I think a little bit about her meeting other guys now, the professors most likely, but I figure I'd have to take my chances. It still worries me a little, especially now that I've decided not to move out.

7. To me she is really okay and attractive—face, figure, her ways. But she turns me off, especially when she is sexually cold to me. She won't even kiss properly—keeps her lips closed.

8. Feel about yourself and mate? I think I'm okay. I'm not so sure about loving Mary but I want to try to make it together. She let me down by not making it easier for me to know I'm okay as a man. It's like I had to do it despite her—I guess I'll resent that for a long time. I think I can give her a lot person-to-person and if she will let herself go I believe I'll get all I want and need from her.

In the area of communication, I know I have problems but so does she. I won't take all the responsibility.

I will try to understand and help her, to communicate, to show affection.

In exchange:

1. I want her to see me as a person—I know I have some insecurities. Instead of ridiculing my orderly ways I want her to understand and I'll try to do the same for her.

2. I want her to try to relax with me sexually. You can help us there, I hope.

3. I will support her at school and in achieving greater independence —although that's mostly up to her. What I have achieved has *not* been at her expense and she enjoys the fruits of it too; I do think I deserve to be respected, but I don't ask for adulation or for love because of what I've accomplished. Love should come from her recognition that I am in her corner—if not it just isn't there and we would do better to quit.

4. We are not kids anymore. We can still achieve a good part of our dreams if we each give a little more.

(Note that each mixed together at the point of *"in exchange"* what they wanted with what they would give—this was characteristic of their relationship and was an early focus of treatment.)

We had talked through their contracts, developing them in the sessions so that it was an interactive and therapeutic experience. I now understood Norman's defensiveness better, and I recognized how often Mary put him off with her own defensiveness—her distancing and provocative remarks. He was rational but somewhat narcissistic too. He was something of a peacock in his manner of dress.

As I thought through their interactions I revised their interactional designation to that of husband, rational-partner; wife, pseudoromantic partner. Mary was at least as distant as Norman, and perhaps in a more pernicious way. She professed to want closeness but withdrew whenever it was offered. When questioned she fell back on reciting old disappointments and injuries from early in the marriage, such as Norman's former premature ejaculation.

Although the terms of their contracts are not as sharp and clear as some other couples', they are illustrative of a common way some patients have of verbalizing and conceptualizing their contracts. These are quite satisfactory for therapeutic work.

THERAPY

In sessions details of their interaction were used in confrontation and to point out their similar desire for love and their fear of injury. Tasks and pleasuring exercises were carried out at home to increase communication. After the first pleasuring session Mary exclaimed to me, "I enjoyed so being active—I never was before."

Confronting Mary with her own distancing maneuvers, as well as getting both to express their feelings toward and resistance to the tasks, moved the couple along rapidly. Both, despite their sophisticated façades, were deeply motivated to work on themselves and their relationship. They realized how close they had been to divorce and both now knew they wanted to stay together, and were able to risk saying this to each other. Both appreciated that they needed room and time for themselves. As Norman said, he would have to take his chances with Mary's going forth into the world and meeting other men. He also added, "I don't swear that I'll always be monogamous." (The effect of this gratuitous remark on Mary and how he created a protective distancing from her just as they came close were made clear.) Both were out in the world a great part of the day—both now seemed to be comfortable about this.

In their last session (there was a total of ten) Norman announced that Mary was going to have the plastic surgery she wanted. He felt it was unnecessary because he loved her as she was, but he could understand that it was important to her so he was now for it. They left with some problem areas unresolved but they had decided jointly that they did not want more therapy at that time, preferring to try to implement and consolidate what they had learned. This was a resistance to further closeness and characterological change for both—a dyadic flight into health that left me with some concern for their future prognosis together.

Mary and Norman had looked over the brink, seen nothing but the same ahead, and decided to turn around and try to find what they wanted at home, not in the "promised land."

THE GRAYS—THE WEIGHT OF THE PAST

Sara and Charles Gray, 24 and 25 respectively, came to therapy with their chief complaint verbalized by Charles as "I pull back from marriage like I don't really want to be closed in or close to Sara." She added, "When I need him he isn't there for me. He holds me off at a distance. At first I was hurt about it but now I get more and more angry. When we lived together we broke up for a few months because of his distance, but we loved one another, came back again and got married 15 months ago." They had had many ups and downs but for the past eight or nine months the trend had been toward less effective and less open communication, more withdrawal by both, less frequent sex, increased depression for Charles, and more anger and sense of frustration for Sara. Nevertheless, they felt that they still loved each other and wanted to make the relationship work.

Sara was a first-year graduate student in biology. Charles, after working in industry for a few years, had returned to business school to get a master's degree. They were financed largely by Charles's parents and their own savings.

Because this couple lived outside New York, we decided at the beginning that we would have an extended evaluation and therapeutic exploratory program of a maximum of ten sessions and that if additional treatment was indicated I would then refer them to a colleague near their campus. I gave each of them one of the marriage contract questionnaires I used at that time to fill out and bring back on their next visit. I later abandoned this questionnaire in favor of the reminder list in Appendix 1, but I shall include the questions here so that readers may compare its greater detail with the reminder list. As with the reminder list, each spouse filled out a separate questionnaire, which they could either discuss together afterward or deal with in the office session as they preferred. So that the mates' responses can be easily compared, they are listed together here.

QUESTIONNAIRE FOR EACH PARTNER

Full Name ....Date ....

Age .... Type of relationship (married, engaged, living together, other—

please specify) ....

Duration of relationship .... Children? (list age and gender)

....

    The following questionnaire is for couples (married and nonmarried). Although the term marriage is constantly used, please understand that the questionnaire applies to any type of close relationship between two persons. It is intended to be filled out at home. Leave plenty of time. It may be done over a period of days.

    Following you will find three series of questions. These questions are meant merely as cues to you. We do not expect you to react fully to all questions, but to focus on those that create problems or that evoke strong feelings. Agreements are as important as disagreements, so please include both.

Instructions

    Write your response beneath each question. If you need more space, use the back of each page and note the number of the question. Respond generally with your ideas or feelings as they are *now, today*, except when the question states otherwise. Add your past thoughts on the subject, too, if you believe that these are important to how you now feel. Try to answer the questions openly and fully. Look deep within yourself.

    If there are thoughts or feelings you *do not want conveyed to your partner* at this time, mark those questions with a large asterisk(*). The staff member whom you are consulting will then respect your preference.

AREA 1. GOALS AND PURPOSES OF THE RELATIONSHIP

People form intimate relationships, including marriage, for a variety of reasons. Some of the reasons are mentioned below. Respond to those that apply to you.

Sara   *Charles*

1. Marriage should make me happy. (How?)

Marriage should make me happy in the sense that I should now have someone who will be real with me, who will give me loving feedback, and who will share himself with me.

I should continue to feel that I made the right choice. Although it shouldn't make me unhappy, it needn't make me happy.

2. Marriage should satisfy social pressures on me. Specify (e.g., "all my friends were doing it," "my family expected it").

There were no social pressures that I was aware of when I got married. In fact, my husband's parents (especially his mother) were *very* much against it.

My goal in marriage as far as I am aware did not and does not involve satisfying social pressures. I am happy that that is not the case.

3. I should have companionship and not be lonely anymore. Explain.

I agree with this statement recognizing that at times my partner is unable to be close to me because he is busy, angry, or wishes distance.

I would never expect marriage to keep me from being lonely anymore. Companionship is, however, a plus for marriage.

4. I want a partner to share some kinds of experiences with me but prefer not to share others (e.g., to share in a home life, but not in my work).

I am willing to share any experiences with my partner that he wishes to be a part of—except in some occasional cases when I wish to do something alone.

The only particular experience that I can't always feel comfortable sharing with Sara is what I write, though often I later decide to read it to her. I do, however, like to be away from her some, either at home while she is away, or when I am out walking, doing errands, occasionally bowling.

Sara	*Charles*

5. I expect our relationship to last until "death do us part." Agree or disagree. Explain your attitude.

Disagree. I expect our relationship to last as long as we both feel love for each other and as long as we satisfy for each other whatever needs we each had when we married.	I don't know what to expect. I do realize the possibility that one or both of us might want out one day.

6. I like family life and want my own family. How does this statement compare to your ideas?

I agree. However, for me this does not exclude a career and other interests.	At this point, given that we are both in school, given financial difficulties and problems with our relationship, I don't want to add to our family. I am also in touch with some uncomfortable (scary, dragged-down) feelings when I think about "settling down," growing old, suburbia.

7. I see marriage as requiring the giving up of my individuality and freedom for a greater goal. Or I wish to be me and to remain an individual and for my partner truly to be herself or himself. Please explain your for, against, or mixed feelings about these statements.

I wish for marriage to allow each of us the greatest possible freedom and opportunity for us to be unique individuals.	Marriage needn't be at the price of one's individuality but it does entail mutual "giving up" of some of our freedom and assuming new responsibilities.

8. Marriage gives me position and status in my own eyes as well as among those people who are important to me. Please explain.

This is not true for me.	I am not aware of a new sense of position and status as a result of marriage.

Sara   *Charles*

9. I want marriage (or other kind of relationship) because I want (or do not want) children. Children are (or are not) the main goal, and having a mate is a means to that end.

Children are not the main goal for me in marriage. The quality of the relationship between the two mates is all-important for me.

My wanting marriage is independent of my wanting children. Having children is definitely not the main goal.

10. Marriage lessens chaos and strife in my life; life tends to be more orderly and reasonable; life now has a purpose. Explain, including the purpose.

True. Ideally, being married provides me with companionship, with immediate access to sex, and provides me with the security of knowing I have someone who cares about me.

Mixed emotions here! Chaos and strife seem to have increased, as well as order and reasonableness. I'm not sure that I was (am) ready for all the orderedness in my marriage. A personal problem that must run over to my marriage is my not having a sense of purpose in life. Difficulties in marriage, doubts about profession, doubts about the efficacy of being in school, spending parents' money, feeling inadequate in social situations, all add up to some real doubts about my sense of meaning.

11. Marriage allows me to have sex without fuss, without constant searching and courting and the risk of rejection. Describe your reaction to this statement.

True. However, I sometimes meet a man with whom I think it would be fun to have sex and then I will fantasize about him for a few days or so. I do not act on my fantasies.

Although it is true, it is without as much of the excitement of courtship. It's obviously more intimate and sometimes the intimacy scares me. Sex without fuss is not high on my scale of values for marriage.

Sara	Charles

12. *I need someone to inspire me to build and to work toward the future. It is easier (and better?) to do this for others (mate and children) than just for myself. Describe your reaction.*

Sara	Charles
I disagree with the part in parentheses. It is easier for me to work toward the future (i.e., to be in graduate school) when I am married for two reasons: 1) I feel more secure, less alone when I have a mate and this frees me to study; 2) my husband is paying for my schooling; otherwise I have no financial resources. I do not feel I need someone to inspire me to work toward the future, nor do I feel it is necessarily better to work for husband and family. It is, however, much easier to work toward the future because of being married. Much more fun to work hard and do something worthwhile and then have someone with whom to *share* the benefits.	I like inspiration for future. I'm aware now of a sense of competitiveness between us, fear that Sara is, or will be, a better student. So I don't feel much inspiration from Sara. Yes, it would feel good to be working for *us*.

13. *I like to share responsibility with a mate. It helps to keep me from making mistakes on important matters. Describe your reaction.*

Sara	Charles
I like to share responsibility—not because I doubt myself but because it is less work to share and because in my marriage I believe most decisions should be made jointly.	I like to share responsibility but at times feel that I have come to depend too much on Sara to take charge in many situations. Then I feel resentful.

Sara   *Charles*

14. I want someone who will look after me on a daily basis, as well as when I am ill—someone who will care about my welfare, as I will about her/his. Elaborate.

True. I do not, however, feel the need for a parent nor do I wish to be a child. I simply like having someone care about my feelings and be willing to give me feedback when I discuss things which are important to me.

I want Sara to *care* about me and want to be freer to reciprocate. I don't know what "looking after me" entails. I think I put Sara in the role of mother too much, don't trust her sometimes, as I never trusted my own mother.

15. Marriage makes things economically more advantageous for me. I do (or do not) expect my spouse to contribute financially or in other ways. Please elaborate.

This statement is definitely true for me, especially right now since I am unable to contribute financially. Once I am out of school, I do expect to.

Marriage hasn't at this point been economically advantageous. I expect my wife to contribute financially when she begins work. When we are both working I expect us *both* to contribute financially and in household duties.

16. Only with my spouse can I feel I am a whole person. Without each other we are less than complete; only together are we whole. Elaborate on how this applies to you and/or your spouse.

This does not apply to me at all. I feel whole whether I am with or without my mate.

I don't feel myself to be whole anyway. I can think of only one brief glimpse I had at feeling at all whole and this occurred several months before I met Sara. I don't feel any more or less whole with or without Sara. I don't want to feel as though I am only whole with Sara or that she is only whole with me.

Sara   *Charles*

17. I love my mate and we have to be together. Life is unsatisfactory without her/him. In what ways and to what extent; will you die without her/him?

Life as a single woman is more difficult for me than married life is because I want to go to school and have no financial resources. However, I would not die without my husband.

I love my mate and I *want* to be with her. Life is painful right now and would be without Sara also and I don't want to always feel this bad. No, I would not die as a result of losing her.

18. Describe other goals and purposes of your relationship that are of significance to you which were not covered above. On which are you and your mate in agreement?

One other important goal for marriage is that I wish for my husband to be a father to my child someday.

Education for both of us to get our degrees. For me real success requires my getting an M.B.A. There's a potential for difficulties if I don't pass my exams.

19. In exchange for what you want from the relationship, what do you feel you are willing and capable of giving to the relationship that was not covered in your preceding answers.

I am willing to give in any way to our relationship that does not compromise my goals for myself (i.e., obtaining a degree) and does not compromise our relationship (i.e., granting my husband sexual freedom as in an open marriage).

Very hard to answer. I'm not sure what it is that I want from Sara that I am not getting. I feel most capable of giving her my honesty as we examine what goes on between us and in return expect hers. I am unsatisfied with this response but don't now know what to say.

AREA 2. INNER NEEDS AND EXPECTATIONS

The second area to be considered covers those needs and expectations based largely on psychological factors within yourself. This may be the most difficult part of the questionnaire for you to respond to because you have to search within yourself. Try to strip away any coverup or mask that you use to hide your deepest wishes and fears about yourself and your mate. Most of us cannot be fully honest with ourselves about these matters, but do the best you can. Your answers should be a combination of what you wish to *receive* and what you want to *give* in exchange.

Sara	*Charles*

20. How dependent are you or would you like to be on your mate? How independent? Perhaps it varies in different situations; if so, explain or illustrate. Be as explicit as you can. Do you want your spouse to be dependent on you? In which ways yes, in which no?

I am dependent on my husband for a quality of interaction which I feel I cannot get—or have not gotten—outside of marriage. I depend on him to listen to me when I am worried or sad or lonely or very happy and excited and to understand me and *be* with me at those times. Sometimes my mate is very good at being with me and simply accepting my feelings; this helps me to accept feelings and situations more easily myself, especially those feelings which are generally unpleasant. I expect my husband to be dependent on me for the same thing I just described above, a special sort of sharing and giving feedback.

I want Sara to be my mother, to suckle me, protect me. I also want to grow up, take care of her, be strong enough so that my ego needn't be shattered as a result of harsh words between us. I don't like my dependence on Sara, nor does she. I blame her sometimes for these wants of mine. We have gotten farther apart emotionally over the last few months and I don't trust her as much with my feelings and don't ask for much. I rarely really trust what I do get. I see less and less chance that I can grow strong in our relationship to the point where I can really take care of her. I seem to be getting weaker, more dependent, and at the same time less willing to accept and more distrustful of what she has for me. I want her more dependent upon me but I want her to like what I give her. As it is she can be dependent (I guess) but never or rarely seems

Sara   *Charles*

to like how I respond to her wants. She then gets mad at me for not being able or willing to give her what she wants.

21. To what extent do you take action, do what you have to do about things and circumstances, make decisions? To what extent do you leave decisions and actions up to your spouse, and just go along with her/his decisions; or do you exercise veto power but not initiate new ideas or projects yourself? Do you assert your desires and take action that will bring about the fulfillment of your goals?

I feel that in general I am an action-oriented person. I often take the initiative in forming relationships and I am generally aggressive in stating my desires about situations. My husband is generally very unclear as regards decisions involving relationships —in our case whether to get married or not, etc. Somehow I feel his indecision is due to his wanting to make me responsible for the outcome; therefore I often feel paralyzed in making decisions when I cannot get some feeling of positive support from him because I know he will blame me if a decision I make is the wrong one. I am in any case manipulative, overbearing, and a bitch—according to him.

Generally, the path of least resistance drives me on. Sara is radically different—highly organized, always ready to act, antennae always extended for new data on which to base new decisions. She appears more logical and better informed. If we disagree, she generally presents a better argument. She is also very clear as to what she wants, why she wants it, what will happen if I don't go along. I'm not very assertive and my goals are not clear to me.

Sara   *Charles*

22a. Can you take charge and use your authority and decision-making power? Or do you abdicate these to your spouse? Or do you visualize sharing control and decision-making in some equitable division of these powers? If so, ultimately how do you want to distribute these powers between you and your spouse? How does your spouse? Be specific.

In general, I would like for all important decisions to be made by us jointly. However, if my husband refuses to participate, I will in general procrastinate about a decision as long as I can until my anxiety pushes me to make an immediate and definite decision. I think my procrastination comes as a result of my hopes that my husband will decide to discuss making the decision with me, and then we will decide rationally what decision would be best.

No, I don't take charge. Sara decides upon the issues, the options. We usually discuss these matters but they are generally matters Sara addresses to me after having decided what needs to be done. I usually go along. I feel as though I've abdicated too much power.

b. What is the source of your power or your mate's? Does one of you surrender a decision-making role out of fear of losing the other? Is it financial power? Is it due to a stronger and more determined personality, or to rigidity? How do you feel about the distribution of decision-making power between you?

I feel my power comes out of my aggressively going after what I want; I am extremely persistent. I am also clear about my values and rarely do something which is inconsistent with them. My husband's power is now primarily financial, since I am not working and my parents are not well off at all. However, originally (in the first one-and-a-half

My power over Sara. That I might leave her. Sara would be financially hard pressed, might be unable to finish school. Sara's power over me—that she might leave me, that she will stop caring about me, ignore me, that she would leave me and I can't take care of myself. She can out-talk me. Talk is her strongest tactical weapon. I don't like the

Sara

Charles

years of our relationship) his power over me lay in his ability to totally mystify me and to perplex me. This kept me excited, interested, and in utter torment. I left him originally because I decided that I no longer needed to keep myself in the pain and frustration of a noncommitted, totally unpredictable relationship. The first four months of our marriage entailed much give and take, much mutual understanding/caring/openness, and only minor upsets and frustrations. My husband's power then was in the way that he so obviously and openly cared for me. That is the way I like it.

distribution of decision-making power between us.

c. How does having the power to make significant decisions make you feel—powerful, uneasy, guilty, too responsible, eager to assume more power?

It has got its problems—i.e., the possibility of having made an important decision which will adversely affect my spouse. However, if I weren't constantly being labeled manipulative I would feel okay about making important decisions on my own. I feel I am getting to that point anyway, in spite of the incessant recriminations.

More powerful also more uneasy. Scary to take responsibility for self or others. My dearest sense of power is my ability to remove myself from situations. It's my first line of defense. It also seems dangerous to me that all I can do to show my power is to leave particular situations; I get feelings of wanting to leave Sara sometimes. I don't know what the answer is.

Sara   Charles

23a. Are you secure in your knowledge of yourself as a female or male? Do you question at times your "womanliness" or "manliness"? Be specific. Do you want your partner to be very much her or his own gender or do you want her/him to have some of the stereotyped characteristics of your gender? Do you need a partner who will reassure you as an adequate woman or man?

I am a woman and do not doubt nor wish to change my sex. I want a partner who is very assured of his masculinity and who, because of his security, is free to experiment with new life styles, i.e., sharing housework, child-rearing, etc., and who is a soft, warm, accepting person.

I'm not secure in my manliness. I don't feel like a man very much. I am insecure, timid, reclusive, and feel practically powerless. I thought I wanted a spunky woman, not a fading violet type. With Sara (who fills that bill) I seem to be losing more of my sense of being a man.

b. Are you concerned about homosexual feelings, tendencies, or impulses in yourself or in your mate? If so, how does this affect your relationship?

I have homosexual feelings; they are most intense when I am receiving no support at home from my husband; I do not feel threatened by these feelings but rather accept them as normal. I am not aware of this as a problem in my mate.

I am aware of homosexual feelings in both of us. I feel okay about Sara's. I don't feel as comfortable with mine. I think they sometimes get in the way of my relations with men, kind of an infantile thing.

24. What are the (a) physical, (b) personality, and (c) character attributes of the sort of person whom you find sexually attractive? Does your mate have these attributes? If not, what would you like to see in her/him that appears to be lacking? What do you believe you offer to your mate as a sex partner that does or does not evoke a response? Details are important.

a) Tall, fair-complexioned, dark hair and eyes, slender; b) loving,

a) Long, thin, Modigliani-type woman with at least moderate-

Sara	Charles
warm, accepting, stable, calm, self-assured, compulsive (i.e., adheres to a regular routine), nonrigid, intelligent, mature, sensuous, optimistic, life-affirming; c) honest, ethical, actively interested in effecting social change either professionally or privately, non-drug user. My mate has every attribute in *a*. When we first married, my mate also had every attribute in *b*. Now those which I do *not* apply in *b* include life-affirming, optimistic, mature, nonrigid, compulsive, calm, self-assured, stable, accepting, warm. In *c*, those which do not apply include ethical and non-drug user. I was much happier during our early marriage, when Charles treated me differently. *Turns him on*: When I act coy, elusive or when I am very aggressive. *Turns him off*: When I am warm and open, more fully myself, wanting to touch his personhood.	size breasts. I generally get involved with women with dark brown hair, but get excited by women with dark blonde. b) It's hard to find a pattern. Intelligent for sure. Sometimes "cool" people comfortable with themselves, sometimes bitchy type like Sara. Generally women who keep some distance, emotionally. I'm in touch with some masochism on my part, wanting women who will not be loving and caring of me. I also like reckless people, women not so passive, spirited. c) I'm not sure what this (character) is. I can't come up with anything here. Sara fits fairly well in terms of physical features. In personality she seems so sure of herself, and sees things as either black or white, and grasps for power. I don't like these qualities too much, especially the latter. Also Sara appears to me to be phony and pretentious a lot. This is the one quality I see in her that doesn't seem so mixed up in my own psychodynamic fuckups. She puts on airs, wears different masks to try to impress people with her erudition. Sometimes I do things overtly sexual without any buildup: grab Sara's tit or crotch, or put her hands on me. She doesn't like this much; I think she says it makes her feel depersonalized.

Sara   *Charles*

25a. What kind of person do you want to love and have love you in return. Are they the same? Be explicit regarding (a) physical, (b) personality, and (c) character attributes. Ideally, how would this person relate to you and treat you? Compare this ideal with what you actually have with your mate. How do you feel about the comparison?

a) The person I want to have love me is described in 24. The person I want to love is also described in 24. However the person(s) I *typically* fall in love with are much like my father: swing between martyrdom and rage, erratic in their behavior, fairly shallow in their feelings and attachments for other people, and extremely infantile and weak—i.e., they can't be trusted. Ideally my spouse would be warm and loving toward me much of the time (with a spicy dash of romanticism thrown in here and there). He would accept responsibility as a matter of course even when it didn't suit him at the moment because he would be in touch with an overall goal of wanting to share experiences with me, of wanting to be my husband. At the very least I would feel that he cared about me all the time. My husband is not at all the way I described my ideal mate above. However he is warm, loving, even a little romantic, and was somewhat willing to accept responsibility when we married. I look back on our marriage—the

a) Physical features would be the same. But I think I want to love a colder, more hostile person than a person would be to love me. I want to preserve the distance and at the same time maintain the passion by being able to love her strongly without her succumbing to me. Sara, when given the opportunity, wants to get too close and when that happens I have less to offer.

Sara   *Charles*

way he came back and proposed to me after a month's separation —and I realize that he must have known I wouldn't have married him the way he was during our previous two-year relationship. He knew what I wanted in a mate, and when he proposed to me, he fit the bill. Anyway, Charles was wonderful to me and with me for four months after we married. Gradually he became more withdrawn, introverted, depressed, and irrational and that's how he is with me now most of the time. How do I feel about it? I HATE IT.

b. What do you understand by the concept of "love" as applied in your own relationship?

I feel that I definitely love my mate—am interested in his thoughts, feelings, what he is doing. I feel concerned when he is down or unhappy and always wish to help if I can. I care about what happens to him more than anyone else in my life. This does *not* mean I enjoy being around him all the time.

If love is unconditional positive regard, then I think we have it some but not too much. We both want things we don't get (maybe conflicting things) and don't want things we do get. We're not giving one another what we want (as for me, I want contradictory things). I am in touch with my capacity to love and to give to Sara much more than what goes on now.

Sara   Charles

26. How close do you really want to be with your mate, and vice versa?
Can you and your mate expose your thoughts, ideas, feelings, and ac-
tions to each other without being made anxious or uncomfortable, or
afraid of being regarded as stupid, crazy, inadequate, etc.? Do you ex-
pect and possibly receive from your mate a type of censure like that from
a parent for the quality of your thoughts and actions? Do you censure
your mate for hers/his?

Ideally, I want a relationship that is so secure that all thoughts, feelings, fantasies could be expressed, and neither spouse would feel any worries or anxieties about this because the primary understanding would be that each partner had the other person's best interests at heart and each partner was securely committed to the relationship. My husband definitely censures any anger or hostility I express toward him. Any time we are having an argument—if he doesn't feel like listening to my gripe —he simply tells me to shut my fucking mouth. That is one case where I always respect his feelings, and I will shut up immediately. His telling me to shut up is typically his signal to me that he can very easily at this point be pushed over the edge into blind and uncontrollable rage. I indirectly censure my mate when he expresses his desire to leave me or his desire to have sex with other women. I do this by getting depressed, feeling hurt, or maintaining some distance from him.

I fantasize about being able to say anything anytime without fear. As it is I don't. One class of feelings, doubts about marriage, produces intense fear and hatred in Sara, which I'm not surprised by. Other less crucial feelings I don't communicate for fear of being totaled and feeling need to justify myself.

Sara   *Charles*

27. *Do you have a deep fear of being deserted or abandoned? Does such a fear motivate your behavior to any extent? How about your spouse's feelings in this area? Does she/he react the way you would like her/him to in view of your feelings about desertion? Specify.*

Yes. I'm not sure how much it motivates my behavior anymore because when I am feeling scared about that now, I try to take care of these feelings by myself. Also I sometimes feel it would be much better for Charles to leave me instead of 1) torturing both of us by being here when he wants to leave or 2) threatening to leave me. Whenever I express (I never do this now) my fears to my husband about his leaving me, he gets very cold and withholds from me completely. He wants to leave me.

As I mentioned earlier, I see my power over Sara in my ability to terminate our relationship. Avoidance and escape are popular with me. I am aware that in the past I might have, short of doing this myself, placed people (e.g., Sara) in a position which nearly forces them to leave. What comes to mind is that I have already been abandoned. Thus fear is replaced by regret. Sara plays out this craziness pretty well. She tends to leave me.

28. *Do you have a great need to feel that your mate "belongs" to you and you to her/him? Does your mate feel possessive toward you? How do you regard the issue of mates belonging to one another? Does it apply or not apply to men as well as to women?*

No one belongs to me and I belong to no one. I choose every day to be with people I care about, and I can only hope they will continue to choose to be with me.

I don't feel "possessiveness" to be a particularly crucial problem for Sara and me. (Maybe that makes it so!?) I don't think either of us feels particularly possessive of one another.

29a. *Do you try to solve questions and problems between you and your mate by talking them through; or do you and your mate go ahead and act on your own ideas?*

I try talking things through; my husband is incapable of rational

At present communication gets broken down very easily when

Sara	*Charles*

Sara

discussion with me.

Charles

we talk things out. Lately we've gotten so distant that problems don't often get talked about. Rarely a meeting of the minds.

b. Can you and your mate express love, anger, conflict, worry, concern, etc., to one another? Or are you loath to or afraid to?

I am very afraid to tell Charles anything. Often if I tell him I love him, he pushes me away, ignores me. If I express any amount of anger toward him, he can always become more angry than I am. He shows this by shouting loudly, slamming things down, curling his lip and leaving the room, sleeping on the sofa bed. All of this is to tell me, "How dare you get angry with me! You're not a good mother after all."

I have become increasingly afraid to express these emotions to Sara. I have not said things that were on my mind for fear that they would make Sara angry and we would get into a fight, in which I never seem to be able to get my position respected.

c. Do you anticipate difficulty because of previous experience with your mate, or is it your usual style to react in this way to a meaningful person of the opposite gender? That is, is it a general pattern or a specific one between you and your mate?

Specific one to me and my husband.

I suppose it's to a large extent a general problem, though Sara in particular is very intelligent and perceptive, and has wanted much from our relationship. She tends to "call my hand," question my behavior and attitudes more than women I've known in the past.

Sara	*Charles*

d. In what ways do you and your mate communicate important ideas and feelings to each other?

I will state that I want to talk to him about something and if I get his okay, I will proceed. Sometimes I will touch him as I talk (I did this often in the past but much less now). My mate communicates to me almost by accident—if I happen to ask the right question or in some cases I overhear what he is telling others.	We tell one another.

e. Are the style, amount, and effectiveness of communication between you and your mate in accord with your desires, or is it antithetical to them and something you really wish to change? If so, what would be the ideal level of communication?

Antithetical. Ideal would be free-flow, honest.	Style, amount okay—effectiveness is not. I can't make my position and feelings clear to Sara. I would like to stop being so afraid of her reactions to what I might say.

f. Do you find it more difficult to talk intelligently and with clarity to your mate than to others? Or she/he with you? Try to explain.

I don't think this is a problem.	I find it almost impossible to talk with intelligence and clarity to anyone since we left home. Sara talks with intelligence and clarity to me much more than I do to her.

Sara	Charles

g. Do you find your mate does not "listen" to you, i.e., does not get what you really mean and does not understand the kind of response you want? Or does she/he complain about you? Try to explain.

My mate listens only until I say something which makes him angry. Oddly, many of the things he takes offense at were never intended to hurt. His reactions to the most neutral statements I might make are totally unpredictable. If the content doesn't irritate him, then he dislikes the way I said it (my tone of voice, choice of words).

She's a pretty good listener. Sometimes her questions in response to my talk seem a bit destructive, she seems sometimes to be trapping me inside broad generalizations. Complain? Yes, she sometimes complains, and so do I.

30a. Do you or your partner frequently respond with anxiety to seemingly small problems? Elaborate on what sets it off for each of you (e.g., when I see the checking account is low I get very nervous).

I respond with high anxiety to a messy house or to my husband's neglecting to do something which I have specifically asked him to do on those occasions when I have to be at school.

A lot of times I'll have a chip on my shoulder, be angry at Sara in which case I tend to get mad over little things, especially if I can blame her.

b. Rate yourself on how much anxiety you generally have and then rate your mate. Rating scale: No anxiety equals 1; great anxiety equals 5. Put parentheses around the number that best expresses the level of anxiety.

	None		Moderate		Great
Self	1	2	(3)	4	5
Mate	1	2	3	(4)	5

	None		Moderate		Great
Self	1	2	3	4	(5)
Mate	1	2	(3)	4	5

c. How would you like your mate to deal with your anxiety in order to make you feel better?

BE CALM AND REASONABLE

1. Not to try to take care of me, mother me.

Sara	Charles

Charles
2. Respect my feelings without patronizing or sympathizing.
3. Not get angry with me for "dragging her down" but instead do what she needs to do for herself.

d. How do you deal with your mate's anxiety? How does her/his anxiety affect your emotional state?

Sara

Charles' anxiety affects me in that I feel like responding to it in a helpful way.

Charles

I'm generally pretty responsive when her anxiety doesn't directly involve me. Unfortunately it usually does. Much of the time I leave her alone. Get her to talk about it. Comfort her, touch her.

31a. Can you accept yourself and your mate as you are today? Enlarge on this.

Sara

I can accept myself. I do not accept my mate when he is irrational or violent or doubting.

Charles

I can't accept myself as I am today. I realize that I can be a real bastard to live with, that my emotional vacillations can and do severely undercut our relationship. I hate the untenable position that with nearly full knowledge I placed myself in (i.e., total financial dependence upon parents). I'm not fulfilled or fulfilling. Surprisingly when I reflect on it, I find that I can accept Sara pretty much as she is today.

b. Can you love your mate, defining love to be as much concerned for the other person as you are for yourself (a state that actually is rarely achieved but often is in part)?

Sara

I think I have felt much this way toward my husband since we

Charles

Yes.

Sara	Charles

have married—until recently. I am now finding that in many cases, if I am to take care of myself I must not allow myself to be concerned for him. I must assume that he can take care of himself. The history of this is that I spent our first two years having negligible regard for my own welfare—at one point tried suicide—and worrying about and caring for him totally. Charles was the only one of us who was important.

c. Do you get that extra special sexual excitement and "turn on" from your mate and vice versa? How has this changed or fluctuated since early in your relationship?

At times I can. In order for this to happen, I must feel very safe, and I rarely feel safe with Charles anymore.

Not very often is my sexual excitement with Sara extra special. Sexual situations which are dark and mysterious, maybe taboo, tend to really turn me on. I remember an expression I used which bothered Sara. I would "steal a kiss"—this hasn't changed much over the course of our relationship.

AREA 3. CAUSES OF DISHARMONY IN THE RELATIONSHIP

The following are the areas that are most commonly cited as causes of friction between mates. They may be considered as external foci of possible disharmony.

Many of the areas may not cause you and your mate any problems. The questions are intended as guides to orient you to various possibilities and are not a complete listing. Add any others that you know are significant for your relationship.

Sara   *Charles*

32. Money. Do you (or your mate) regard money as power? Do you use money against each other? Who is expected to make what percentage of it? How are decisions made regarding expenditures and investments? Who is the bookkeeper? Is there financial independence of both mates? Is either on an allowance from the other? How do you feel about these questions and what do you want?

My mate and I both regard money as power. At present he has all the resources and at times he has definitely used it against me. I have been the bookkeeper (he hates math and doesn't care whether books are kept or not). I did the work for our income tax this year but I really do not care whether the books are kept or not.

We haven't in the past. Due to the really horrible financial situation we're in (where my parents are supporting us), plus marital unhappiness, I feel that it is being used more like that. I wonder if *one* of the reasons Sara stays with me is the fact that she's getting to go to graduate school via my parents' money. There's no allowance business, but I think I exercise more control over money as a result of its coming from my parents.

33. Child rearing. Are there differences in philosophy and methods between you and your mate? If so, what significance do these have for you? As a family are you and your mate oriented primarily toward the children, toward the adults, or toward an equal and democratic esprit de corps? Or any others?

I do not know my mate's philosophy on child rearing.

No essential difference in philosophy.

34. Children. Is any child in your family used as a symbol or substitute for you or your mate? Are you or your mate unusually loving or hateful toward any child? If so, why? Which children identify with which parent, and vice versa?

Does not apply.

I imagine I might be jealous of a child.

| *Sara* | *Charles* |

35. Sex

a. Is your mate a suitable sex partner for you by your standards, and vice versa? What do you like and not like as far as sex with your mate is concerned? Do you "turn each other on" sexually? Are there any dysfunctions on your part or your partner's? Ideally what do you want your sex partner to be like? Sex play? Responsiveness of partner? Frequency, etc.?

My mate is a sexual athlete and is very aware of his prowess in bed. He is also very cold. For example, he rarely talks to me at all; he is rarely tender and in three years he has never said my name while we were in bed. The minute we start to have sex, I become an object to him. I feel that he is "working out" on me; I also feel that he would rather be working out on someone else most of the time. He has told me repeatedly in the past that my breasts are too small and my hips too large. His suggestions are that I take birth control pills to improve the former and exercise to diminish the latter. I feel totally dehumanized.	Yes, she is pretty much, though for her sex is more of a communicative act where she wants to be closer after sex than I. Sex for me is powerfully scary and sometimes I feel almost hypnotized and detached in it. I would like her to turn me on more. She is generally pretty passive in sex. No dysfunctions. I would probably feel more comfortable if she had more of a sex for sex's sake rather than a sex for love's sake attitude. I would like more sex play, less love play. I would like her to be more responsive. Frequency maybe three times a week.

b. Can you express your wishes and fantasies to your mate and vice versa? Do you act some of them out together?

I have done this twice. Both times it was hard for me to do with him—although I have done this with other partners—and both times he took me seriously. I won't do it again for a while.	I can, but I get a lot of fear and disapproval from Sara. She can and does to me, apparently comfortably, except that she's afraid I'll want to realize them.

Sara	*Charles*

c. Are there questions of sexual fidelity that concern you and your spouse? What is the understanding you have regarding monogamy, other sexual relationships, shared sexual experiences with others, etc.?

My husband would prefer shared sexual experiences with others. I want traditional monogamy. I feel that monogamy, far from being a drag, can be a highly satisfying, creative state of affairs. I consider my sexual participation with another as having a special and particular meaning which, in marriage, I wish to communicate only to my husband.

I trust Sara's fidelity. I don't think that she trusts me. We understand that Sara insists upon monogamy and that I (with mixed emotions) would like to include other people at least once in our sex lives.

36. *Families of origin. How do you both feel about wanting to continue close relationships with your original families? Did you marry in order, at least in part, to get into your spouse's family? Are you jealous of her/ his close relationship or dependency on her/his mother or father? Do you argue about visiting parents, etc.? If families of origin cause problems for you (e.g., "in-law trouble," etc.), what do you think the difficulty is? Specify.*

The only in-law trouble we have is that Charles turns me into his mother and responds to me as if I were dangerous and cruel.

Neither of us wants particularly close relationships with our families. I didn't (I don't think Sara did either) marry to enter my mate's family. I am sometimes jealous of her father, compare myself unfavorably with him, as I am sure Sara does too.

37. *Friends.*
   a. Can you accept each other's friends?

I have no strong negative feelings about any of his friends. In fact most of them are also my friends.

Yes.

Sara	*Charles*

b. Should each of you have friends you see alone? Same sex? Opposite sex?

Yes—same and opposite sex.	Yes, if we want to.

38. Intelligence, etc.

a. Do you believe your mate is smart enough, intuitive enough, well spoken enough, cultured enough for you, and vice versa? Do any of these areas create problems between you?

No problems.	These qualities are dwindling in me. Sara now appears to be smarter, more intuitive, etc. I am jealous of this in her, to some extent seek to blame her, and often feel competitive with her.

b. Do you think you will grow and develop in a way that will allow you to continue to be interesting to one another? Or is this area not significant for you?

No problems that I can foresee.	The gulf seems to be increasing between us and it appears to be an increasing problem.

39. Interests. What interests do you and your mate share? How important is it to you both to have similar or different interests? Does one always feel she/he can't get into an activity without the other either participating or taking over? Do you or your mate have a need to include or exclude the other? What's involved if you do?

I have a need to include Charles in most (but not all) of my interests. I don't think it matters to him whether I am included or not in what he does. We share interests in movies, traveling, music (especially jazz), books, cats, plants, and *sometimes* he shares my interest in cooking. In regard to the latter, he often tries	Interest in people, music, books, general liberal arts stuff. I don't think that our particular interests should be dependent upon the other's participation. I don't think either of us does much taking over. No particular need to include or exclude.

Sara	*Charles*

to take over—criticizes and complains about what I'm doing. Reminds me of his father, who likes to say that his wife (Charles' mother) is trying to poison him.

40. Roles. This is an important question, particularly in these days of changing values about male and female roles in the home and at work. What roles, tasks, and responsibilities do you want for yourself and for your mate? Are these gender determined or determined in another way? Be specific. Try to discuss fully how this works out for you in regard to household chores, money, social arrangements, child care, and other areas important to you.

Sara	*Charles*
I want Charles's cooperation and *initiative* and participation in sharing household chores, pet care, planning of activities. As for money, he is afraid that every woman is out to get his money (his parents told him this). I don't know how this can be worked out; he is very withholding.	I *think* that our student roles, responsibilities, etc., should be shared. Sometimes, though, I like Sara to do more "feminine" things for me as a kind of symbol that she cares for me (e.g., bake me a cake). When I want to show my caring for Sara I'll often do something in a more traditionally masculine role (take her out, etc.). I feel comfortable with that. It works out pretty well.

41. Energy level, intensity, absorption.

   a. Are you dependent upon or irritated by your spouse's higher or lower energy level?

Sara	*Charles*
I am irritated by my spouse's lower energy level.	No.

Sara	*Charles*

b. Are you bothered by her/his intensity and absorption in matters that might exclude you?

Not so long as his absorption is not keeping him oblivious to the need to do things at home when I'm not there.	Occasionally, but it is not a particular problem.

c. Do you complement each other well in the above areas and utilize each other's qualities in a positive way? Or do these areas bug and irritate you ("His intensity over petty things drives me up the wall")?

I don't know. I would like for our skills and interests to be complementary.	Sara's compulsivity bothers me. I feel as though we are running a race and I must keep up.

42. Criticism. Do you or your partner try to make each other "perfect"? How well can you give and take criticism? Is it motivated by constructive objectives, or by anxiety, power struggles, or manipulation? Is it done in a constructive, acceptable way or does it put down or destroy? Do either of you use psychological concepts as a weapon?

There is no way for me to constructively criticize Charles; he becomes inflamed and defensive and feels blamed and put down almost every time I say *anything* to him personally. Sometimes I get so frustrated with his non-responsiveness, I will tell him that I think he's acting crazy—not to put him down but to say, "Hey, look, I think you're bent out of shape, inappropriate to the situation, blind to what I said." I often want to shout, "Get hold of yourself!" If Charles starts to feel very anxious, he will not hesitate to shut me up.	Hard to say. Sara has an ideal picture of "husband" which I think she wants me to reflect. She may have given this up by now. I don't take criticism well at all these days, always feel on the defensive. Most of the time I feel put down. This, of course, may be my projection. Sara occasionally tells me I'm crazy, which pisses me off. I don't know about manipulation. Sometimes I feel I'm being manipulated. I'm aware that I want more power with her and want to take some of hers. Thus I belittle more than I should.

Sara	Charles

43. *Leisure time. Are there conflicts over how, where, when, and with whom to spend your time? What part may be spent in separate activity? Is a desire for separate activity regarded as showing lack of love? Cultural interests as well as needs for particular types of friends are important considerations. What is involved in these areas for you and your spouse? Are these areas over which you disagree? Specify.*

Sara	Charles
This is not a problem.	We have few conflicts here. We both seem to be fairly comfortable engaging in activities apart from one another, without feeling unloved. But most of our lives are spent very close to one another.

44. *Life style. Do both of you have essentially the same life style? If it varies, specify. If not similar, can you work out a compromise? Are you casual or formal; planner or nonplanner; esoteric or prosaic; avant-garde or conservative; seashore or mountains; stay put or travel; intellectual or emotional; open or closed to new ideas? What do clothes mean to you? What is important in home decoration styles, in cars, books, etc.? Discuss similarities and differences and how you deal with them.*

Sara	Charles
Our life styles are similar; we like to do most of the same things for entertainment, and we both have aspirations in our work. We agree on most political issues. Our differences are that I am a planner, an extrovert, an entertainer. I am physically affectionate and seek meaning through relationships with other people. My husband is a nonplanner, an introvert, and seeks the periphery of social situations. He is quiet, restrained, and seeks meaning through his own suffering and	Sara is an organizer, highly methodical, into routines much more than I. I am not nearly so organized, methodical, etc. She likes a clean, tidy apartment. I don't care about that nearly so much. We work out compromises for shared household responsibility which work fairly well but eventually break down to be later reinstated.

Sara   Charles

through metaphysical ideas. I am
afraid of being alone; he is afraid
of not being alone. I am active,
he is passive.

45. What (if any) image do you want to maintain before the world regarding yourself, your mate, and the relationship? Are there myths that are important to maintain (the perfect couple, the swinging couple, etc.)?

If we have a good relationship, it will show. I am not interested in myths.

I don't want to give the appearance that either of us drags the other down. I'm sure that Sara and many of her friends feel I do drag her down. I'm less concerned with the image, though, than the fact.

46. And the last question

a. What would you be willing to do, give up, or change in yourself in order to maintain a continuing relationship with your partner?

I don't know how to answer this question. I honestly believe that the only way that a woman can have a relationship with Charles is to be away, absent. This is because Charles' most intense relationships are those with women he cannot have except in fantasy.

To try to be more patient, more understanding, more reasonable, to assume with less of a begrudging attitude my share of household responsibilities. I will also be willing to give up what threads of dependence on my parents I still have.

b. What do you believe she/he would do to keep you as a partner? Review what you have written and, wherever appropriate, be sure you have included what you would give or do in exchange for what your partner would give or do for you.

I don't believe he wants me as a partner in spite of anything he might say to the contrary during therapy. From what I can tell, my husband is in great emo-

Sara has told me that she would do anything short of 1) polygamous sex; 2) jeopardizing her career; 3) making her less than a whole human being. I don't

Sara

tional pain all the time. His pain is intensified when a woman gets close. I think he would like to find some way to resolve this pain but he has so far been unable to do this—in therapy, alone, or in his relationship with women. Until he can find a way to take care of his pain, I do not see that he has any room for anyone else. I look at his marrying me as a desire to be touched and to touch, but eventually the old problems, fears, and desires came back, and I think he hates me because my presence intensifies these feelings. I have tried everything I can think of to help him—from being very close, very supportive and nurturant, to being very distant and leaving him totally alone. When I am close, he pushes me away. When I am distant, he's angry that I've deserted him. I am tired of getting nothing from him but anger and hatred, and I am tired of his rejection of every moment of closeness that I offer him. From what I have written on this questionnaire I think you can see that I value and enjoy warmth above everything else in a marriage. I did not marry Charles for his money; with it or without it I would have married him. Now I find I am very dependent on it since I have no other

Charles

know how she-we would operationalize this. But I believe what she has said.

One of my needs that directly involves Sara is in severing as much as possible financial dependence upon my parents. It has gotten so bad that Sara, after one of our big fights (which began with my not knowing whether I wanted to be married), dropped out of school to get a job to save money to leave me. My mother found out and sent Sara a check for the amount of money Sara had staked in our moving and entering graduate school. Sara, more financially secure and less dependent upon me, immediately returned to school. My mother (almost contradictorily) might have averted our breakup, but I don't like her having that kind of power.

Sara   *Charles*

means of support. It is of great importance to me that I stay here; I feel I started to grow, change, become more myself almost from the moment we arrived. I feel good about it, and I want to experience more growth. To go back home would be unmitigated hell.

I also want to say that I hate our constant fighting, bickering. I always feel that if a problem comes up, we should be able to discuss it, analyze it, and decide how we can overcome it together. I do not feel that I want to use Charles and twist him for my own purposes. I feel I have a high respect for where he is, for his feelings, his wishes, and I want to take care of his needs whatever they are. I want him to utilize my resources.

I am hurt and bewildered by his recriminations and misinterpretations of almost everything I say or do. He doesn't trust me, he withdraws, and withholds from me. I can take his anger, rage, fear—anything—except this one major way he has of relating to me—avoidance. It is very hard for me to remain warm, soft, honest, and open with him when he is telling me he wants to leave, have sex with other people, or being utterly irrational—*yet I think this is what he wants from*

Sara   *Charles*

me. I don't want to have this
type of childish behavior from a
husband. With him I want something entirely different. I am
selfish.

DISCUSSION

My assessment of their profile was that Sara was an equal (with
parental secondary) partner and Charles a parallel (with childlike
secondary) partner. They described their own interactional dynamics well. The equal-parallel combination did not work well,
nor did Charles' childlike adaptation when he would abdicate his
adulthood and try, often with success, to maneuver Sara into being
parental. She then became angry and hurt; he would feel injured in
turn. His judgments of himself were as harsh as hers and he then
became depressed. His depression and withdrawal would then compound the downhill escalation. At this point the prognosis for their
marriage was poor.

These lengthy contracts indicate how much usable material can
rapidly be made available for therapeutic work, and how much
couples themselves can learn about their relationship by the work of
preparing their contracts.

The Grays wanted to help themselves and to salvage their marriage
if they could because there were genuine feelings of love between
them. After a little exploration it was clear that etiologically remote
factors, especially for Charles, would have to be dealt with if any
positive movement were to take place in the relationship. I had confronted them with elements of their contracts and quickly realized
that a dyadic approach would not be productive at this time. Charles
was in too much conflict and reacted to Sara too transferentially.
Her anxiety and defensiveness might be dealt with satisfactorily but
not in therapy with Charles. I therefore recommended an individual
therapist for Charles. Sara said she wanted individual therapy too
and that she would seek a woman therapist. I concurred with her
decision.

I sent the Grays a follow-up letter a year after referral for individual therapy. Sara Gray responded. She stated that a week after my referral she had started analysis with a woman therapist, and Charles with another, male therapist. She considered leaving Charles but did not; she then thought she might have a sexual relationship and fantasized a great deal about it, trying to convince herself she did not love Charles. Several men approached her in this period—"I guess that I was so needy for male attention and companionship (and sex) that it was written all over me." After several luncheon and drink "dates" she realized that she wanted Charles "and I finally gave the whole thing up (without ever having even kissed anyone!)."

Six months after I had last seen them, Charles had returned from an analytic session "and he looked at me and started to talk . . . I could hardly believe *he* initiated it." Since then they had had some downs but it had been mostly up. Sara expressed pleasure at their current situation and gratitude to me and to the other therapists. My letter had caused her to re-evaluate their situation and she was acutely aware of how far they had come in the past year.

In some instances, individual therapy is an appropriate modality for changing the marital system. At some future time Sara and Charles may turn again to conjoint therapy.

12

General Applications and Education for Marriage

IN THIS VOLUME THE CONTRACT CONCEPT has been focused on the marital pair and their dyadic system, as well as on the use of these formulations in treatment. The same contractual and therapeutic principles have validity for any situation that involves two committed people, or even an individual and an organization.

Within families there are unspoken contracts between parents and children or a parent and a child, and between generations and other family subgroupings. I have often used the contract concept in family therapy by dealing with essential contractual parameters during therapy sessions. On some occasions, especially when the children are adolescents, I have asked parents and children to write out contracts. The terms of these contracts deal not only with behavior, family rules, duties and responsibilities, but also with items from category 2, such as closeness-distance, power and authority, sexuality, life styles, defenses, and so on. At the appropriate time any parameter may be dealt with openly in the family.

I have also used the contract concept to good advantage with business partners. One situation that worked out particularly well was that of two business partners, each with a reasonably good marriage, whose strong negative reactions to each other were expressed in frustration and disappointment. It became apparent that each wanted to be dependent on the other—in essence they were two childlike partners in search of a parent. This was clarified and worked through, with emphasis on each partner's desire to maneuver the other into a fatherlike role and each one's father transferential feelings toward the other.

The concepts of this volume can be fruitfully adapted and applied to the relationship between an individual and an organization. People tend to carry over family expectations to the other important areas of their lives. Employers, schools, political groups, and many other entities are recipients of these transferential expectations.

For centuries political leaders have been father or mother images and have carefully groomed themselves to be experienced as such by the population. Such "contractual" arrangements work both ways, but often with different contracts for each of the two parties. Labor unions have often found it more difficult to win workers' rights from paternalistic (good father) companies than from the more obviously exploitive ones. Sports coaches exploit the "family" or team concept to its fullest, as do most businesses. Schools and colleges, hospitals, and other institutions often have "contractual" arrangements with the individuals involved with them that go far beyond whatever written or spoken agreements actually exist. Such contracts also vary for staff members and consumers. These unspoken or implied terms are often different for the two concerned parties, which leads to a great deal of difficulty and misunderstanding, just as we have observed with couples.

Sometimes there is a conscious use of unwritten contractual terms for exploitive reasons. In other instances both contracting parties have unrealistic or mistaken expectations. The reader will think of numerous other areas where the contract concept may be useful. In a marriage there is a greater potential for equality than in more obviously unequal relationships such as employer-employee, hospital-patient, school-student, and so on. It is useful to inspect one's own unspoken contracts with all individuals and institutions. Certainly the therapist-patient contract is a most important one for the professional and the patient or client.

EDUCATION AND PREVENTION

I hope that eventually the most important application will be in education and prevention. Some of this work is now being done in the area of sex education, but that is only one part of the whole.

There is much to be done on the therapeutic front—but ultimately prevention of misery is more constructive than trying to repair the damage. Marital therapy is primary prevention in relation to family life because it so deeply affects the children of the marriage, but there is a broader possibility for prevention at several points in the individual and marital life cycles.

Young people now are simply not taught what is truly involved in an intimate person-to-person relationship, whether it is a marriage or a living-together arrangement. They are or have recently been children in their parents' home. Their parents' marriage may or may not be a salutary model; even when it is, the children have rarely had an opportunity to discuss or think about the purpose and meaning of a dyadic relationship and its truly important parameters. What is absorbed nonverbally is of the greatest import but it is not necessarily the most constructive for the child.

Premarital counseling, as most commonly practiced, is often not an effective approach except when specific problems have emerged in the courting period for which the couple is ready to seek help. The vast majority of people who already have decided to marry or live together do not want, at that point, to examine and question their own or their partner's feelings and motivations, or how the two of them interact together. They tend to deny the sound of any subliminal warning bells that ring. Under the pressure of their own urgency to marry, the fear that an opportunity will be lost, the reassurances of parents and friends that everyone "gets the jitters," the *wanting* to be in love, plus the societal compulsion to complete marriage plans once they are in motion ("I can't disappoint Mom and Dad now," "the guests are invited," etc.), the couple are on a roller coaster they can't stop. One or both individuals are frequently too fearful to closely examine themselves and their interrelationship. At that time they are afraid to examine behavior that ordinarily would be questionable, or to confront their own misgivings. Most individuals or couples do not at such times have access to a person or group with whom misgivings or the underlying sources of such questions could be discussed from a helpful, nonpartisan viewpoint.

The clergy, in their traditional role in premarital counseling, have attempted, with varying degrees of success, to reinforce humanistic values and the importance of the two betrothed people to each other. The clergyman reminds the couple of their new duties and responsibilities to God and to themselves. In many churches, when such premarital religious counseling is utilized by the couple, it is brief and pro forma. Many clergymen feel the need for more effective approaches, as do family life educators, marriage guidance counselors, and related professionals.

Somehow, in all our vast system of educational, religious, and social institutions, there is no place for young people to learn about and explore their own ideas about what they want and expect from love, from marriage, from sex, from intimacy; nor do they feel and think through what they really want and *do not want* from a mate, and what they will give in exchange. They have no opportunity to learn about what responsibilities they will have (or want) and how the marital system may, in turn, affect them individually. They are not given the means with which to explore transferentially determined perceptions and expectations, questions and unsureness about themselves, the role of genuine complementarity between self and mate, value differences, methods for discussing, fighting, determining basic sources of conflict, and working toward resolutions.

I should like to see us move toward a broad educational program of preparation for living together and marriage that would begin with the first year of high school. The concepts of this book might be among the sources for such a program. Marriage has grown like Topsy; now that it is changing so rapidly, it has become imperative that we try a new kind of educational program, one that would deal realistically with what is involved when two people make a commitment to each other. Young people would become conscious of their contractual demands and of their biological and intrapsychic needs. They would be encouraged to think about and discuss with one another in classes or groups their feelings and reactions in past and present relationships and what they hope for in future ones. They would become aware of what being "in love" means in terms of oneself and one's mate, of closeness, intimacy, and sharing, and of their individual balance between commitment and integrity of self.

I do not wish to attempt to set forth a curriculum for such a program, but rather to establish that a new kind of education-discussion program is urgently needed within the school system for our youth.

Any point in a couple's life cycle that is approaching change or at which change has recently occurred provides another ready opportunity for prophylactic intervention. Here the overall problem is how to get couples to perceive their need for help and realize that others face similar situations. Once we stimulate interest in the need for such help, then as professionals we must be prepared to provide or to help develop the programs that are needed by the target population.

Some new phases for intervention, in addition to the usual "normal" ones in the marital cycle, have evolved as a result of changes in society. Two of these are related to the mobility and rootlessness of many contemporary families. When adults and children are uprooted, it makes little difference whether they travel from the East Coast to the West Coast or from the "old neighborhood" to a new housing development a mile away—similar problems and alienating effects take place. Separation and divorce provide another area for counseling of adults and children. The increasing divorce rate, in turn, leads to the problems inherent in the single-parent family and to the problems of remarriage, with or without children. Counseling should be available not only for the concerned adults but for the children too.

The health care system offers many ways to reach people at crucial points in their marital cycle. Clinics that deal with illnesses of the older population—cardiac disease and hypertension, arthritis, cancer and others—provide a point of entry at the time when the couple, in addition to adjustments demanded by the aging process, are past the age of having children at home and have to adapt to a new kind of interdependence.

A time of particular importance at which prophylactic entry can be made via the health care system is when young couples are preparing for their first child. It is important for them to examine their contracts and marital system and prepare for the inclusion of the yet unborn child into their system. For many of them, it will be very helpful to think, talk and feel through the problems that emerge. To some extent this is done in terms of the physical aspects of prenatal and neonatal care, with the husband often being included as much as possible. This, of course, helps with the emotional aspects, too. But the vast majority of young couples are not prepared for the emotional stress that is entailed in shifting from a dyadic to a triadic system.

We now have data from research sources, in addition to clinical experience with the contract concept, to formulate conceptual approaches for undertaking a preventive and educational program that has promise of being constructive.

Appendix 1. Reminder List for Marriage Contract of Each Partner

THE REMINDER LIST that follows outlines the more common subjects covered in marriage contracts. The subjects fall into three general categories as described below. The reminder list may be used by the therapist to remind him or her of pertinent areas to be covered. It may also be given to the couple to fill out at home. The worksheet, a page of which is included here, can readily be duplicated. When it is used, six copies of the worksheet may be given to each couple so each partner has one for each of the three categories.

"Marriage Contract" is a misnomer as the term is used here because we are not referring to formal contracts. These are not legally written contracts or agreements that both mates write out and subscribe to openly. You each have your own "contract" that probably differs from the other. Do not be surprised if your contract is inconsistent because you simultaneously may have strong contradictory wishes or needs. For example, you may have the desire to be independent and yet at the same time also require your spouse's approval of your actions. Contradictions are usual for most of us.

Each "contract" has three levels of awareness:

1. *Verbalized*—these are discussed with each other, although not always heard by the receiver.
2. *Conscious but not verbalized*—the parts of your contract that you are aware of but do not verbalize to your spouse because you fear his/her anger, disapproval, or you feel embarrassed, etc.

3. *Beyond awareness or unconscious*—aspects that are beyond your usual awareness. You may have an idea of what some of these are. They are often felt as a warning light in your head or a fleeting feeling of concern that gets pushed away. Do the best with these you can.

Each person acts as if the other knew the terms of the contract (which were never really agreed upon) and feels angered, hurt, betrayed, etc., when they believe the spouse did not fulfill his/her part of the contract. In each area note down where you believe your spouse failed in his/her part of the bargain. Do not worry about being fair. How do you *really feel* about his behavior.

Contractual terms, i.e., desires, expectations and what you are *willing to give* as well as want from marriage and your mate, fall into three general categories. This reminder list consists of these three categories. Following under each are listed several common areas that are sources of marital and personal trouble. Some you may have thought of before, others not.

INSTRUCTIONS FOR REMINDER LIST FOR MARRIAGE CONTRACT

The following is a guide to help you write out *your* marriage contract. Do not compare with your spouse until *after* you both have completed your own.

1. Use the worksheets provided. Use as many sheets as you need. If you run out make some extra for yourself. Start each category on a new sheet.
2. Respond to all areas that are meaningful to you. Skip the others.
3. Include those areas where you feel your spouse did not keep his/her part of the bargain. Be specific. State how you feel about it.
4. Answer in terms of today. If something is a sore point from the past indicate this.
5. Make your answers as long or as short as you wish but if they are to be useful they must convey your feelings, not just "Yes" or "No."
6. Write out answers (type if possible) clearly on the worksheets. Use the same numbers for the category and item numbers such as 1.3; 2.5; etc.
7. Do not try to do all three categories at one time. One at a sitting is recommended.

1. CATEGORIES BASED ON EXPECTATIONS OF MARRIAGE

Each partner marries for their own purposes and goals in relation to our institution called marriage. The marital system itself generates other purposes of which the individuals may have originally been unaware. Keep in mind that this list is meant only to remind you to consider these possibilities. Others may be important for you, if so put them in.

Among the most common expectations (a person may have several) of marriages are:

1. For a mate who will be loyal, devoted, loving and exclusive.
2. To provide constant support against the rest of the world.
3. Insurance against loneliness.
4. Marriage is a goal in itself rather than a beginning.
5. Panacea against chaos and strife in life.
6. A relationship that must last "until death do us part."
7. To provide sanctioned and readily available sex.
8. To create a family.
9. Persons aside from the spouse who may be included with you in your new family: children, parents, friends, etc.
10. To marry a family rather than just a mate.
11. To have my own home-refuge from the world.
12. To have a respectable position and status in society.
13. To be an economic unit, a social unit.
14. To be an umbrella image to inspire you to work, build, accumulate.
15. To serve as a respectable cover for aggressive drives (everything I do is only for my family, not for me).
16. Others, list.
17. Have you included those areas where you feel your mate let you down?—Please do so and add how you feel.
18. Please write out a summary of what you *want* from your marriage that relates to the above areas and what *in exchange* you will give.

2. CATEGORIES BASED ON PSYCHOLOGICAL AND BIOLOGICAL NEEDS

These areas are determined in large part by psychological and biological factors rather than by the marital system as such. They arise largely from within the person. The needs and desires germinated by these factors often are beyond the individual's awareness. Yet you do have some ideas about them. Among these major areas that are common sources of trouble are:

1. Independence-dependence—this has to do with feelings. The general conduct of yourself in relation to your mate. Do you set the style and pattern for yourself?

2. Activity-passivity—this has to do with initiative and action.

3. Closeness-distance—how much closeness and intimacy do you really want? Your mate? How much do you want to include each other in what you think and do? How does either pull away when you want or feel you have to? Are you aware of putting distance between you?

4. Power—its use, abuse and abdication. Who controls what? How do you feel about who is in charge? Are you competitive with your spouse?

5. Submission and domination—who submits, who dominates in the relationship? Is there an equal give and take of leadership in the relationship?

6. Abandonment and loneliness fears.

7. Possession and control of spouse or vice-versa.

8. Level of anxiety—what triggers it and what are your main coping or defensive patterns to reduce anxiety. Answer for self and mate.

9. How do you feel about yourself as a man or woman?

10. Physical and personality characteristics desired or required in your mate—how does he/she measure up? Does he/she turn you on? If not, what is lacking? Do you like his/her attitudes about sex? How do they compare to your own? Are there any sexual problems?

11. Ability to love and to accept yourself and your mate. Do you?

12. How do you and your mate approach problems—are your styles the same or different? Can you accept and appreciate the differences or are they cause for trouble?

13. Have you included those areas where you feel your mate let you down or which cause trouble? Be specific.

14. Other areas not mentioned.

15. Please write out a summary of what you want from your mate that relates to the above areas and what *in exchange* you will *give.*

3. CATEGORIES THAT ARE DERIVATIVE OR THE EXTERNALIZED FOCI OF OTHER PROBLEMS

These externalized foci usually are the apparent cause of marital trouble, but in reality they are the symptoms of something wrong in an area of category 1 or 2. These most common problem areas and stimuli of marital arguments are:

1. Communication—is there openness and clarity in the sending as well as the receiving? Can you talk and listen to each other?
2. Intellectual differences between you and your spouse.
3. Energy level—intensity, absorption, enthusiasm.
4. Interests—work and recreational life style.
5. Do you fight about your families of origin? What is involved?
6. Child rearing practices (a common battleground).
7. Children—are children used in alliance against either parent? Is any child identified particularly as yours or your mate's? Do your children come between you and your spouse? Specify.
8. Are there family or personal myths or pretensions that are important to maintain? Specify.
9. Are there differences over control, spending, saving or the making of money?
10. Sex—the "turn-on"—who initiates, frequency, alternative sex partners, practices, etc., feeling desired and loved. Is sex pleasurable, fun, gratifying? Why so or why not?
11. Values, including priority systems and those related to gender, equality, cultural, economic and social class, etc.
12. Friends—do you share and does each have their own? Do you and your mate each have friends of the opposite gender as well as of the same?
13. Gender and interest determined roles and responsibilities at home, socially, making and spending money, leisure time, etc.
14. Include those areas where you feel your mate let you down or caused trouble. Be specific. Include your feelings.
15. How do you most often react when you feel you have been let down or deceived? How does your mate?
16. Other areas not mentioned.
17. Please write out a summary of what you *want* that relates to the above areas from your mate and what in *exchange* you will *give*.

Final Question—add any additional comments or thoughts about yourself, your mate and your marriage that have occurred to you. A summarizing paragraph would be a good idea as the questions above may have missed the flavor or did not get to how you really see things. Be as lengthy and detailed as you care to.

WORKSHEET FOR MARRIAGE CONTRACT
(see reminder list before filling out)

Please Start Each Category On A New Page

Category No. (Circle one)   1   2   3   Name   Date

Number	Your Statement--include what you want, and what you would give in exchange, and what if any problems these items cause between you.	Check one		
		Verbalized	Conscious (not verbal)	Unconscious

Appendix 2. Intrapsychic and Biological Determinants

APPENDIX 2 CONSISTS OF CODES for loosely quantifying the more common characteristics of the 12 parameters of the second category of the marriage contracts, a code for indicating the common mechanisms of defense and a chart that lists the commonly found characteristics for each of the seven types of behavioral (interactional) profiles. The chart is designed to indicate the trend or consensus of commonly found characteristics that contribute to the Gestalt of each profile type; these may be descriptively useful to the clinician and researcher.

Code for Twelve of the Areas of Category Two
of the Marriage Contracts

All scales, 1-9. Each end indicates a polarity along a continuum.

	1	5	9
1. Independence-Dependence	Overly Independent	Midpoint	Overly Dependent
2. Active-Passive	Active	Midpoint	Passive
3. Closeness-Distance	Closeness	Midpoint	Distance
4. Power	Abdicates and/or Submissive	Midpoint	Must Have Power Obsessed with It; Dominates
5. Possess and/or Control Mate	Has Need to Be Controlled	Laissez-Faire	Extreme Need to Control
6. Fear of Abandonment	None	Midpoint	Extreme
7. Anxiety Level	Almost Never	Average	Extreme
8. Defense Mechanisms	(See separate scale A, B, C, etc.)		
9. Gender Identity	Certain	Loose But Not Anxious	Very Confused on Physical Sex and Gender Identification
10. Does Mate Have Desirable Physical and Emotional Characteristics for Sexual Turn-on?	Terrific	Fair	Leaves Cold
11. Capacity to Love Self and Mate	Excellent	Moderate	None
12. (A) Cognitive Style	Same as (or Accepts) Mate's	Accept Difference or Similarity and Use to Complement Each Other	Angered by Difference; No Respect for Mate's
(B) Cognitive Style	Scattered, "Intuitive," Chaotic	Mix of Organized and Emotional	Needs "All" Data; Highly Organized; "No" Emotions; Intellectualizes

CODE FOR MECHANISMS OF DEFENSE

A. Sublimation
B. Altruistic surrender
C. Repression
D. Regression
E. Reaction formation
F. Denial (and/or perceptual defense)
G. Inhibition of impulses and affect (aggressive, hostile, loving, affectionate, sexual, etc.)
H. Introjection, incorporation and identification
 I. Reversal (turning against self)
 J. Displacement
K. Projection
L. Intellectualization and isolation
M. Undoing (magic)
N. Fantasy (to sustain denial)

Interactional Profile	Independ- ence/ Dependence 1	Active/ Passive 2	Close/ Distance 3	Power 4	Abandon- ment Fear 5	Possession/ Control of Mate 6	Anxiety Level 7	Defense Mechanisms 8	Gender Identity 9	Sexual Response to Mate 10	Love of Self and Mate 11	Cognitive Style 12 A	Cognitive Style 12 B
1. Equal Partner	2-6	3-7	1-6	4-6	2-6	4-6	3-7	A,C,F,H, K,L	1-4	1-5	1-4	1-6	2-7
2. Romantic Partner	4-9	1-8	1-3	1-8	6-9	5-9	4-9	A,B,C,D, E,F,H,I,K,N	1-7	1-3	1-3	1-5	1-7
3. Parental Partner	1-5	1-5	1-9	6-9	6-9	6-9	1-9	C,E,F,J, L,N	1-7	1-7	1-9	5-9	5-9
4. Childlike Partner	6-9	5-9	1-9	1-5	1-9	4-9	5-9	B,C,D,E, H,I,J,K, M,N	2-7	1-6	1-9	4-9	1-6
5. Rational Partner	1-7	1-7	4-8	3-8	1-9	3-8	2-6	C,E,F,G, J,L	1-6	1-9	3-9	3-9	6-9
6. Companionate Partner	3-7	2-7	2-7	3-7	3-7	3-7	2-7	A,C,E,F, L,N	1-6	3-7	1-7	1-6	4-9
7. Parallel Partner	1-4	1-6	7-9	4-9	7-9	4-9	2-6	A,C,E,G, J,L	1-9	1-9	5-9	1-9	6-9

Most Common Characteristics Found With Each Interactional Profile

Bibliography

1. The Concept of Marriage and Its Applications to Therapy

Berman, E. M., and H. I. Lief (1975), "Marital Therapy from a Psychiatric Perspective: An Overview," *Amer. J. Psychiat.*, 132:6, 583-591.

Olson, D. H. (1975), "Marital and Family Therapy: A Critical Overview." In A. S. Gurman and D. G. Rice, eds., *Couples in Conflict*. New York: Jason Aronson, pp. 7-62.

Raymond, H. (1971), "A Woman's Lib Parable—of 449 B.C." *New York Times*, Oct. 1, 1971, pp. 43 and 81.

Sager, C. J. (1966a), "The Treatment of Married Couples," Chapter 15 in S. Arieti (ed.), *American Handbook of Psychiatry*, Vol. 3. New York: Basic Books.

Sager, C. J. (1966b), "The Development of Marriage Therapy: An Historical Review," *Amer. J. Orthopsychiat.*, 36:456-467.

Sager, C. J., H. S. Kaplan, R. H. Gundlach, M. Kremer, R. Lenz, and J. Royce (1971), "The Marriage Contract," *Family Process*, 10:311; also published in C. J. Sager and H. S. Kaplan (eds.), *Progress in Group and Family Therapy* (1972). New York: Brunner/Mazel, pp. 483-497.

Sussman, M. B., B. E. Cogswell, and H. A. Ross (1973), "The Personal Contract—New Form of Marriage Bond," mimeographed. Dr. Sussman is Professor of Sociology at Case Western Reserve University.

2. The Individual Contract

Duhl, B. S., and F. J. Duhl (1975), "Cognitive Styles and Marital Process." Paper presented at the Annual Meeting of the American Psychiatric Association, Anaheim, Calif., May 9.

Greene, B. L. (1970), *A Clinical Approach to Marital Problems*. Springfield, Ill.: Charles C Thomas, p. 33.

Money, J., and A. A. Ehrhardt (1972), *Man & Woman, Boy & Girl*. Baltimore, Md.: Johns Hopkins University Press, p. 284.

325

3. The Interactional Contract

Bateson, G., D. D. Jackson, J. Haley, and J. Weakland (1956), "Towards a Theory of Schizophrenia," *Behavioral Science*, 1:251-264.

Bateson, G., D. D. Jackson, J. Haley, and J. Weakland (1963), "Note on the Double Bind," *Family Press*, 2:154-161.

Dicks, H. V. (1963), "Object Relations Theory and Marital Studies," *Brit. J. Med. Psychol.*, 37:125.

Dicks, H. V. (1967), *Marital Tensions*. New York: Basic Books.

Fenichel, O. (1945), *The Psychoanalytic Theory of Neurosis*, New York: Norton.

Freud, A. (1966), *The Ego and the Mechanisms of Defense*, New York: International Universities Press.

Tiger, L. and R. Fox (1971), *The Imperial Animal*, New York: Holt, Rinehart and Winston, pp. 68-84.

Von Bertalanffy, L. (1952), *Problems of Life*, New York: Wiley.

Von Bertalanffy, L. (1956), "General Systems Theory." *General Systems*, 1:1.

Suggested Additional References

Those interested in general systems theory as applied to human behavior will find the following books helpful: W. Gray, F. J. Duhl, N. D. Rizzo (eds.) (1969), *General Systems Theory and Psychiatry*, Boston: Little, Brown; P. Watzlawick, J. Beavin and D. Jackson (1967), *Pragmatics of Human Communication*, New York: Norton; and W. Buckley (ed.) (1968), *Modern Systems Research for the Behavioral Scientist*, Chicago: Aldine. For the mechanisms of defense: the books of A. Freud and Chapter IX, Mechanisms of Defense, in the volume by Fenichel referred to above. For further investigations into love: M. E. Cristen (ed.) (1973), *Symposium on Love*, New York: Behavioral Publications; A. Fromme (1971), *The Ability to Love*, New York: Pocket Books, and O. F. Kernberg (1976), "Boundaries and Structures in Love Relations" a paper presented at the Academy of Medicine, New York, January 6. Dr. Kernberg presents a psychoanalytic formulation of love. W. R. Fairbairn made a significant contribution with his development of object relations theory. This concept is explicated in his *Psychoanalytic Studies of the Personality* (1952), London: Tavistock Publications, and "Synopsis of an Object Relations Theory of the Personality," *Int. J. Psychoanalysis* (1963), 44:224. Mate selection is discussed from the object relations perspective in Dicks' book *Marital Tensions* (1967), referred to above, as well as in Chapters 11 and 12 of R. F. Winch and G. B. Spanier (eds.), (1974), *Selected Studies in Marriage and the Family*, New York: Holt, Rinehart and Winston, and from the sociological viewpoint by R. O. Blood, Jr. (1964), *Marriage*, New York: The Free Press of Glencoe. Those interested in further data regarding male-female, male-male and consanguinal bonding will find L. Tiger and R. Fox's book, cited above, interesting and controversial.

5. The Smiths: A Marriage in Transition

Sager, C. J., H. S. Kaplan, R. H. Gundlach, M. Kremer, R. Lenz, and J. Royce (1971), "The Marriage Contract," *Family Process*, 10:311.

6. Behavioral Profiles

Money, J. and A. A. Ehrhardt (1972), *Man & Woman, Boy & Girl*, Baltimore: Johns Hopkins University Press.

BIBLIOGRAPHY 327

7. Partnership Combinations

BERNE, ERIC (1961), *Transactional Analysis in Psychotherapy*, New York: Grove Press.

O'NEILL, N. and G. O'NEILL (1972), *Open Marriage*, New York: Avon.

PITTMAN, F. and K. FLOMENHAFT (1970), "Treating the Doll's House Marriage," *Family Process*, 9:143-155; reproduced in C. J. Sager and H. S. Kaplan (eds.), *Progress in Group and Family Therapy* (1972), New York: Brunner/Mazel, pp. 509-520.

WELCH, M. S. (1974), "Secret Expectations," *Glamour*, May, 1974, p. 179.

8. Congruence, Complementarity, and Conflict

ACKERMAN, N. W. (1958), *The Psychodynamics of Family Life*. New York: Basic Books.

LEDERER, W. J., and D. D. JACKSON (1968), *The Mirages of Marriage*. New York: Norton.

Additional References and Readings

For a technique and system for predicting the antagonistic and collaborative potentials of couples I suggest R. A. Ravich and Barbara Wyden, *Predictable Pairings*, Wyden, New York, 1974. R. N. Kohl's classic paper on "Pathologic Reactions of Marital Partners to Improvement of Patients," *American Journal of Psychiatry*, 1962, 118:1036-1041, demonstrates the pathological interdependent complementarity of couples. R. G. Tharp, "Psychological Patterning in Marriage," *Psychological Bulletin*, 1963, 60:97-117, is an important study of marital patterns. Those interested in differences and changes in marital and family structure are referred to pp. 48-208 of *Selected Studies in Marriage and the Family*, edited by R. F. Winch and G. B. Spanier, Holt, Rinehart, and Winston, New York, 1974. Those interested in alternative styles of living are referred to L. and J. Constantine's article, "Counseling Implications of Comarital and Multilateral Relations," in *Progress in Group and Family Therapy*, edited by C. J. Sager and H. S. Kaplan, Brunner/Mazel, New York, 1972, pp. 537-552. A. Skolnick explores the changing marital scene in *The Intimate Environment*, Little, Brown, Boston, 1973.

9. Therapeutic Principles and Techniques

ACKERMAN, N. W. (1968), *The Psychodynamics of Family Life*. New York: Basic Books.

ACKERMAN, N. W. (1966), *Treating the Troubled Family*. New York: Basic Books.

BERMAN, E. M., and LIEF, H. I. (1975), "Marital Therapy from a Psychiatric Perspective: An Overview," *Amer. J. Psychiat.*, 132:6, 583-592.

DICKS, H. V. (1967), *Marital Tensions*, New York: Basic Books.

CUBOR, J. F. and P. B. HARROFF (1966), *Sex and the Significant Americans*. Baltimore: Penguin Books, pp. 43-65.

FAIRBAIRN, W. R. (1952), *Psychoanalytic Studies of the Personality*. London: Tavistock.

FAIRBAIRN, W. R. (1963), "Synopsis of an Object Relations Theory of the Personality," *Int. J. Psychoanalysis*, 44:224.

FENSTERHEIM, H. (1972), "Behavior Therapy: Assertive Training in Groups." In C. J. Sager and H. S. Kaplan (eds.) *Progress in Group and Family Therapy*. New York: Brunner/Mazel.

FERBER, A. and J. RANZ (1972), "How to Succeed in Family Therapy: Set Reachable Goals—Give Workable Tasks." Chapter in A. Ferber (ed.) *The Book of Family Therapy.*" New York: Science House.

GOLDSTEIN, M. (1974), "The Uses of Dreams in Conjoint Marital Therapy," *Journal of Sex and Marital Therapy*, 1:75-81.

GOULDING, R. (1972), "New Directions in Transactional Analysis: Creating an Environment for Redecision and Change." In C. J. Sager and H. S. Kaplan (eds.), *Progress in Group and Family Therapy.* New York: Brunner/Mazel, pp. 105-134.

GREENE, B. L. (1970), *A Clinical Approach to Marital Problems*, Springfield: Thomas, pp. 257-259.

HALEY, J. (1963), *Strategies of Psychotherapy*, New York: Grune and Stratton.

HORNEY, K. (1939), *New Ways in Psychoanalysis.* New York: Norton.

HORNEY, K. (1950), *Neurosis and Human Growth.* New York: Norton.

KAPLAN, H. S. (1974), *The New Sex Therapy*, New York: Brunner/Mazel.

KAPLAN, H. S. (1975), *The Illustrated Manual of Sex Therapy.* New York: Quadrangle, pp. 29-59.

LEDERER, W. J. and D. D. JACKSON, (1968), *The Mirages of Marriage*, New York: Norton.

LINDNER, ROBERT M. (1955), *The 50-Minute Hour.* New York: Rinehart.

MENNINGER, K. (1958), *Theory of Psychoanalytic Technique*, New York: Basic Books, pp. 15-24.

MINUCHIN, S. (1974), *Families and Family Therapy*, Cambridge: Harvard University Press.

MITTELMAN, B. (1944), "Complementary Neurotic Reactions in Intimate Relationships," *Psychoanalytic Quarterly*, 13:479-491.

MITTELMAN, B. (1948), "The Concurrent Analysis of Marital Couples," *Psychoanalytic Quarterly*, 17:182-197.

POLLAK, O. (1965), "Sociological and Psychoanalytic Concepts in Family Diagnosis." In B. L. Greene (ed.), *The Psychotherapies of Marital Disharmony.* New York: Free Press, pp. 15-26.

RAVICH, A. A., and B. WYDEN (1974), *Predictable Pairing*, New York: Wyden.

SAGER, C. J. (1966a), "The Development of Marriage Therapy—An Historical Review." *Amer. J. Orthopsychiat.*, 36:458-466.

SAGER, C. J. (1966b), "The Treatment of Married Couples." In S. Arieti (ed.), *The American Handbook of Psychiatry*, Vol. 3, New York: Basic Books, pp. 213-224.

SAGER, C. J. (1967a), "The Diagnosis and Treatment of Marital Complaints," *Amer. J. Psychoanal.*, 27:139-156.

SAGER, C. J. (1967b), "Transference in Conjoint Treatment of Married Couples," *Arch. Gen. Psychiat.*, 16:185-193.

SAGER, C. J. (1967c), "Marital Psychotherapy." In J. Masserman (ed.), *Current Psychiatric Therapies*, Vol. 7, New York: Grune and Stratton, pp. 92-102.

SAGER, C. J. (1976), "Sex Therapy in Marital Therapy," *Amer. J. Psychiat.*, 133: 5, 555-558.

STUART, R. B. (1972), "Operant-Interpersonal Treatment of Marital Discord." In C. J. Sager and H. S. Kaplan (eds.), *Progress in Group and Family Therapy*, New York: Brunner/Mazel, pp. 495-508.

SULLIVAN, H. S. (1945), "Conceptions of Modern Psychiatry." Reprinted from *Psychiatry*, 3:2, 1940 and 8:2, 1945. Distributed by Norton, New York.

SULLIVAN, H. S. (1953), *The Interpersonal Theory of Psychiatry.* New York: Norton.

WHITAKER, C. A. and M. H. MILLER (1969), A Re-evaluation of 'Psychiatric Help' When Divorce Impends," *Amer. J. Psychiat.*, 126:611-616.

WOLPE, J. (1973), *The Practice of Behavior Therapy*, New York: Pergamon Press.

Additional Readings

Those interested in marital group therapy will find useful M. Markowitz's and A. Kadis' "Short Term Analytic Treatment of Married Couples in a Group by a Therapist Couple" in C. J. Sager and H. S. Kaplan (eds.), *Progress in Group and Family Therapy*, Brunner/Mazel, New York, 1972, pp. 463-482. In the same volume H. P. Laquer's article "Mechanisms of Change in Multiple Family Therapy," pp. 400-415, discusses multiple family dynamics in systems terms that apply equally well to couples groups. E. Leichter, who has pioneered in work with couples groups, summarizes her work in an excellent paper titled "Treatment of Married Couples Groups," *The Family Coordinator*, Vol. 22, 1973, pp. 31-42. For those interested in additional behavioral approaches to marital therapy there is a good section (pp. 207-278) in A. S. Gurman and D. G. Rice (eds.), *Couples in Conflict*, Aronson, New York, 1975.

Those wishing a broader reference base for marital therapy should consult the bibliography above as well as the bibliographies in Sager, 1966a, Greene, 1970 and Berman and Lief, 1975 above.

In addition to the references already mentioned, the following are suggested: R. V. Fitzgerald, *Conjoint Couple Therapy*, Aronson, New York, 1973; I. Charny, *Marital Love and Hate*, Macmillan, New York, 1972; C. R. Rogers, *Becoming Partners: Marriage and Its Alternatives*, Delacorte Press, New York, 1972. A classic volume is V. Eisenstein (ed.) *Neurotic Interaction in Marriage*, Basic Books, New York, 1956. This is an excellent collection of papers for its time. Emphasis on the use of communication theory will be found in D. D. Jackson and J. H. Weakland, "Conjoint Family Therapy," *Psychiatry*, 1967, 24:30-45, and Lederer's and Jackson's book, already referred to. *The Psychotherapies of Marital Disharmony* edited by B. L. Greene, New York, Free Press, 1965 has many superb articles that run the gamut of theory and technique up to that date. For Gestalt therapy the reader is referred to F. Perls, *Gestalt Therapy Verbatim*, The Real People Press, Lafayette, California, 1969; *In and Out of the Garbage Pail*, 1969, same publisher; and Erving and Miriam Polster, *Gestalt Therapy Integrated*, New York, Brunner/Mazel, 1973.

10. SEX THERAPY IN MARITAL THERAPY

KAPLAN, H. S. (1974), *The New Sex Therapy*, New York: Brunner/Mazel.

KAPLAN, H. S. (1975), *The Illustrated Manual of Sex Therapy*, New York: Quadrangle.

MASTERS, W. H., and V. E. JOHNSON (1966), *Human Sexual Response*, Boston: Little, Brown and Company.

MASTERS, W. H., and V. E. JOHNSON (1970), *Human Sexual Inadequacy*, Boston: Little, Brown and Company.

MICHAEL, R. D., R. W. BONSALL, and P. WARNER (1974), "Human Vaginal Secretions: Volatile Fatty Acid Content." *Science*, Vol. 186, No. 4170, pp. 1217-1219.

SAGER, C. J., H. S. KAPLAN, R. H. GUNDLACH, M. KREMER, H. LENG, and J. R. ROYCE (1971), "The Marriage Contract," *Family Process*, 10:311-326.

SAGER, C. J. (1974), "Sexual Dysfunctions and Marital Discord." Chapter 24 in H. S. Kaplan, *The New Sex Therapy*, New York: Brunner/Mazel.

SAGER, C. J. (1975), "The Couples Model in the Treatment of Sexual Dysfunction in the Single Person." Chapter in *Sexuality and Psychoanalysis*, E. T. Adelson (ed), New York: Brunner/Mazel.

SAGER, C. J. (1976), "Sex Therapy in Marital Therapy," *Amer. J. Psychiatry*, 133:5, 555-558.

Additional Readings

The first four references above are recommended for basic reading. Those interested in the components of a good sex history may read the report of the Group for the Advancement of Psychiatry *Assessment of Sexual Function: A Guide to Interviewing*, Vol. 8, No. 88, 1973, New York or R. Greene's chapter on interviewing in the volume he edited, *Human Sexuality*, Williams and Wilkins, Baltimore, 1975. The American Psychiatric Association's volume, *Human Sexuality*, American Psychiatric Association, Washington, D. C., 1972 summarizes a great deal of important information. E. T. Adelson edited a volume, *Sexuality and Psychoanalysis*, Brunner/ Mazel, 1975, that is broader than its title and has some excellent papers. *Sexual Conduct* by J. H. Gagnon and W. S. Simon, Aldine, Chicago, 1973; *Perspectives on Human Sexuality*, edited by N. W. Wagner, published by Behavioral Publications, New York, 1974; and *Contemporary Sexual Behavior*, edited by J. Zubin and J. Money, all deal with broad aspects of sexuality including the sociological, anthropological and physiological.

Index